Public Policy
and the Arts

Westview Special Studies in Public Policy and Public Systems Management

Public Policy and the Arts
edited by Kevin V. Mulcahy and C. Richard Swaim

Like wilderness areas, the environment, and in an earlier time parks and schools, the arts now have vocal constituencies among local community leaders and national opinion makers. The issues raised along with this growing public support are by no means resolved, nor are the available solutions universally accepted. But the recent well-publicized attack on public culture by the Reagan administration (with proposed budget cuts approaching 50 percent) and the spirited counterattack by various cultural interest groups (successfully reducing these cuts to 25 percent) testify to the political significance of arts policy.

This text--a collection of original essays--defines the field of arts policy and explores the various issues involved in arts policy-making. The authors point out that the issues raised--in particular challenges to certain basic assumptions about "high" culture, standards-setting, eastern and urban cultural hegemony, regional and institutional funding patterns, the composition of program evaluation panels and the national councils, etc.--are similar to those raised in all public policy areas. The consensus is that the arts world has discovered, among other things, that public support is a mixed blessing; that politics, i.e., questions about what is in the public interest, always follows public money, and that resolutions of these questions will occur in the public arena, not in board rooms or opera boxes.

Dr. Kevin V. Mulcahy is an assistant professor of political science at Louisiana State University and a founder of the Conference Group on Government and the Arts of the American Political Science Association. Dr. C. Richard Swaim is an assistant professor of political science at the University of Baltimore currently on leave as a faculty fellow with the Administration on Aging. He was formerly an intern fellow with the National Endowment for the Arts.

In memory of
James A. Mulcahy

For
Catherine Swaim

Public Policy
and the Arts

edited by Kevin V. Mulcahy
and C. Richard Swaim

Westview Press / Boulder, Colorado

Westview Special Studies in Public Policy and Public Systems Management

Copyright © 1982 by Westview Press, Inc.

Published in 1982 in the United States of America by
     Westview Press, Inc.
     5500 Central Avenue
     Boulder, Colorado 80301
     Frederick A. Praeger, President and Publisher

Library of Congress Catalog Card Number: 82-050069
ISBN 0-86531-115-3 (hc)
ISBN 0-86531-288-5 (pb)

Composition for this book was provided by the editors
Printed and bound in the United States of America

Contents

Tables

Preface

Collections of essays are often a suspect commodity in the academic world. And cultural policy is admittedly not widely perceived as a major political concern. This book seeks to correct that misperception, and to abate some of the suspicions about edited works. Although the United States government has provided direct support for the arts since 1965 (and even earlier during the New Deal), this activity has only recently come under scrutiny. Dick Netzer's The Subsidized Muse (Cambridge University Press, 1978)--a very thoughtful, if somewhat critical, study of the economics of public support--is the only book-length treatment of the subject. Michael Straight's Twigs for an Eagle's Nest (Devon Press, 1979) is a highly anecdotal "insider's view" of the National Endowment for the Arts and Michael Mooney's The Ministry of Culture (Wyndham Books, 1980) is a bad effort at journalistic "muckraking." Netzer's book is limited (albeit intentionally) to economic questions; he largely excludes those areas that are political, administrative, and historical.[1] Twigs for an Eagle's Nest is essentially a memoir, although one that provides a highly informative account of bureaucratic politics at the Arts Endowment. Mooney's book is a failure because what he claims to expose has been already documented as minor peccadillos and his normative arguments are overblown, unfocused, and seemingly indifferent to matters of fact.[2]

We hope that Public Policy and the Arts will correct at least some of the deficiencies in our understanding of cultural policymaking. The well-publicized attack on public culture by the Reagan administration (with proposed budgetary cuts approaching fifty percent) and the spirited counter-attack by various cultural interest groups (successfully reducing those cuts to about twenty-five percent) testifies to the political significance of arts policy. This intensity is all the more surprising given the miniscule amount of the federal budget that is involved. But culture has emerged as one of the areas where segments of the public do not simply accept what the market provides; they expect the government to guarantee the availability of culture. Like parks and schools, wilderness areas and the environment, arts organizations (museums, orchestras, opera companies and dance groups) are judged part of the quality of life. And all of these policies have vocal constituencies that include both local community leaders and national opinion-makers.

Apologists for government support of the arts have discovered (somewhat to their dismay) that public culture is no less political (and perhaps more so) than other policy areas. During the Carter administration, political spokesmen for those outside the traditional cultural consensus challenged certain basic assumptions about high culture versus popular culture, standard-setting versus community-oriented arts organizations, and the general character of funding patterns and the decisionmaking process. In the Reagan administration, the entire philosophy of public subsidies, including those for culture, has come under question as have cultural policies that seek to expand the arts audience and to increase its aesthetic diversity. In short, the arts world discovered that public support is not an unmixed blessing, that political debates--that is, questions about what is the public interest--always follow public money. Moreover, political resolutions will be made in the rough-and-tumble of the public arena, not in the rarefied atmosphere of board rooms and opera boxes.

All of the contributors to Public Policy and the Arts see arts policy as inherently political and thus similar to broader social policies concerning education, social, and environmental values. All but two of the contributors (an economist and a sociologist) have been acquainted with one another since 1976 as members of the Conference Group on Government and the Arts of the American Political Science Association. Consequently, while each contributor worked independently, and his or her contribution reflects an individual subject matter and viewpoint, most contributors share intellectual assumptions and analytical methods. To insure regularity in style and usage, the editors have taken many liberties with the contributions for which the authors may rightly wish to plead innocence.

Like all books this one has incurred a list of debts in its production that demand acknowledgement. Dr. Ralph Smith of the University of Illinois published different versions of chapters three and six in the Journal of Aesthetic Education; we are grateful for his editorial generosity. Our editors at Westview, Lynne Rienner and Miriam Gilbert, showed remarkable patience and forbearance. Kim Bourgeois, Kim Cormier, Lisa Naquin, Joan Payne, and Sharon Roberts of the Text Processing Center at Louisiana State University demonstrated even more remarkable perseverance through the many revisions, as did Linda Gray and Joanie Palmer of LSU's Political Science Department. Most important, Adam Hayward, while a graduate student at LSU, coordinated the entire editorial process from first

typescript to final proofing. It was a truly "awful"
responsibility for which he deserves only the credit.
He did his best to save us from our worst mistakes.

Kevin V. Mulcahy   C. Richard Swaim
Louisiana State University   University of Baltimore

NOTES

[1] The same deliberate limitation of scope applies to
William S. Hendon, James L. Shanahan, and Alice
MacDonald, eds., Economic Policy for the Arts
(Cambridge, MA: ABT Books, 1980) and Mark Blaug, ed.,
The Economics of the Arts (Boulder, CO: Westview, 1979).

[2] For fuller discussions of the Straight and Mooney
books, see reviews by Kevin V. Mulcahy in the American
Political Science Review 75 (June 1981) and 75
(December 1981). See also, Kevin V. Mulcahy, "Public
Culture and the Public: A Review Article," Western
Political Quarterly 34 (September 1981): 461-70.

1
Public Culture and Policy Analysis: An Introduction

C. Richard Swaim

Arts policy is an appropriate area of concern for policy analysis and does not differ greatly from education, science, or health as a matter for public concern and inquiry. But public patronage raises political questions regarding matters of the costs and benefits which characterize the policy's distribution; and, perhaps of greater consequence, answers to these questions have implications for the character, content, and development of culture. A former Deputy Chairman of the Arts Endowment reasons, "[G]reat art is sustained and strengthened by great patronage. Poor patronage discourages and diminishes art."[1] The beginnings of direct patronage of the arts by the public sector in the United States were modest indeed when compared to the National Endowments for the Arts and the Humanities which grew so dramatically in the dozen years between 1968 and 1980. What is unclear, however, is whether this commitment to public culture will continue in the next decade in the face of serious budgetary cutbacks.

Culture has emerged as one of those areas where segments of the public do not accept what the market provides; rather, they expect government to guarantee greater cultural availability and protection from the vagaries of the market.[2] Museums, opera, dance, and symphony concerts are thought to be part of the quality of life. Like wilderness areas and the environment, the arts have constituencies among local community leaders and national opinion makers. Yet, the issues raised by public support are not simply resolved and solutions are not universally accepted. The politics of culture questions basic assumptions about high culture, standard-setting institutions, Eastern/urban hegemony, peer review of grant proposals, the quality of political appointees, geographic distribution of appropriations, and intergovernmental relations. In short, the issues raised by arts policy are similar to those raised in all policy discussions; and, as in other realms, the art

1

world has discovered that public support is a mixed
blessing. Politics--that is, pointed debate over the
public interest--follows public support. And, as the
Reagan administration is demonstrating, what the
government gives can also be taken away.

> Perhaps the major lesson to be learned by arts
> organizations is that public subsidy requires
> entry into the political process. They must
> learn the techniques of lobbying by other
> special interest groups that are competing for
> funds.[3]

Further, nothing is sacrosanct, not even the highest of
"high" culture. Nor is high culture meritorious by
definition alone.[4] Indeed, as many lament, culture must
demonstrate its economic impact, it must play in Peoria,
and it must cater to congressional whim and presidential
fancy.[5]

As a collection of original essays, this book
discusses ideology, government as patron, comparative
and foreign policy perspectives. This first chapter
provides an overview and introduces in a general way the
subsequent contributions. What I have tried to do is
indicate the significance of the questions posed and
embroider analysis in the process. As noted, support
for the arts has only recently become a matter of public
policy concern. Hence, the political debate is intense
and unresolved. As Margaret Wyszomirski presents the
case, the debate centers on three major themes: (1) a
fundamental ambivalence over whether government should
be in the business of supporting culture with public
funds; (2) the elitist-populist controversy over how
support should be distributed, and; (3) the myth that
public policy for the arts is apolitical.[6] Drawing on
her experience as a former Fellow at the Arts Endowment
and as a political scientist, Wyszormirski presents the
contemporary arguments and offers a social scientist's
perspective on the debate and the probable manner of its
resolution.

Advancing the case for public culture, the
subsequent chapter by Kevin Mulcahy begins with the
spectre of a "tax-cutting, no frills in government"
mentality which threatens to cut the budgets allocated
for public culture. Mulcahy's message is reinforced by
the probable effects of the Reagan administration's
skepticism about many social programs as well as the
neo-conservative critique of public support for the
arts.[7] Mulcahy asserts that what public art agencies
need is a statement of purpose that will enable them to
assert their claim to public support. The typical
argument for subsidy, he observes, is economic. But
what if cultural institutions, much less individual

artists, make no economic contributions? Can one still make the case for their public support? The difficulty of a stance that goes beyond economics is exacerbated by a strong American tradition that public culture should serve a useful purpose. This utilitarian theme, as former National Endowment for the Humanities Chairman Ronald Berman writes, requires that the arts and humanities be socially useful and a possible cure-all for crime, inner-city tension, and economic malaise.[8] Mulcahy concludes that supporters of public culture need to make the case based on the principle that culture is "good for you," and that society has a duty to secure its cultural achievements.

If Mulcahy nibbles at the inadequacy of economics as a basis of support, David Cwi devours the economic arguments for support of the arts. Cwi examines the economics of art and culture and reexamines the traditional economic arguments made on behalf of arts support.[9] First, he discusses the finances of the arts, especially the patterns of expenditures, income, and existing labor-intensive employment patterns. He then presents the arguments for public support of culture: the failure of the market-place, arts as a merit good, and the beneficial economic impact of the arts for communities. Cwi argues that the use of such economic reasoning is not dispassionate analysis but rather advocacy. These economic rationales, he argues, present the arts as socially desirable, susceptible to market failure, and thus deserving of support. This becomes a political argument. The merit-good argument reduces to "spend more on the arts because the arts are important." The market-failure argument is a contribution only if there is agreement on how much consumption and production ought to be provided by the private market, of what quality, when, and how often. These are judgments about what we should do and are based on values and political ideology and not economics.

Derral Cheatwood continues the multidisciplinary investigation by providing the reflections of a sociologist. Cheatwood casts the artists as a private muse in a public world and cites problems which artists cannot avoid in modern American society. First, the production of culture requires resources which are often beyond the market-value return of the product produced. Second, the production of art in modern times is increasingly an organized, cooperative venture requiring a large coterie of support personnel. Further, when these factors are combined with the traditional rebellious nature of artists and traditional schemes of public support, a paradox emerges. This paradox requires an examination of the relationship of artist to society, past and present, in order to understand the emerging social structure. Such a backdrop is necessary

to appreciate the analytic modeling of the relationship
among art, artists, and our political, socio-economic
structure.

As already noted, government is an important part
of the cultural world. Government can encourage,
support, constrain or censor. This takes on additional
importance as government becomes patron. Lawrence
Mankin presents an historical overview of government
patronage in the United States.[10] Mankin discusses the
various approaches that the national government has
taken in its relation to practicing artists from the
early days of the nation until the establishment of the
National Endowments for the Arts and Humanities. We
find a mixed review of the federal government's relation
with the arts, perhaps not surprising in a society where
"art appreciation is not part of the interwoven value
foundation."[11] Mankin notes that throughout our
history, government has fulfilled the role of patron
through rhetorical support, symbolic gestures of
support, and specific, though minor, programs of
support. While government can nourish the arts (the
European case is proof enough), Mankin demonstrates that
it can also harass, retard, and manipulate the arts as
well.

In his discussion of the Kennedy administration and
the arts, Milton Cummings analyzes the political arguments for a national cultural agency. Cummings claims
that the national government has had an impact on the
nation's literature and other art forms since the
beginning of the republic. However, these early experi-
ments--most notably those of the New Deal era--widened
the gulf between culture and government. Support for
artistic activities in the United States came largely
from the box office and a truly remarkable system of
private patronage encouraged by tax deductible provi-
sions. There was not yet large-scale, direct support
for culture on the European model. This would change.
The election of John Kennedy brought to Washington a
large number of individuals wanting more federal support
for the arts. The creation of a presidential assistant
for cultural affairs, and the subsequent Heckscher
report recommending the creation of an arts foundation,
helped to establish the political and intellectual base
for such support. Cummings's contribution represents an
evaluation of the influence of domestic politics,
ideology, and presidential personalities on cultural
policymaking. These are important because they are
precisely what continue to influence the development of
arts policy in the United States.[12] Both Mankin and
Cummings present the historical and ideological setting
for the targeted discussion of the National Endowment
for the Arts which follows. What is obvious throughout
these chapters are the following continuities: the

pointed references to history and the impact of political imperatives and personalities on policy.

The National Endowment for the Arts is the federal agency charged with the direct support and promotion of the arts and its character and growth is the focus of Swaim's chapter. The chapter's main concerns are the policy implications stemming from the budgetary success of the agency, its structure, and the chairmen who have headed the agency. The Arts Endowment is described with specific attention to program proliferation, budgetary processes, and the institutionalization of experts within the bureaucratic structure. Swaim's assessment of the intraorganizational policy process has implications for arts policy in terms of federal impact, specific consequences for private support of the arts, state and local government support, and for the nature of art itself. An important facet of the structure of government's support for the arts is the intergovernmental focus. This is, of course, required in the federal system as policy is seldom within the purview of a single level of government. The arts are not an exception. Swaim presents an introduction to this intergovernmental aspect of government arts patronage; a more focused and comprehensive view follows in subsequent chapters by Svenson and Mulcahy.

Arthur Svenson presents a number of themes common to state arts agencies and deserving of critical analysis. He first discusses the motives which inspired the institutionalization of state arts patronage noting that the states, though much maligned, have often ventured into policy areas before the federal government. Svenson devotes considerable attention to the desires of state legislators to promote artistic opportunity and quantity of artistic production. He then examines the characteristics associated with the administrators and administration of state arts agencies. Finally, Svenson reviews the programmatic approaches adopted by state arts agencies and concludes with a discussion of the political and financial structure of state arts agencies and the problems awaiting these agencies in the future.

Local flavors of the arts are viewed in a more ideological vein by Kevin Mulcahy as he examines the historical relationship between culture and the cities. Mulcahy demonstrates the contributions that arts institutions make to the urban economy and environment and judges them to be invaluable resources meriting a status similar to national parks. As manufacturing sites shift to the urban periphery, cultural production and related services, such as retailing and tourism, emerge as ever more important factors in the urban economy. The Northeast, particularly New York City, is the prime example although Mulcahy gives considerable attention to Seattle, Los Angeles and New Orleans as well. He goes on to say that for many cities--for example, Boston, Baltimore and Salt Lake City--the cultural quotient is often their main attraction. He further argues for the necessity of culture as a determinant of the quality of urban life.

A quite different tack is presented in the succeeding two chapters as Katz and Mulcahy view culture in a comparative and international perspective. Richard Katz considers the relationship between public broadcasting and the performing arts with specific reference to the United States and Great Britain. Among the topics discussed are issues which cut across the broad spectrum of support for public culture. For example, consider the implications of these issues as they relate to the future of patronage. Broadcast performances can bring the arts to a wider audience than ever before. Further, television and radio can introduce high quality artistic productions to people who would never consider attending such performances live. What will this mean for future arts policies? Can a political compromise be found in subsidizing high culture for an elite attending-audience and a great mass-audience sitting at home enjoying the performance on radio or television? Clearly, these are questions which spark debate and need much more discussion. On a different note, Mulcahy's chapter on "cultural diplomacy" examines a little known aspect of American foreign policy--its programs of cultural exchange. This discussion cuts across issues as he raises the implications of culture for export. What kind of culture is exported? he asks. Is it representative of the American scene and is it what we want others to see? Is it indicative of the "American way of life?" To whom are culture exchanges presented? Is an exchange different from propaganda? Mulcahy wraps his chapter around a basic policy question: What foundation is there for cultural diplomacy--propaganda or understanding?

The concluding chapter by Kevin Mulcahy evaluates arts policy in light of the Reagan administration's drastic budget cuts. It brings together several of the issues discussed throughout the book as many of the assumptions underlying public culture have been seriously challenged. It is our hope that these chapters present arts policy in some coherent way so as to spark interest among the cultural public, the academic public, and the public-at-large. The question of arts patronage is a complex one; for patron, artist, and analyst. The implications of patronage extend to the very heart of the arts, their content and development, and their centrality to the society that they mirror. "The truth is that the way an artist is paid profoundly affects his product, whether he's an opera producer, what used to be called a lyric poet, or anything in between."[13]   With increased public support for the arts, this concern is magnified.   A host of questions arise. How does one support and nourish without disturbing or unduly influencing?   Indeed, what is undue influence?   In addition, when support is public, do artists cater to what is popular--that is, what the "public" wants or thinks is good? Must artists cater to such whims though that public be ignorant?   Is the situation analogous to the Medici or the Church when one painted what the patron wanted in order to pay the bills or stay alive? Is this the situation today?

Do artists produce what the government (that is, "we the people") wants, or do they accept the support and produce what is good for the public even if that public cannot accept, much less appreciate, symmetrical boulders geometrically placed in a town square as art-- even modern art?[14]   Can we ask the public to wait two centuries before discovering that what they did not like will be revered as classical twentieth century art? Do we let the arts die of neglect? If so, which arts? Do we allow the market place of taste to decide? If so, what kinds of art will survive? Is it probable that the same art which survives with public support would survive without it?   Is this survival dependent on the quality of the art or on the quality of the elite support--public and private--for certain forms of cultural expression? Policy analysis is initially most exciting when raising questions. We hope this book raises some of those questions, or leads the reader to raise those questions. The discussion should continue; it is in the best tradition of the policy sciences. This book was not designed to answer definitively such questions, or the many more which should be raised. Our hopes are more modest.   We wish only to bring the discussion to the table.   Responsible and thoughtful patronage of the arts requires that much and much more.

NOTES

[1] Michael Straight, Twigs for an Eagle's Nest (Berkeley, CA: Devon Press, 1980).

[2] William J. Baumol and William G. Bowen, The Performing Arts: The Economic Dilemma (New York: Twentieth Century Fund, 1966). They are responsible for the popularity of the "market failure" and "labor intensive" arguments for public support of the arts.

[3] Sara P. Garretson and Carol B. Grossman, "The Arts in the United States: Inflation, Recession and Public Policy," paper prepared for the West Berlin Conference on Culture, Economics and Politics, Germany, 1975.

[4] Herbert Gans, Popular Culture and High Culture: An Analysis and Evaluation of Taste (New York: Basic Books, 1974).

[5] C. Richard Swaim, "The Arts and Government: Public Policy Questions," Journal of Aesthetic Education 12 (October 1978): 43-48. For a sociological perspective, contact the Social Theory and the Arts Organization (Derral Cheatwood, University of Baltimore.) The Journal of Cultural Economics (Bill Hendon, University of Akron) devotes its issues to economic analysis of the performing arts. For additional economic perspectives see, of course, Baumol and Bowen; and Dick Netzer, The Subsidized Muse (New York: Cambridge University Press, 1978). Political scientists have lagged behind the others. However, contact the Conference Group on Government and the Arts (Richard Katz, Johns Hopkins University) for manuscript information and conference activities. The Journal of Aesthetic Education is increasing its attention to matters of cultural and educational policy. See for example, the special issue, "The Government, Art, and Aesthetic Education," 14 (October 1980), edited by Kevin V. Mulcahy.

[6] For a full story of the politiciztion of the arts see C. Richard Swaim, The Fine Politics of Art (Boulder, CO: Westview Press, forthcoming.)

[7] The neo-conservative critique can be gleaned from Ernest van den Haag, "Should the Government Subsidize the Arts," Policy Review 10 (Fall 1979): 63-73; see also Kingsley Amis, "An Arts Policy", Policy Review 12 (Fall 1980): 82-94; and Charles L. Heatherly, ed., Mandate for Leadership (Washington, DC: The Heritage Foundation, 1980), pp. 1039-1056. This formed much of the transition report received by President Reagan. A predictive document for the Reagan's administration plans for the arts and humanities can be seen in the "Stockman Hit List" which requests a fifty percent cut in each Endowment's appropriations and very incremental increases for the following five years.

[8] Robert Brustein, "Can the Show Go On," New York Times Magazine, July 10, 1977, p. 59.

[9] Netzer also attacks the so-called "Baumol and Bowen" thesis on the economic plight of the arts.

[10] See Lawrence Mankin, "Government and the Arts: From the Great Depression to 1973," Ph.D. dissertation, University of Illinois, 1976.

[11] Alexis de Tocqueville was particularly optimistic in this regard, saying that culture will become the province of the many and not only the few.". . . [N]ot only will the number of those who take an interest in the production of the mind be greater, but the taste for intellectual enjoyment will descend, step by step, even to those who, in aristocratic societies, seem to have neither time or ability to indulge in them." Writing later, Thorstein Veblen sharply disagreed and thought that high culture would remain the province of the elite. See Paul DiMaggio and Michael Useem, "Cultural Democracy in a Period of Cultural Expansion: The Social Composition of Arts Audiences in the United States," Social Problems 26 (December 1978): 179-197.

[12] For an interesting view see, Joan Simpson Burns, The Awkward Embrace (New York: Knopf, 1975).

[13] Amis, "An Arts Policy."

[14] The story of the Hartford "rocks" is well known in some circles as an excellent example of the problems of public patronage. A sculptor, charged with the task of providing a piece for the Hartford town square, created a series of huge boulders placed geometrically about the square. The "people" as well as the mayor failed to see any "art" and protested loudly about "misuse" of public money. Similarly, city governments have rejected works by such noted artists as Alexander Calder and Diego DiRivera as too "controversial."

2
Controversies in Arts Policymaking

Margaret J. Wyszomirski

Historically, American attitudes towards the arts have been ambiguous and contradictory. On the one hand, Americans have long envied and sought to imitate or import Western European culture. Since colonial times, Americans have felt themselves to be in "the backwash of European artistic and cultural achievements."[1] On the other hand, American culture in the past generation has come of age and become a dynamic center of artistic creativity, innovation, and excellence in fields as diverse as dance and opera, popular music and architecture. This new-found artistic maturity, however, has not been matched by the development of a clear public philosophy regarding the value and place of art in society or about the "proper" relationship between government and the arts.

While Americans have traditionally envied the European tradition and achievements in the arts, we have also recognized the roles that monarchies, aristocracies, and churches have played in providing public patronage for the arts. The close historical relationship between the arts and these elite institutions has created a cross-current of American opinion which suspects that artistic excellence may not be compatable with secular, democratic values. Alexis De Tocqueville put it well when he observed that:

> . . . the democratic principle not only tends to direct the human to the useful arts, but it induces the artisan to produce with great rapidity many imperfect commodities. . . . In aristocracies, a few great pictures are produced, in democratic countries a vast number of insignificant ones . . .[2]

The tradition and legitimacy of public patronage of the arts that was established in Europe by aristocratic and clerical patrons is not only absent from the

11

American milieu, it is at variance with democratic principles and a traditional commitment to the separation of church and state. Furthermore, there still remains a residue of puritan disregard for much art as wicked frivolity and of a frontier society's inhospitability to, and isolation from, most artistic activity. These various historical forces have contributed to a strong American perception that the arts, and therefore a public policy regarding the arts, can only be justified if they serve a useful purpose. This utilitarian theme has had many expressions. De Tocqueville noted that "democratic nations . . . will . . . cultivate the arts that render life easy, in preference to those whose object is to adorn it. They will habitually prefer the useful to the beautiful, and they will require that the beautiful should be useful."[3]

More recently, Anthony L. Barresi has argued that the involvement of American government in the arts has always been motivated by necessity--by practical necessity at first, by economic necessity during the Great Depression era, and by cultural necessity since World War II.[4] Ronald Berman, former chairman of the National Endowment for the Humanities (NEH), has written that the arts are now regarded as "socially useful"--as a possible cure-all for everything from adolescent violence and anomie to drug addiction, inner-city tensions, crime, and the problems of old age.[5] As America (and American art) has come of age and its populace has become better-educated and more widely exposed to aesthetic values other than the traditional utilitarian perspective, an audience has developed with a very different approach to artistic activity and to public support for the arts. It is these two aesthetics which have constituted the deep, and often treacherous, undercurrents of public debate about a public policy regarding the arts.

THE ELITIST-POPULIST DEBATE

It was during the Carter administration--the administration of non-Washingtonian, non-establishment outsiders--that public debate about how to implement an arts policy came to center on the themes of elitism vs. populism and of politicization. During the late 1970's, these twin themes often went hand-in-hand as charges that political appointees to head both the National Endowments would effect a policy shift towards populism. Although the two debates are related, each is distinguishable in its own right.

In the realm of arts policy, the elitism vs.

populism controversy emerged in full bloom during 1977. The terms are characterized differently by advocates of each position. To proponents of the "elitist" position, elitism means that public policy on the arts should stress artistic quality as a criterion of support and that quality is most consistently found in, or associated with, the established cultural institutions. This position assumes that there are "strong boundaries between performer and audience, amateur and professional"; and that art is "distinct from 'popular' forms of creative endeavor."[6] Furthermore, the elitist concept of the arts tend to be creator-oriented.[7] Elitists are likely to be creative artists in the traditional fields of the fine arts, cultural critics, and the typically well-educated upper and upper-middle class supporters and attenders of the established institutions of the arts. Detractors of the elitist position are likely to use the term pejoratively as the equivalent of "snobbism" and its adherents are disparaged as "highbrows" and "eggheads"; conservative and undemocratic.

On the other side, populists advocate a public arts policy that stresses the widest possible availability of the arts. An example might be the following policy statement of the National Endowment for the Arts(NEA):

> To insure that all Americans have a true opportunity to make an informed, an educated choice to have the arts of high quality touch their lives so that no person is deprived of access to the arts by reason of
> a) geography
> b) inadequate income
> c) inadequate education
> d) physical or mental handicaps
> e) social or cultural patterns unresponsive to diverse ethnic or group needs.[8]

This approach tends to endorse a less traditional, more pluralistic notion of artistic merit and consciously seeks to create a policy of cultural diversity. The populist tends to emphasize the user or consumer of arts, and hence is concerned with the broad dissemination of the arts and with the promotion of cultural products that meet diverse constituent demands. The focus is on participation and experience and, therefore, perceives only weak boundaries between audience and performer, between amateur and professional.[9] Indeed, in merit considerations, populists are willing to give potential great, perhaps even equal, weight with existing quality. Such a view is expressed in the NEA's statement of mission as including " . . . assist[ance to] those who have the potential to achieve 'profes-

sional excellence' in their art."[10]   Proponents of
populism are frequently advocates of minority arts, folk
arts, crafts, ethnic arts, or counter-culture activities.   Fundamentally, they argue that art means
different things to different people and that any public
definition of art should be broad enough to include
alternatives and supplements to traditional concepts of
the fine arts.   Critics of populism contend that such
policies will dilute, homogenize, vulgarize, and
popularize the arts[11]--sacrificing concerns for
excellence to the political expediency of geographic,
racial, sexual, and/or ethnic parity. Of course, each
camp exaggerates its own virtues and its opponents's
vices.   Public agencies funding the arts have, therefore, attempted to take a fencesitting, logrolling
position.   For instance, the NEA, through Chairman
Livingston Biddle and its official statements and publications, has asserted that it gives equal weight ". . .
to fostering of excellence in the arts and to insuring
that the arts are available to the public . . ."[12]
Indeed, Chairman Biddle has consistently emphasized that
the NEA's mission is to foster "access to the best" in
the arts.[13]

     Such a combined policy of quality and dispersion is
not without precedent. Indeed, it was implemented in New
York State.   Ever since its creation in 1960, the New
York State Council on the Arts (NYSCA) has been a
harbinger of national arts issues and policies. In New
York, the elitism-populism issue had a downstate-upstate
flavor that was resolved in policy decisions legislatively enacted between 1973 and 1975. In 1973-4, the
state legislature mandated that arts funds be propor-
tioned geographically, with each county getting seventy-
five cents (now fifty-five cents) per capita.   This
dealt with populist claims.   The following year, the
legislature mandated that fifty percent of all Arts
Council funds go to "primary" institutions. This spoke
to elitist demands.

     To date, no such strict formulas have been imposed
on the NEA.   The New York case is, nonetheless,
interesting for a number of reasons.   It demonstrates
that the controversy has roots that reach beyond the
Carter administration and outside the Washington
political scene. It is even possible that the New York
case set the stage for the emergence of the national
elitism vs. populism debate in 1977. Furthermore, New
York State's resolution of the conflict suggests that a
similar policy will probably not be possible at the
national level. A close look at budget figures in New
York in the early 1970's shows that between 1970 and
1974 state arts funds increased nearly ten-fold. This
dramatic increase apparently helped touch off the New
York elitist-populist debate because it raised the level

of what was at stake. During the years when the debate
prevailed and was gradually resolved by legislative
action, the budget held steady at approximately $16
million. Once the resolution which combined both
elitist and populist demands was put into effect, the
budget more than doubled from $16.4 million to $35.6
million.[14] In other words, to accomplish policies of
both quality and dispersion, New York had to find twice
the resources.

Similarly, the present national elitist-populist
debate was preceded by a period of dramatic budgetary
increases for the NEA. Between 1970 and 1974, the NEA
budget nearly doubled three times in four years--rising
from $8 million to $15 million to $29 million to $38
million to $60 million. Thereafter, budgetary growth
continued, but at an incremental rate.[15] In its recent
general plan, the Endowment projects another doubling of
its budget--from $150 million in 1980 to $300 million by
the year 1984.[16] At first glance, this suggests that
the NEA may be attempting to replicate the New York
strategy. Such a strategy, however, may not be politically feasible and, if realized, is unlikely to be as
successful either in resolving the political debate or
in providing an adequate level of support for the arts.
One drawback to the NEA's plan for budgetary growth is
that it spreads out the process over a five year period.
This will dilute the impact of the increase--particu-
larly as inflation continues to diminish the value of
NEA funds and their ability to offset (or even match)
the rising costs of producing the arts. Clearly, the
eventual doubling of NEA funds will not have the same
impact as an immediate doubling. Any discussion of the
relative impact of gradually, as opposed to immediately,
doubling the NEA budget presupposes the political feasibility of large-scale increases. Yet such an assumption
is very questionable in these days of tight budgets and
efforts to reduce government spending. The chances of
obtaining major funding increases in the Reagan administration are extremely remote. Under a fiscally conservative administration the NEA will find it has all it
can do merely to stave off budget cuts. The political
prospects of obtaining major funding increases are anything but promising.

Tabling for the moment the problems of political
feasibility and timing, a major question remains as to
whether a doubling of the present NEA budget would have
the same effect as the doubling of NYSCA's budget in
1975. The New York increase injected a large amount of
money into a limited geographic, demographic, and
economic market at one time. Adjusted for a conservative inflation rate of eight percent per a year for the
five years since then, New York's $1 million increase in
1975 would translate into a $26.6 million increase

injected into the larger national arena. If funds were spread equally among the fifty states, this would mean that by 1984 each state would only see a total of an extra three million dollars--at a rate of approximately $750,000 each year. Even if this projection could be finely adjusted to variations from state to state and to discount the value of the money for the continued, deteriorating effect of inflation, the impact of $750,000 a year for five years or of $3 million after five years would not be of the same order of magnitude as a $19 million increase in one year in one state.

In addition, there are other arguments that indicate that a mere doubling of national funds to support the arts cannot adequately meet the needs of existing arts institutions and activities as well as encourage more and broader activities. According to a 1974 Ford Foundation study of major, non-profit performing arts organizations throughout the country, it was projected that production and operating costs would double by 1980-81. While earned income would also increase, it would be at a slower rate--leaving a larger income gap to be filled by public and private support. Indeed, this study projected that the income gap would increase at least four and a half times if the annual inflation rate were assumed to be four and one-half percent.[17] Hence the need for support is growing at a faster rate than the mere increase in production costs. Part of the income gap might be filled by increased support from business. However, corporate contributions are unlikely to be a willing, able, or advisable means of filling the gap.[18] There are also limits on additional money that can be raised from the audience. Earned income can only be incrementally increased since ticket prices cannot be raised continually without an arts organization pricing itself out of the market. Furthermore, the quest for foundation and private donor money is fiercely competitive in today's tight-money and inflationary world.

Since the outlook for significantly increasing funds from private sources looks dim, public funds assume a greater importance. Dick Netzer, in The Subsidized Muse, estimates that total public funding (national, state, and local) would have had to increase over 400 percent between 1975 and 1980-81--from $300 million to $1.1 billion--if government was simply to maintain its proportion of the contribution budgets of arts organizations.[19] In other words, public support would need to quadruple simply to maintain the status quo. Any attempt to expand supportive or fostering activities would necessitate budgetary increases over and above the aforementioned quadrupling! It appears that the NEA and other government agencies involved in the arts will have to begin making difficult policy decisions and establishing priorities rather than continue fence-straddling between the elitist and populist perspectives. Any attempt to resolve the controversy is very difficult because the roots of the debate entail fundamental philosophical choices.

The elitist-populist debate is really a contemporary version of what John W. Gardner has called "the democratic dilemma"[20]--the tension between the quest for excellence and the quest of equality. In earlier times, the debate was generally framed in terms of democracy vs. republicanism; aristocracy vs. Jacobinism. The commitment to equality--in this case, of opportunity to experience and to create art that speaks to the various dialects of this pluralist nation as well as to the world--is a strong motive force in public policy decisions in America. Compound this concern for traditional support of grassroots activism with a federal political system, and you have generated a potent and deep-rooted support for cultural populism.

Conversely, the elitists voice an opinion at least as old as Jefferson's belief in a "natural aristocracy of virtue and talent.[21] A society generally wishes to foster the growth of, and benefit from the services of, its best and brightest but such a "natural aristocracy" of talent implies that intellect and ability are not equally distributed among the populace. This is particularly true of the arts, where quality is the equivalent of elitism[22]--in the original sense of the word. Lincoln Kirsten argues the point eloquently:

> . . . if there is one single primacy which can be presently considered, accepted, and then fought for, it is the assertion or admission that there is in fact and indeed an elite, that this elite . . . deserves to be legitimized, fostered, preserved, encouraged, and that the root meaning of the word elite is election, which implies also selection . . . This involves further 'the choice or flower of society, or of any body or class of persons' . . . the elite is, perforce, an aristocracy; however impotent politically, culturally it is imperial . . .[23]

While substantial agreement could be secured for the notion that the talent to create or perform quality art is the province (and the gift) of a "natural aristocracy", the catch still remains that the verdict of "quality" art is an essentially subjective judgment; or, as Mary Beth Norton put it, "excellence [is] . . . in the eye of the beholder."[24] What has less of a consensus is the idea that the consumers, as well as the creators, of culture are an elite. The arts audience as an elite is a perception apparently common among prominent creative artists and their community. Julius Rudel, former artistic director of the New York City Opera, has written: "Art is not and never has been for everyone: it is for an elite." Schuyler Chapin, former general manager of the Metropolitan Opera, asserted that: "Opera is after all essentially aristocratic and elitist in that it requires intelligence, interest and involvement on the part of its audience." Dance and theater critic Clive Barnes has observed that: ". . . most of the arts are fundamentally elitist . . . [and that] while the arts may be for all the people, not all the people are for the arts."[25]

Students of the sociology of culture also lend support to this perception of the arts audience as an elite. For instance, when discussing the prospects for democratizing the arts, Paul DiMaggio and Michael Useem point out that: ". . . appreciation of and familiarity with the arts is a capacity requiring prolonged training. . . . Individuals must learn to 'read' a painting or a piece of music just as they must learn to comprehend the printed word . . . ."[26] To view the arts audience as an elite is not necessarily at odds with democratic sentiments if it is a sort of open-door exclusivity. As both Julius Rudel and Martha Graham note: ". . .[T]he wonder, the miracle of America is that . . . an elite exists, ready for discovery, in every class, race, religion, ethnic group, and even sex." ". . .[E]litism in the arts is much frowned upon but increasingly necessary. We need a mandarin approach with the special American provision that anyone who wants to can elect him or herself a mandarin. . ."[27]

The present elitist-populist debate also has roots in old, geopolitical issues. Artistic creativity is predominantly an urban phenomenon. Cities provide that critical mass of humanity that allows artistic communities to coalesce, intermingle, and "cross-pollinate" in ways that generate and refine individual creative impulses. These communities act, in turn, as magnets attracting other artists or budding artists. The creative atmosphere sustains and maintains itself-- experimenting for the future and preserving the best of the past. Cities encompass diverse, large populations capable of providing an interested and informed audience for artistic activity. Individual artists may appear and choose to work anywhere; but the arts thrive and flourish in the cities. This has always been the case-- not just in contemporary America, but throughout the world history: from Thebes to Athens to Rome; through Florence, Salzburg, Paris and London; to New York City, Boston, and San Francisco. (For related a discussion, see Chapter 10 on "Culture and the Cities.")

As a mercantile and industrial nation, America has accepted urban life as a natural fact of life, but its dreams have idealized the country life. Many of the Founding Fathers lived and endorsed the life of a country squire--a transplanted British ideal. Jefferson rhapsodized over the virtues of "yeoman farmer" life--a condition that was to be preferred to the clamor, bustle, and congestion of the city. To this day, a cornerstone of the American dream is to have one's own little kingdom--a home, a place in the country or at the shore. During the nineteenth century that desire propelled millions across the frontiers as homesteaders. Since at least World War II, it has propelled millions more into suburbia to build their castles and call it home. One might say that America's heart lies in the country while its mind is drawn to the city. As a child of the city, the arts often suffer from a form of "guilt by association". They are maligned (as cities often are) for decadence, wickedness, frivolity, and snobbishness. Hence when populists rant against the "big" arts institutions and the superiority complex of New York City, or argue that Cedar Rapids has as much right to an opera company as San Francisco, they are voicing a modern version of an old American suspicion of the urban and a sentimental preference for the rural.

This city vs. country axis is also expressed in coastal vs. heartland terms. Artistic activity thrives and proliferates along the coasts of the nation-- spreading out from the major cities to form concentra- tions of artistic activity that span the eastern seaboard from Boston, through New York and Philadelphia, to Washington, and recently sparking substantial activity farther south--to Charleston and Atlanta. On the West Coast, the original bipolar cultural centers of Los Angeles and San Francisco have spurred Seattle and San Diego into an arts boom. The Gulf Coast too has seen artistic growth, especially in Houston/Galveston, New Orleans, Tampa/St. Petersburg. The coastal flourishing of the arts is not matched, however, by activity in the heartland.[28] The heartland is not devoid of the arts, it simply provides less fertile soil for them. Some of the major cities of the midlands-- Chicago, Salt Lake City, Dallas, Minneapolis, St. Louis, Cleveland, and Cincinnati--are oases that can all boast of major artistic achievements. Frequently these cities have first-rate orchestras and musical communities, occasionally good regional opera, dance, or theatre groups. But, by and large, even the cities of the heartland cannot sustain the artistic scope, size or diversity of the coastal cities. So the elitist- populist debate can be seen as a variation of the old feud that pits the "establishment" from Beacon Hill or Nob Hill against the populist farmers, frontiersmen, and pioneers.

The most extreme manifestation of this tension, in

all its varied vehemence, paints New York City as the
epitome of everything that is elitist, coastal, urban;
and, therefore, suspect. Some high officials at the
Arts Endowment apparently believe that the New York City
arts community has an egomanical superiority-complex,
and a virtual paranoia about losing its preeminent position in the cultural world. These attitudes, according
to some voices at the NEA, have driven the New York
artistic community (through its house organ--the New
York Times) to invent a phantom elitist-populist controversy as a tactic designed to secure a disproportionate
amount of public funds. As a recent article in the
Saturday Review noted: ". . . staff members [of the
NEA] call elitism/populism a 'false issue' and are quite
defensive about allegations of an anti-New York
bias."[29]

Funding figures, however, would seem to indicate
that, under Biddle's chairmanship of the NEA (which is
perceived as populist or at least populist-leaning), the
arts institutions of New York City (as well as other
coastal metropolitan centers in Massachusetts and
California) have lost government support. Instead,
public money has been channelled into heartland cities
with less-established activities and organizations. A
report by the Cultural Assistance Center found New York
to be "a principal victim of . . . the federal governments's new direction in giving support on the basis of
geography rather than on artistic quality."[30] John
Friedman writing in the New York Times concluded that
"it is possible to say that there is now a discernible
and growing trend towards the politically popular policy
of assisting newer, more regionally dispersed 'populist'
groups rather than traditional 'elitist' cultural
institution."[31] New York City's percentage of federal
funds for the arts has declined under the Biddle regime
and so has the percentage of panelists from New York.
Indeed, when testifying before Congress, Mr. Biddle
stated that when he assumed the leadership of the
agency, "there was a concentration of grants and monies
in New York, California, and Massachuetts . . . [and
that] . . . we would [now] see a shifting. It would be
my wish to see a greater shifting as time goes
on. . . ."[32]

Livingston Biddle believes that a trend toward
"greater regional dispersion" of grants has not led to
"diminished support for larger organizations."[33]
Certainly no final judgment on that can be made since
the long-range effects of a shifting pattern of federal
arts support cannot yet be clearly discerned. However,
if a populist funding trend continues and/or expands and
this proves to "victimize" major cultural institutions,
we may find that public cultural policy is implying a
rather surprising opinion. In essence, it would be

saying that the more recognized an arts institution becomes and the more it grows--in size, in repertory, in reputation, in length of season, in touring schedule-- the less it merits public patronage. In other words, such a governmental policy would seem to imply that too much artistic success may lead the NEA to declare an arts institution financially independent. While it is true that that major arts institutions have a significant capability to raise funds in the private sector, it is equally true that their operating costs are substantial and increasing. For instance, the Metropolitan Opera's annual operating budget of approximately $38 million amounts to one-fifth of the Arts Endowment's annual appropriation!

Furthermore, to argue that federal money can be "better" spent supporting the arts in areas where there is little activity or support proposes something like a compensatory theory of federal support. New York state and city governments do more to support the arts than any other state or city in the country. Together, the state and the city support the arts with an annual amount equal to one-third of the NEA's national funding commitment. If the state and city of New York are willing to support the arts so vigorously, why should this become a rationale for the reduction of federal support for the arts in their area? New York--and other major metropolitan centers like Boston, Philadelphia, and San Francisco--have supported and cultivated the arts more successfully and longer than other areas of the country. Since this development and support is dispersed disproportionately throughout the nation, federal support--if it is to follow quality--cannot be equally or proportionately dispersed.

The arts have never been a profit-making enterprise. The arts, particularly the best of the fine arts, have always required patronage. If government is to assume some of the responsibility for supporting the arts, then it seems inconsistent for it to penalize those organizations that have been most successful at consistently producing and presenting quality art. The elitist-populist debate is unlikely to be resolved because it is a manifestation of a fundamental, and still unresolved, debate within the American sociopolitical system. Instead of resolution, support for each perspective will vary at different times, affected by social, economic, artistic, and political developments.

THE POLITICIZATION OF THE ARTS

A controversy often related to the elitism/populism
debate concerns what is called the "politicization" of
the arts. Here again, the very term at issue has no
common or consistent meaning. In one sense, the arts
become politicized whenever they are a subject of public
policy. Certainly an ongoing political element was
introduced into the arts when a bureaucratic entity, the
NEA, was created to support them. It is easy to see how
politics is likely to have some effect on artistic affairs when the bureaucratic agency established requires
yearly funding from Congress and is directed by
presidential appointees who must secure senatorial
confirmation. In this sense, politicization of the arts
is an inevitable consequence of making support of the
arts a public responsibility. Livingston Biddle sought
to enunciate an essentially neutral perspective about
the arts and politics when he stated that "I find
'politics' difficult to give a derogatory meaning to
because our whole government is based on the political
process as translated through our democracy."[34] Anything that becomes a subject of public decisions becomes
affected, in either substance or procedure (or both), by
politics.
Critics of the "politicization" of the arts use the
term differently--usually implying the intervention of
political and/or partisan considerations into personnel
and grant decisions. Indeed, such charges of politicization were raised early in the Carter administration in
response to the NEH appointments of new chairmen for the
NEA and the NEH. The opening salvos of this controversy
were fired over the appointment of a new chairman for
the NEH. The character and timing of the exchanges
demonstrated that "politicization" could be a complex
blend of issues concerning political patronage and
cultural ideology.
President Carter had inherited an NEH headed by
Ronald S. Berman, whose reappointment to a second term
as chairman had been blocked during 1976 by Senator
Claiborne Pell--chairman of the Higher Education, Arts,
and Humanities Subcommittee of the Labor and Human
Resources Committee. Senator Pell criticized Berman for
practicing elitism and his agency for financing
"esoteric programs that had not reached a broad enough
segment of the population."[35] Hence the first "politicization" controversy concerned elitism compounded by
apparent consideration of political patronage as the
appointment was caught in the transition between the
Ford and the Carter administrations. The search process
that the Carter administration undertook to find a new
NEH chairman turned into a long, intensely controversial
affair that one White House staff member compared to a

"Marx Brothers movie". The President himself once quipped that "he was spending more time on the Endowment appointment than on the early SALT talks."[36] The long search ended in the nomination of Joseph Duffey--a former Assistant Secretary of State for Education and Cultural affairs, former chairman of the Americans for Democratic Action, a candidate for senator from Connecticut, an early Carter supporter; and, husband of a Carter White House staff member, Anne Wexler. His selection was seen by many observers as "political" and it served to set the political stage for an aroused public awareness of the issues involved when a vacancy arose at the NEA.

Nancy Hanks had served as chairman of the NEA for eight years when she announced her resignation in 1977. She was generally well-regarded for having provided outstanding leadership--both in supporting the arts throughout the nation and in building up the Endowment administratively.[37] The process of replacing Mrs. Hanks proved to be shorter, but no less controversial, than the transition effected at the NEH. Within weeks of her resignation the deputy chairman of the NEA, Michael Straight, blasted the Carter administration by asserting that "the cancer of political interference has begun to undermine the credibility of the endowments."[38] Straight not only charged that the appointment of Livingston Biddle (formerly the staff director of Pell's Senate oversight committee and his old college roommate) was "political", but that the administration's failure to appoint a senior White House advisor on cultural policy was also political by giving the Vice President's wife, Joan Mondale, a "free hand as spokesman for the arts." Furthermore, he charged that "pressure groups" and "vested interests" (including blacks, women and performing arts unions) had succeeded in imposing virtual representation and funding quotas upon the Endowments. This constituted further evidence of politicization.

These charges escalated the politicization debate as both administration defenders and opponents joined the fray. In an impassioned article in the New York Times on the following Sunday, Hilton Kramer decried a "catastrophic shift in government policy in cultural affairs" and the beginning of "a new era marked by an aggressive politicization of federal cultural policy." These events were apparently being initiated by the appointments of Biddle and Duffey--both of which bore "the stigma of cynical political convenience."[39] Three days later, the administration retaliated through Vice President Mondale who, while officiating at the swearing-in ceremony of Joseph Duffey as the new chairman of the Humanities Endowment, delivered a strong defense of the appointments and of the administration's

avowed aim of making the two endowments less elitist.[40]
Although the controversy cooled after this flash-point,
it later reemerged as part of the elitist/populist
controversy as charges of politicization suggested that
quality considerations in awarding grants and in select-
ing panelists were being sacrificed to concerns for
geographic dispersion, ethnic, racial and minority
representation, and aesthetic diversity.[41]

The argument for geographical dispersion, in particular, has an old and respected basis. As Dick Netzer
puts it, "a general rule of public finance . . . is that
the geographic area in which the benefits from a
particular expenditure are realized should correspond
roughly to the geographic area within which taxes are
collected to finance that expenditure. . . ."[42] As
applied to NEA funding policies, this philosophy
supports wide dispersion, rather than the concentration,
of funds in support of the arts. This argument may also
be phrased in terms of accountability. For example,
Douglas Fox asked whether arts institutions which are
granted large public subsidies did not bear an obligation to make themselves more available (responsive) to
the publics that could not afford their normal ticket
prices.[43] It is also evident that dispersion is seen
not only in geographic terms, but in what might be
called "affirmative action" terms. This aspect of the
argument was well put by Joan Mondale when she commented
that ". . . you've got to remember that most dancers and
actors and musicians are white, educated, middle class
people. And you can't help them when there's this big
social problem to be solved with the blacks and other
minority groups."[44]

Politicization of arts policy has also occurred in
two other ways that seem to have touched off less public
outcry. Nevertheless, they demonstrate that any subject
of public policy becomes a matter of politics. The
first development has been the linkages among arts
policy and other, larger, well-entrenched public policy
issues. From its earliest days, arts policy--indeed,
the very establishment of the National Endowment for the
Arts--has been linked to educational interests. The
power of the educational/academic community was an
important, perhaps crucial, element in securing the
creation of the two endowments.[45] The Arts Endowment's
educational programs, particularly the Artists-in-
Schools program, testified to the continued relationship
between art and education and was designed to "raise the
consciousness of all about the values of the arts as an
integral part of the general education of all children"
and as a means of enriching and intensifying the
educational experience.[46] Although this program is
currently in the process of being redirected toward the
development and training of artists and arts educators,

it still illustrates the commonality of policy interests between arts and education.

If the arts/education policy nexus has been somewhat deemphasized, it has become supplemented by the rise of other policy connections--namely to economic and urban policies. Indeed, a spokesman for the Carter administration pointed to the administration's efforts "to assist and encourage the many other federal agencies, such as the Department of Education, the Department of Labor, the Veterans Administration, and the Small Business Administration to incorporate the arts in their efforts to effect social, environmental, and economic progress.[47] The connection to economic policy has been developing since the mid-1960's and emerged vividly during the Carter administration. This argument links arts activity to economic vitality, presenting evidence that arts activity has an impact on the economic life of the cities that ripples to the county and state level. As a 1978 report from the U.S. Commerce Department stated, cultural activities act as "people magnets" which stimulate tourism and expand demand for attendent restaurant, hotel, and transportation facilities. Economic benefits may also be generated from construction and business interest attracted by cultural activities. The impact of Lincoln Center on the surrounding area is frequently used as an example of this phenomenon. In the twenty years since the establishment of Lincoln Center, the neighborhood has been transformed from a slum into "one of the city's most fashionable residential quarters," and has stimulated over $600 million of new construction that has brought the city a 400 percent increase in real estate tax revenues.[48]

The popularity and political utility of the economic impact arguments to justify support for the arts was demonstrated to the incoming Carter administration which recognized the possibility of linking a policy of support for the arts with the larger campaign issues of jobs and the economy. Thus, it found a rationale for a policy which might otherwise have been difficult to support in a period of tight money and budgetary cutbacks. The Carter administration adopted the economic impact argument and used it to strengthen the economic arts relationship by portraying the arts as an industry that gave a very "profitable" return for the money invested therein.[49] This perspective was further underlined by the creation of the post of Special Assistant for Cultural Resources in the Commerce Department as a tactic to "legitimize" the validity of the economic impact argument and of the arts as industry.[50] Recently this linkage has become a frequent refrain among art administrators. For example, Beverly Sills, managing director of the New York City Opera, argued that "the arts are meat and potatoes . . ." and, "we are no longer frills, we are big business and we must be taken much more seriously."[51]

A natural extension of the economic impact argument links the arts to employment issues and the urban economy. Since the arts are essentially a labor-intensive, service industry, they can be easily tied to the general issues of jobs and employment. The extension of CETA job training opportunities in the arts has become a means of not only coping with artist unemployment (and underemployment), but also an indirect subsidy by underwriting administrative costs.[52] Regarding the urban economy, the Lincoln Center case dramatically demonstrated that the arts can play an important role in urban revitalization efforts. During the Carter administration, this policy linkage was developed primarily through the Economic Development Administration which encouraged the inclusion of a cultural element in urban planning. This has, in turn, stimulated the interest of state and local groups--like the U.S. Conference of Mayors, the National League of Cities, the National Governors' Association, and the National Conference of State Legislators--to establish arts task forces for disseminating information about funding arts projects as tools of economic development.

Finally, arts policy has been politicized through the mobilization of an arts constituency. In the last five years, elected officials of all varieties have discovered that the arts community can mobilize a vocal, visible, and effective lobby. In 1977 Congressman Brademas (D-Ind.) declared that:

> The arts [had become] politically saleable. Now a Congressman could get into more difficulty voting against the arts than for. All the evidence points to the fact that Federal support has become not only acceptable but popular.[55]

Arts groups have learned the power of organization and numbers and have taken steps to enhance their effectiveness as advocates. Arts interests, like other special interests, have learned that the key to continued political support is the ability to represent their private good as the public good.

Virtually every art form has a national association that can pursue and protect its political interests; for example, the Association of Art Museum Directors, the Association of Dance Companies, and OPERA America. Professional journals, like Museum News, inform their members on effective lobbying techniques.[55] The National Committee for Symphony Orchestra Support has designed a pamphlet manual on lobbying entitled

"Orchestras and Advocacy: How to Structure a Public Affairs Committee on Your Board." While these organizations are capable of acting independently to protect their special artistic interests, they have also recognized the possibility of cooperative efforts. Late in 1977 museum, dance, music, opera, and theatre interests joined to form the American Alliance for the Arts. Leaders of the alliance emphasized that by pooling their efforts the arts hoped to "have a much more powerful impact on Congress, the White House, government agencies and the general public" and that an "assertive voice was necessary not only for legislation on the arts . . . but also for such seemingly unrelated matters as energy, tax reform, social security, and the postal system."[56]

National associations have also been established to link and mobilize public arts agencies. Within two years of the creation of the last of the state arts agencies, the National Association of State Arts Agencies (NASAA) was established. Initially, NASAA's primary responsibility was facilitating communication between the field and Washington; later it coordinated inter-state communications among state arts agencies. In 1979 NASAA officially registered as a lobby. There is also the National Association of Community Arts Agencies facilitating communications and coordination among municipal and county arts agencies. In addition, a multitude of citizens groups have begun to appear on behalf of the arts. Groups such as the Ohio Citizens Committee for the Arts or Concerned Citizens for the Arts of New York State focused their lobbying efforts on Washington, D.C. as well on their own state capitols. These activities are establishing a reservoir of knowledgeable arts advocates across the country which has the potential of national mobilization in the future.

The 1960's saw the establishment and acceptance of the principle of public support for the arts. The 1970's saw a heightening of both public and governmental awareness of, and support for, policies central to that principle. The 1980's are witnessing a continuing controversey over public arts programs in a setting of ideological conservatisism and fiscal austerity. While few public policies attract unanimous political support, issues of arts policy seem to generate a disproportionate amount of controversy. But few governmental activities can affect personal values as dramatically as cultural programs. Controversies over how we support the arts invariably involve questions of what art is supported and at whose expense. The determination of such value-laden issues is rarely an uncontroversial matter.

NOTES

[1] For a brief discussion of art in colonial America, see Carl N. Degler, Out of Our Past (New York: Harper and Row, 1962), pp. 40-42.

[2] As quoted in Bernard Rosenberg and David Manning, eds., Mass Culture (New York: Free Press, 1964), pp. 28, 30.

[3] Ibid., p. 27.

[4] Anthony L. Barresi, "Federal Commitment to the Arts: An Historical Tracing," American Arts 2 (May 1980): 22-25.

[5] Ronald Berman, "Art versus The Arts," Commentary 68 (November 1979): 46-48.

[6] Paul Dimaggio and Michael Useem, "Cultural Policy and Public Policy: Emerging Tensions on Government Support for the Arts," Social Research 45 (Summer 1978): 369.

[7] This is derived from a combination of Herbert Gans's "high" and "upper middle cultures". He differentiates the two as distinct "taste cultures". Here, however, they seem to share policy proclivities and certaintly have more in common with each other than with other cultures. See Herbert Gans, Popular Culture and High Culture (New York: Basic Books, Inc., 1974), pp. 75-94.

[8] National Endowment for the Arts, General Plan, 1980-84 (Washington, D.C., April 1979), p. 5.

[9] Dimaggio and Useem, "Cultural Policy," p. 369.

[10] National Endowment for the Arts, General Plan, p. 6.

[11] Former Deputy Chairman of the Arts Endowment, Michael Straight, speaks to this point in Malcolm Carter, "The NEA: Will Success Spoil Our Biggest Patron?" Arts News 76 (May 1977): 32-40.

[12] National Endowment for the Arts, General Plan, p. 6.

[13] See for instance "The Year in Review" in the Annual Report, 1978, National Endowment for the Arts, (Washington, D.C.: September, 1979), p.7.

[14] For New York State Council on the Arts budgetary data, National Endowment for the Arts, The State Arts Agencies in 1974: All Present and Accounted For (Washington, D.C., April, 1978).

[15] For a detailed description and analysis of the Arts Endowment's budgetary history, see C. Richard Swaim, "The Budgetary Process of the Arts Endowment," paper presented at the American Political Science Association Annual Meeting, Washington, D.C., 1977. According to this study, Arts Endowment funds increased at a rate that varied between twenty-three percent and ninety-seven percent during 1971 through 1975 and that before and after this period funds increased

incrementally in a range of three to ten percent.
   [16]National Endowment for the Arts, General Plan, p. 150.
   [17]The Ford Foundation, The Finances of the Performing Arts, Volume 1, (New York, 1974).
   [18]Some of the problems or drawbacks of more corportate funding for the arts became evident during 1980 when New York City proposed decreased funding for cultural affairs. During the spring of 1980 as the cut was debated, the arts community made an attempt to solicit increased corporate funding. This effort, as a headline from the New York Times made clear, caused business to bristle at the prospect of making up for cuts in public financing because to do so would, in the words of Robert F. Longley of Morgan Gauranty Trust, "mean cutting back on contributions to education and other worthy recipients."
   Also, as part of the debate, Martin E. Siegel, a former New York City Commissioner of Cultural Affairs argued in the editorial section of the New York Times that it was inadvisable for the city to expect cooperations to take up the slack in public funding. He argued that this could set the city in competition with cultural organizations for corporate and foundation support and, furthermore, that such an effort amounted to special corporate tax.
   [19]Dick Netzer, The Subsidized Muse (New York: Cambridge University Press, 1978), p. 41.
   [20]John W. Gardner, Excellence, Can We Be Equal and Excellent Too? (New York: Harper and Row, 1961), especially, pp. 109-126.
   [21]For expressions of Thomas Jefferson on the "natural aristocracy" see "Letter to John Adams" dated Monticello, October 28, 1813, The Writings of Thomas Jefferson, Volume XIII, (Washington, D.C.: The Thomas Jefferson Memorial Association, 1904), pp. 396-397.
   [22]Barbara Tuchman recently made this point in general about quality implying elitism and the disrepute that quality has recently acquired, see "The Decline in Quality," New York Times Magazine, November 2, 1980, particulary p. 41.
   [23]Lincoln Kirstein, "The Performing Arts and Our Egregious Elite," in W. McNeil Lowry, ed., The Performing Arts and American Society (Englewood Cliffs, NJ: Prentice Hall/Spectrum Books, 1978), pp. 156-196.
   [24] Quoted in the New York Times, April 27, 1978.
   [25]The remarks by Barnes, Rudel, and Chapin were all included in an article by Clive Barnes, "The Arts in America: Optimism Tempered by Need," New York Times, August 29, 1976, sec. 2, p. 16.
   [26]DiMaggio and Useem, "Cultural Policy," p. 282.
   [27]Barnes, "The Arts in America."
   [28]Joan Mondale, a Carter Administration advocate for

the arts, spoke in a 1977 interview about rediscovering artworks in the American heartland. See Robert Brustein, "Whither the National Arts and Humanities Endowments," New York Times, December 18, 1977, sec. 2, p. 35.

[29] Ben Yagoda, "Uncle Sam as Impresario: Are We Funding Junk?" Saturday Review, July 1980, p. 15.

[30] New York Times, January 29, 1980.

[31] John Friedman, "A Populist Shift in Federal Cultural Support," New York Times, May 13, 1979, sec. 2, p. 1.

[32] Ibid., p. 35.

[33] Ibid.

[34] As quoted in the New York Times, October 12, 1977.

[35] For a discussion of the controversey surrounding the replacement of Berman with Duffey, see Grace Gulek, "Filling the Humanities Post Is An Art," New York Times, June 28, 1977.

[36] See John S. Friedman "Mr. Duffy Goes to the Humanities Endowment," New York Times, August 21, 1977, sec. 2, pp. 1, 12.

[37] On Hanks's resignation, see the New York Times, August 30, 1977.

[38] New York Times, October 19, 1977.

[39] Hilton Kramer, "The Threat of Politicization of Federal Arts Programs," New York Times, October 16, 1977, sec. 2, pp. 1, 36.

[40] New York Times, October 19, 1977.

[41] For a general discussion, see John S. Friedman, "A Populist Shift," New York Times, May 13, 1979, sec. 2, pp. 1, 35. See also Robert Mayer, "The Arts Debate: Elitism versus Populism," Grants Magazine, March 1979, pp. 25-30.

[42] Netzer, The Subsidized Muse, p. 167.

[43] Douglas M. Fox, "Government Support for the Arts: A Review Essay," Public Administration Review 36 (August 1976): 451-454. Dick Netzer also addresses the accountability issue in The Subsidized Muse, pp. 34-35.

[44] Quoted in Brustein, "Whither the National . . . Endowments?" New York Times, December 18, 1977, sec. 2, p. 35.

[45] Interview with Congressman Frank Thompson, July 16, 1979, Washington, D.C.

[46] National Endowment for the Arts, General Plan, pp. 58, 59.

[47] American Arts 11 (May 1980): 19.

[48] New York Times, May 21, 1979.

[49] This is often called the multiplier effect. For example, Amyas Ames estimated that every dollar spent on the arts in New York City generated another $1.40 in other business revenues, see the New York Times, March 5, 1980. New York State Arts Council Chairman Kitty

Carlisle Hart, estimated that "every dollar for arts comes back three or four-fold." See the New York Times, February 5, 1980. An econometric model depicting this multiplier effect has been developed. See David Cwi and Katherine Lyall, Economic Impact of Arts and Institutions: A Model for Assessment and A Case Study in Cultural Institutions of Baltimore (Washington, D.C.: National Endowment for the Arts, 1978).

[50]Interview with Louise Wiener, July 27, 1979, Washington, D.C. See also a January 3, 1977 article in the New York Times regarding a transition study group on the arts.

[51]New York Times, February 5, 1980.

[52]For a brief discussion of CETA and the arts, see the National Journal December 15, 1979, p. 2106.

[53]Jerry Hagstrom, "Bring People Back Downtown With A Little Help From the Arts," National Journal, December 15, 1979, pp. 2104-2107.

[54]New York Times, September 4, 1977, sec. 2, p. 18.

[55]See, for instance, the article by Carole R. Achterhof, "How to Lobby for the Arts," Museum News 57 (May-June 1979): 19-22.

[56]New York Times, November 15, 1977.

3
The Rationale
for Public Culture

Kevin V. Mulcahy

Save for the brief, noble experiment with public culture in the New Deal era, the United States has no record of significant government patronage of the arts. Indeed, the record points to a separation between state and culture that has been justified as republican simplicity, democratic restraint, and nonpartisan parsimony. Worse, the Works Progress Administration (WPA) arts programs during the New Deal left a legacy of suspicion between the governmental and cultural worlds. The estrangement between government and public culture in the United States ended in 1965. While the establishment of the National Endowment for the Arts (NEA) did not exactly herald the arrival of a full-blown public culture, it did signal the end of hostilities. Although the Reagan administration has cut the NEA's budget drastically, a public commitment to culture still exists--however tenuously.

If the federal government was not exactly to be a patron of the arts, it was willing to be a season subscriber--that is, a guarantor of support for cultural activities on a regular basis. More important, our large cultural institutions, especially the museums and orchestras, had succeeded in persuading the government that the financial conditions of culture required a public subsidy to survive. They also argued that culture was deserving of such a subsidy because of its economic contribution to the local economy and because of its social contribution to the local environment. Cultural policy now became part of a larger commitment to social policy. Culture deserved support because it contributed to the public good.

But is this an adequate justification in support of public culture? I would argue that a public arts policy needs a stronger basis for its existence than the somewhat vague and, often unsupported, assertion that it is an incontestable public good. The need for some rationale for public support is especially necessary given the growing mood of budget-cutting. The double-barrelled attack--that "public arts programs are frills," and "the culture funded is unrepresentative"-- has made continued support for public culture difficult and politically controversial.

In the past twenty years, public culture has gone from being unthinkable to popular to questionable. Such volatility may be inherent in the nature of cultural policymaking. Since it touches on our basic societal values, public support for culture can elicit strong public reactions. This discussion examines the various arguments that are offered in favor of government subsidy for the arts. Not all the arguments are of equal importance; but each one provides an insight into how the case for public culture is perceived by its various supporters. By examining each of the arguments (economic, educational, moral, political), I hope that a rationale for public culture will become clearer. In effect, this is a public commitment to the principle that culture is a good in itself and government subsidy is necessary to guarantee its preservation and to increase its accessibility.

THE ECONOMIC ARGUMENT

Requests for public subsidies stem from the financial deficits incurred by most cultural institutions. All houses of culture lose money; great houses, like the Metropolitan Opera, lose money on a truly grand scale. (The exceptions are theatres and movie houses which are almost always profit-making, although there are subsidized repertory theatres and art houses.) It is not that seats are empty. The Metropolitan Opera, for example, averages a ninety-three percent of capacity house but ticket sales account for less than half of the revenue needed. Many companies lose money even when there is standing-room-only. The costs of artistic production are simply so high that they cannot be matched by reasonable admissions prices. Moreover, production costs tend to rise geometrically while ticket prices can only be raised arithmetically.

Admittedly, cultural institutions are somewhat conditioned to "cry wolf" financially in order to scare up donations, both public and private. This is an argument that Dick Netzer makes in his study of public support for the arts in the United States.

> Like all other industries, the performing arts generally fall short of maximum efficiency. Hence, they have significant unexploited

> opportunities to increase technical effi-
> ciency. . . . And in fact there is abundant
> evidence that productivity in the arts is not
> completely stagnant, in part because of new
> technology, in part because of more efficient
> use of existing technology.[1]

Netzer concludes that subsidies are difficult to justify
for arts organizations that are not operating in the
most efficient and economic manner possible. This is
true enough and certainly recognized by arts organizations themselves. What the organizations also realize
is that the criteria of economy and efficiency have
peculiar limitations in the delivery of a cultural
product as they do in the delivery of other public
programs such as education, welfare, and health care.
    Indeed, there are many similarities between arts
organizations and these social service agencies: labor
intensity, limits on standardization and technical
innovation, increasing employee militancy resulting from
unionization and professionalization. All add up to
higher labor costs and greater capital investment. As
Netzer acknowledges, a string quartet requires four
players; they can only play the Beethoven Op. 132 so
fast; a film or recording of the Guaneri or Julliard
Quartets is not the same aesthetic experience as a live
hearing. Or consider the case of grand opera. Even
within the performing arts world opera is regarded as
both rara avis and dinosaur-rare because only found in
full plumage (that is, a complete season) in New York,
Chicago, and San Francisco; anachronistic because its
production costs (and, to some extent, its aesthetic
sensibility) are completely off-scale by contemporary
standards. The Rockefeller Report on the Performing
Arts put it this way:

> Of all the performing arts, grand opera can
> clearly be the most spectacular, the most
> aristocratic, and the most expensive . . .
> With huge production costs and sizable reper-
> tory, a grand opera company can stand in
> magnificent solitude, dwarfing by sheer magni-
> tude dramas . . . orchestras . . . and even
> ballet.[2]

    Even so, the Metropolitan Opera, the grandest of
the grand opera companies in the United States, received
75 percent of its operating expenses from box office
receipts--compared to 30 percent at the Vienna Statsoper
and 20 percent at La Scala. Professor Netzer makes the
following concession:

> The Met's financial problems cannot be traced

> to management sloth, lethargic fund raising,
> unwillingness to invade capital, or any of the
> other all-too-common characteristics of
> venerable non-profit organizations; the basic
> difficulty is the inherently high cost of
> presenting high-quality grand opera.[3]

Why then do we continue to produce an art form whose
audience appeal is so highly select? Wagner observed
that opera was the synthesis of all other art forms:
music, drama, poetry, dance, architecture; hence, it
must be the best art form. This is certainly a debatable proposition. However, opera is recognized as a
unique and invaluable expression of our cultural heritage: it is an expression that we wish to see continued
despite a cost that cannot be supported by market
economics. Again, I think that Netzer puts it very
well.

> The Metropolitan Opera is one of perhaps a
> half-dozen such companies in the world today,
> the only one in this hemisphere and, arguably,
> the best in the world. It is, in two senses,
> the United States counterpart to the Royal
> Shakespeare Company: our premier national
> theater and our entry into an art form in
> which we do as well as or better than anyone
> else. The evidence of the past fifteen years
> indicates that the Met cannot be supported at
> the box office or on the basis of the box
> office plus private contributions. If it is
> to survive, it will require government support
> on a large scale.[4]

What is true of the Metropolitan Opera in so
dramatic a fashion is true of all cultural institutions.
These institutions are weak in the market place because
of characteristics inherent to their organizational
structure.[5] (1) Since labor costs increase yearly,
production costs rise constantly. (2) Cultural production does not lend itself to assembly-line methods but
requires single-unit production. (3) For the most part,
audiences cannot be substantially increased without
incurring further costs: larger halls or extra performances. (4) Since it is very difficult to judge
audience reaction to new productions, risk estimation is
very difficult. (5) And, since the performing arts are
"live," the organization cannot build up an inventory
for the reduction of risk.

The Committee for Cultural Resources observed that
this leads to a paradox: "The more technologically
advanced we become as a nation, the greater the economic
burden on arts organizations." As its <u>National Report</u>

on the Arts concluded, the only solution to this problem is a government subsidy of twenty percent of the total costs of arts organizations (ten percent each from state and federal sources). This is needed "to maintain the quality and stability of the nation's arts organizations and to enable them to provide full service to the public."[6]   In fact, public support today probably accounts for about fifteen percent of the total operating expenses of museums and performing arts organizations in the United States.   That this is insufficient is clear to the cultural world.   That the formula for distributions of funds needs evaluation is increasingly evident.   What is also painfully apparent is that this subsidy will face continued cuts in the face of budgetary austerity and political criticism.

The existence of a public subsidy does not necessarily eliminate incentives for economizing or finding private sources of support.   But since there will increasingly be more arts organizations needing support than money available, grantmaking agencies will have to establish criteria for rewarding organizations that keep their costs under control.   This means that public arts agencies will have to rank cultural objectives according to some standard of public support.   Public subsidy has softened some of the economic realities of artistic production while making our cultural heritage more widely available.   The assisted arts organizations have an obligation on their part "to maintain the highest possible production standards;   serve the community as broadly as possible;   perpetuate the finest in our artistic heritage; develop new and experimental works; provide opportunities for new talent; maintain educational programs."[7]

The Rockefeller Panel that first studied the contemporary condition of the performing arts saw an analogy between box office proceeds and tuition charges in the financing of universities and arts organizations.   The Report observed that, if tuition were raised to the point where it covered costs, "the broad diffusion of higher education would be impossible."[8] This is also true of arts organizations.   Indeed, the importance of people's access to their cultural heritage "provides as strong an argument for public support as did the arguments that led to the historic development of universal public education in this country."[9]   Few would argue that public support for education is without socioeconomic biases.   As one moves up the income scale, one finds greater success in school and greater use of learning resources.   For that matter, a visit to the public library would disabuse anyone of the notion that it is being used by the population-at-large;   so too would a survey of the users of national parks and wilderness areas.

The point is that national parks, libraries, and colleges are all unrepresentative in that they are not used equally by all social groups. But to say that a subsidy is unrepresentative does not mean that it is undesirable. Culture should stop claiming to be what it is not and arts organizations should stop apologizing for their public support. Public support for the arts--especially given the recent vintage of that support--should come under scrutiny after, not before, all the other "unrepresentative," "undemocratic" subsidies that have a claim on the public purse have been reevaluated.

THE SOCIAL ARGUMENT

That public support for the arts should stand on its own, without buttressing by claims of utility or equity, seems difficult for its advocates to allow. It takes a skeptic such as Dick Netzer to make the straight-forward argument for culture as a good-in-itself worthy of public subsidy. In the following example, he speaks again of defending public support for the Metropolitan Opera.

> But this support cannot be justified as building audiences, educating the young, or making grand opera accessible to people with low incomes. No matter how vigorously reduced-price ticket schemes, special youth programs, or media exposure are promoted, the typical audience for grand-opera live performances at the Metropolitan Opera will remain relatively small and (as long as there is any real effort to defray a significant part of the Met's costs from box office receipts) relatively affluent. The decision to subsidize the Met from public funds must be based on a straightforward "merit-goods" argument: the Met is a good thing that should be perpetuated and can be perpetuated only with fairly large amounts of public subsidy.[10]

While this seems a farly simple assertion, it is not one with which the cultural world seems comfortable. Much time has been taken to justify arts organizations as socially responsible and much cant spoken about how public subsidy has increased, and more public subsidy will further increase, the numbers of the young, the poor, and members of minority groups in cultural audiences. To argue the social utility of the arts has been an enduring theme with cultural institutions in the

United States. Museum leaders, for example, have gone out of their way to preach a gospel of cultural uplift--improving the lot of the working man through exposure to high culture. Joseph C. Choate, a trustee of the Metropolitan Museum of Art, declared in 1880 that the museum had been founded in the belief "that the diffusion of a knowledge of art in its higher forms of beauty would tend directly to humanize, to educate and refine a practical and laborious people . . . " No longer the exclusive preserve of the rich, art now belonged to the general populace; it "has become their best resources and most efficient education" and was now "the vital and practical interest of the working millions."[11]

Much of the contemporary argument for public support has had such a missionary zeal about it. Arts organizations argue that government subsidy allows them to offer "out-reach" programs to those currently outside the cultural world. Public arts agencies defend their appropriations before legislative committees with examples of the breadth of appeal that the funded programs have to the the population-at-large (or, more especially, to the constituents of the elected official before whom they are testifying). In reporting on the "results of a ten-year investment" by the National Endowment for the Arts, then Chairman Nancy Hanks highlighted the following:

> (1) An effective Federal-State partnership program is one way to achieve our legislative mandate of making the arts more available."
> (2) Endowment-sponsored programs have helped to make the arts more available through arts programming in the neighborhoods and in the schools.
> (3) The Expansion Arts program has encouraged "the creative vitality of our citizens in inner cities, in geographically isolated communities, rural areas, among those less privileged than others. Because of Endowment initiatives, these needs are receiving a new national focus as are the needs in jazz and in folk art and crafts, the arts indigenous to our heritage.[12]

Mrs. Hanks also addressed herself to the Endowment's other goals of developing the nation's cultural resources and of advancing its cultural legacy. Throughout her testimony the theme of the Endowment's social utility sounds clearly. This is not to fault what was in fact sound political judgment, nor to suggest that this programmatic emphasis on "cultural outreach" is not well-intentioned (if at times a bit patronizing). The problem is that these elaborate efforts to justify cultural policy as a subset of social policy--that is, cultural equity is to social equality as the redistribution of artistic opportunities is to the redistribution of economic opportunities--have not been borne out by the empirical evidence.

Audience composition is the focus for most of the uneasiness of supporters of public culture. This audience should not be too well-to-do, too white, or too "elitist"; policy should be directed at achieving an audience that is more "representative" of the public-at-large. After fifteen years of attempting to "democratize" the cultural audience, the data strongly indicate that this goal has not been achieved (although the Endowment has shown no want of effort). The basis for these conclusions is an independent evaluation commissioned by the Research Division of the National Endowment for the Arts in 1978.[13] This report examined 270 audience studies of the performing arts and museums to determine the general characteristics of the "culture-consuming public." This arts public was found to differ from the general public on several measures of socioeconomic status.

Educational attainment is the single most salient characteristic of the cultural public. Over 50 percent of its members had college degrees (compared to 24 percent of the adult population); about 30 percent had post-graduate training. Similarly, the employed members of this public were largely professionals: 56 percent of those surveyed (compared to 15 percent of the employed work force). Teachers made up 21 percent of museum-goers and performing arts attenders but only four percent of the workforce. High income is associated with cultural participation but not to the same degree as education and occupation. Given the strong correlation between social status attendance at cultural events, it should not be surprising that racial and ethnic minorities are underrepresented compared to their proportion of the population-at-large.

But it should be noted here that differences exist in attendance among the cultural institutions. Racial and ethnic minorities are estimated to account for seven percent of cultural attendance while making up twenty percent of the total population; these minorities, however, constitute eleven percent of the attendance at non-art museums (those devoted to natural history, science, history, technology). Museums in general, and non-art museums in particular, are more "representative" than performing arts institutions. Compared to the other performing arts, theatre-goers were also more representative in that they were less wealthy, well-educated, and less likely to be professionals than other audiences.[14]   "In sum, the studies show that the culture-consuming public is more educated, has higher incomes, and has higher status jobs than the general public."[15]

There is no evidence from studies conducted over the past fifteen years that cultural audiences are becoming more "democratic," that is, representative of the population-at-large in educational level and socioeconomic status. This should not be so startling nor need it be distressing. While culture may speak to everyone, not everyone chooses to listen; nor is everyone conditioned to listen. Moreover, the strongest association with cultural attendance is educational attainment--not income level. Doubtless, this is because schools provide training in artistic skills and encourage cultural understanding. Increased educational attainment may be associated with greater awareness of aesthetic values, creating a habit of cultural participation. Indeed, the heavy representation of teachers in the cultural public affirms the importance of education as a determinant of artistic awareness. As the transmitters of our cultural heritage, teachers are quite likely to be sensitive to the arts.

To be aesthetically self-conscious, artistically aware, culturally active is a specialized type of behavior as is political involvement or, for that matter, voting. Yet, we do not reject elections because voting behavior is unrepresentative although we are disturbed about the shrinking size of the electorate. It was the defenders of public support for the arts who argued their case on the grounds that such support would result in a more democratic audience. Despite great efforts by both public arts agencies and cultural organizations, this has not occurred; nor is it likely to do so given foreseeable social and economic arrangements. The advocates of public culture are well rid of that line of argument: an overly defensive, somewhat tiresome search for justification by claiming to serve a civilizing influence or to provide cultural socialization for the masses. In fact, public support for culture has increased access to the art world even if it has not broadened the sociological composition of the audience. Meaningful cultural participation is less dependent than ever on geography, place of residence, and income. Great progress has been made toward equality of cultural opportunity. What has not been realized is an equality of result that would mean universal cultural participation.

THE EDUCATIONAL ARGUMENT

Some of the social arguments for culture are reminiscent of certain instrumental arguments in favor of higher education, especially the claim that a college education pays off in higher earnings. Thus, there was consternation in educational circles when economic studies demonstrated that the money spent (direct and indirect) on a college education would yield a higher return to the student if invested in things other than tuition. Higher education did not seem to produce the profits claimed. All of the tortured explanations to the contrary were rather silly. As most college students—particularly those who are the first-generation to attend—are aware, the diploma is really a passport into a world of middle-class values and taste preferences. A college education means that a whole array of life opportunities (if not realities) becomes available. It is the quality of one's life that will be enhanced, not just the quantity of material goods. Education can thus be viewed as a means of social uplift by which more people may acquire the aesthetic concerns that make them part of the cultural public.

Increasing educational attainment has been shown to be strongly associated with attendance at cultural events. Some have interpreted this association as an example of social class stratification and exclusionary policies.

> The upper class can be expected to make efforts to exclude other classes from acquiring its artistic interests as a means of preserving elite boundaries and dominance from generation to generation. At the same time, as a strategy for gaining access to the positions, economic resources, and social community of the upper class, individual members of other classes, especially the upper-middle class, are likely to strive to acquire the cultural style necessary for upward mobility. Enrollment in elite universities and cultivation of "high brow" artistic tastes are both means for achieving this end.[16]

The problem with such a theory of cultural stratification is that there is little evidence of class-exclusionary policies by artistic organizations. As we have discussed, the American cultural establishment seems rather uncomfortable with its elitism and seeks to expand its appeal to as broad a spectrum of social classes as possible. However unsuccessful "cultural

outreach" may have been in changing audience configuration, cultural organizations cannot be faulted for want
of effort or good intentions. Cultural critics are
correct, however, when they suggest that divergent life
experiences and cultural traditions seem to influence
one's receptiveness to, and familiarity with, high
culture. A cultural sensibility (like other affective
attitudes) is a habit of the mind, a conditioning
developed through early exposure and encouragement and
there is a distinct advantage in coming from an
artistically sophisticated background.

> In the case of the high arts, the correspond-
> ing cultural codes are most strongly
> established and cultivated in the upper and
> upper-middle classes, particularly certain
> professional sectors and old-line patrician
> fractions. For the latter, high arts consump-
> tion is a matter of unconscious deciphering
> with an ease that is rooted in prolonged
> family socialization into the world of elite
> culture. In the absence of such a family
> background, others can self-consciously though
> sometimes awkwardly acquire the necessary
> training through other means, particularly
> schooling. Still others, lacking either
> appropriate family background or educational
> experiences, remain deprived of the means for
> appropriating the high arts throughout their
> lives.[17]

But this puts too much emphasis on a class propen-
sity for cultural excellence. Only prodigies acquire
artistic skills with ease; for the rest of us it is a
slow and self-conscious process regardless of class
background. What this analysis correctly emphasizes is
the importance of early childhood experiences for the
acquisition of cultural values. The findings in
Americans and the Arts provide strong evidence of the
close connection between attendance at museums and the
perfoming arts and early exposure to the arts through
cultural attendance when growing up. In particular, the
most frequent attenders of cultural events (people going
more than four times a year) are overwhelmingly those
who first attended before age twenty. This suggests
that early arts education can compensate for some of the
cultural limitations associated with income and
class.[18]

When surveyed about their attitudes concerning the
arts and children, people responded overwhelmingly (91
percent) that it is important for school-age children to
be exposed to cultural activities. On the other hand, a
substantial proportion (43 percent) said that school

children in their locality lacked sufficient opportunities to attend cultural events.[19]   Respondents also
reported strong support for arts teaching as part of the
regular school curriculum: 80 percent said that training in a musical instrument should be given for credit;
70 percent thought that credit should be given for art
appreciation; 79 percent said that the funding for arts
courses should come from the regular school budget.

> In conclusion, the public feels very strongly
> that children should have opportunities to go
> to arts events and performances and to study
> arts subjects in the schools.   The increasing
> support for the teaching of the arts as credit
> courses is evidence of the importance people
> attribute to this area.   This finding is
> especially significant at a time when, in some
> areas, suggestions are being made that school
> budgets should be cut in such subjects as the
> arts.   If these cuts were to be made, they
> would go completely counter to the public's
> views.[20]

But the arts curriculum is very often the first
area for massive retrenchment when public school budgets
are reduced and "unnecessary" programs abolished.   That
this is a shortsighted judgment should be clear.   That
it can also be cruel to deprive children of the one
source of artistic and aesthetic stimuli to which they
might have access should be equally clear.   It consigns
children, particularly poor children, to a future of
cultural poverty, artistic isolation, and limited
horizons.

Educators have also observed that there is no
distinction between the arts and general learning.   "In
fact, a student who really gets an appreciation for
beauty is much more apt to be able to read than one who
doesn't."[21]   These remarks were expressed during
proceedings of the Panel on Arts, Education and
Americans chaired by David Rockefeller, Jr.   The panel's
report argues for a heightened importance of the arts as
part of the American educational system.

> Perception and communication--both fundamental
> learning skills--require more than verbal
> training.   And since the arts (painting,
> dancing, singing, acting, and so forth) can
> send important nonverbal messages from a
> creator or performer to an observer, they are
> ideal vehicles for training our senses, for
> enriching our emotional selves and for
> organizing our environment.[22]

There is a strong argument that the educational
system has been delinquent in neglecting unconventional
modes of learning--whether because these are considered
irrelevant or subversive is a debatable issue.[23] The
National Endowment for the Arts has sought to remedy
some of these deficiencies through the Artists-in-
Schools Program which places professional artists in
elementary and secondary schools to demonstrate their
skills. However, since the NEA does not have arts
education as one of its legislatively defined purposes,
such a commitment will always be a peripheral interest.
Indeed, when confronted with an almost fifty percent cut
in its budget, the NEA proposed to virtually terminate
Artists-in-Schools programs.

The Rockefeller Panel recommended an expanded
cultural curriculum based on the principle that "the
fundamental goals of American education can be realized
only when the arts become central to the individual's
learning experience."[24] The goal of such a "cultural
program" is to broaden the cultural horizons of school
children, especially those from less-privileged
backgrounds. Increased emphasis on arts in education
may also provide opportunities for the artistically
gifted who might not otherwise have an awareness of, or
training in, their talent. Resident artists can
heighten self-awareness, stimulate students and
teachers, and help improve general learning skills and
conceptual abilities. At the very least, cultural
offerings can complement structured learning and logical
analysis and allow an opportunity to exercise creativity. What culture in the schools cannot do is
guarantee universal artistic appreciation.

Many supporters of public culture have been suspicious of school-arts programs on the grounds that they
do not foster true artistic achievement. Without
diminshing support for culturally-innovative programs,
greater emphasis on cultural education would help to
create an audience receptive to artistic excellence and
innovation. Arts education can also compensate for some
of the disparities in cultural opportunities that exist
because of socioeconomic differences. While education
cannot remedy the problems of cultural disequality, it
offers a vehicle for increasing opportunity that is
consonent with the traditional mission of American
schools.

THE MORAL ARGUMENT

Cultural advocates have often had a strong sense of
mission, and culture is for many a form of secular

religion. Attending concerts and going to museums can be a ritual replacing church attendance. Arguments in favor of public support for the arts can have almost theological (as well as moralistic) overtones. In his <u>Ministry of Art</u>, Ralph Adams Cram wrote in 1914 that art should serve "as an agency working toward the redemption of human character."[25] For Cram, culture is not important for aesthetic and intellectual reasons alone.

> Above all this, it is the touchstone of life, the power of standards, the director of choice. Accepted, assimilated, it becomes one of the great builders of character, linked indissolubly with religion and philosophy toward the final goal of right feeling, right thinking, and right conduct.[26]

After sixty-five years Cram's claims for the significance of culture seem either quaint or nonsensical depending on the reader's disposition. These words, and much of the sentiment behind them, must have seemed exaggerated to many of Cram's contemporaries. Yet, they do point to an assumption that, albeit infrequently expressed, does surface now and again in debates over public support for the arts. This is the belief that artists should not have to "grovel" for public support but should receive it as a matter of right and because of the inherent quality of artistic endeavors. Some artists, frustrated by the grant-making procedures of public arts agencies, demand that the money simply be distributed upon request and used as the artist deems best.

What is more disturbing than the political naivete is the political insensitivity, or indifference, that lies behind the words. It suggests an arrogance about having to justify claims to public money and a condescension to those who run the political process. Given the values of artistic organizations, such an indifference to politics is perhaps understandable. As one arts administrator put it: "The purpose of the not-for-profit artistic institution is to enable artists to create and communicate their output to the society-at-large according to their artistic conscience."[27] To be overly attentive to politics would require an arts organization to follow trends rather than to create them; to reinforce existing levels of aesthetic sensibility rather than to provide alternatives. Artists are conditioned to oppose outside control and to be hostile to what they see as interference with the creative process.

While the attitudes discussed above are a healthy safeguard against any limitations on artistic autonomy, they can lead to a moralistic assertion that "high"

culture is superior to other cultural expressions and
thus "deserves" to be supported. High culture is seen
as a creative process in which artists work to fulfill
personal ends by producing a unique, individual work.
This is contrasted with the mass-produced, consumer-
oriented product produced for public consumption.[28]
However, as Herbert Gans points out, many of our
cultural judgments are deeply rooted in educational
privilege and have distinct class biases. Moreover,
many opponents of mass culture have translated this
personal evaluation into a public policy position "which
not only ignores other people's private evaluations but
seeks to eliminate them altogether."[29] Gans argues that
such a stand is analytically indefensible and socially
unjustifiable. He would seek to replace such an
exclusionary cultural policy stand with a more
comprehensive approach.

> American society should pursue policies that
> would maximize educational and other
> opportunities for all so as to permit everyone
> to choose from higher taste cultures. Until
> such opportunities are available, however, it
> would be wrong to expect a society with a
> median education level of twelve years to
> choose only from taste cultures requiring a
> college education, or for that matter, to
> support through public policies the welfare of
> the higher cultures at the expense of the
> lower ones. Moreover, it would be wrong to
> criticize people for holding and applying
> aesthetic standards that are related to their
> educational background, and for participating
> in taste cultures reflecting this
> background.[30]

This judgment, which calls into question the claim
of high culture to a superior status, has caused some
discomfort among advocates of public support for the
arts. There is perhaps an inevitable uneasiness about
spending taxpayers' money to support cultural activities
with limited popular appeal. But this goes back again
to the assumption that public subsidy is justified only
if its beneficiaries constitute a perfectly normal
distribution--one in which all classes are represented
in proper proportions. One would be hard-pressed to
find any public policy which could demonstrate such an
outcome. Indeed, public policymaking is a process for
representing the plurality of societal interests, not
that elusive public interest.
As American society becomes increasingly well-
educated, high culture will enjoy an even larger
audience. The so-called "cultural explosion" of the

1960's was the demand of a new generation of better-educated Americans for artistic offerings consistent with their educational background. But artistic talent can also spring up in unlikely places with little regard to socioeconomic determinants. This suggests an important contribution that public support makes to high culture. As children of all classes are exposed to culture in the schools, it increases the likelihood that artistic talent will be recognized and developed among children of all backgrounds. In general the greater availability of the arts that is made possible through public subsidy makes more probable a culture that cuts across class barriers.

THE POLITICAL ARGUMENT

Given the atypicality of high culture, the extent of public support for government subsidy is all the more striking. The table below summarizes the magnitude of public support of the arts by level of government and type of cultural activity based on a 1975 survey of the American public.

TABLE 3.1
Attitudes Toward Government Support Of The Arts

CULTURAL ACTIVITY	LEVEL OF GOVERNMENT		
	LOCAL	STATE	FEDERAL
Art Museums	56%	55%	43%
Theatre Groups	38%	28%	22%
Symphony Orchestras	37%	27%	22%
Opera Companies	33%	26%	21%
Ballet or Modern Dance Companies	33%	26%	22%

Source: National Research Center for the Arts, Americans and the Arts, 1975: Highlights (New York: Associated Councils of the Arts, 1976), p. 21.

The public's ordering of the cultural activities preferred for subsidy suggests a relationship between level of support and degree of familiarity with a cultural activity. Museums, the most accessible of cultural institutions, rate most favorably in a claim for public support. Not surprisingly, people are most likely to support public programs with which they have had past (presumably favorable) experiences. Active, out-reach programs to expand museum attendance would seem to pay off in public popularity even if they do not succeed in "democratizing" the composition of the audience. Performing arts institutions, of course, have higher thresholds to casual attendance (ticket prices, scheduled programs) but they might benefit from further expanding such efforts. Surveys have also reported that "the best predictors of individual willingness to endorse government involvement are the individual's educational level (already shown to be one of the best indicators of arts attendance) and whether the individual is an active arts consumer."[31] Consequently, there is reason to believe that as educational levels increase and as culture is made generally more available (largely because of government subsidies), support for public culture will increase.

Despite this reassuring evidence of support for public culture, the arts are still a low public policy priority for most Americans. When asked to evaluate the importance of various community services, the arts ranked after health, transportation, education, law enforcement, housing, and recreation facilities.[32] This is easily understandable, given the importance of these programs for one's physical well-being. The ease with which the Reagan administration cut the NEA's budget suggests the political vulnerability of public culture. In California, a large majority approved of state government aid to cultural organizations in need of financial support. Yet, in the aftermath of the passage of Proposition 13, the budget of the California Arts Commission was cut by over fifty percent. California, home to the nation's largest concentration of artists, now ranks fifty-third (out of fifty-five) among states and territories in per capita support for the arts.

The public supports government subsidy for those cultural activities with which they are the most familiar. This underscores the importance of the milieu in which an artistic activity takes place. The barriers inherent in high culture itself are heightened by the social context and milieu in which the works are performed. For instance, open-air arts patrons have been found to be more representative of the local population in socioeconomic terms than are indoor audiences for the same type of artistic performance.[33] But perhaps the lowest barrier to participation in

cultural activities is found in public broadcasts. The
medium offers almost universal accessibility and an
absence of social intimidation; it is familiar,
unthreatening, and free. While not the same experience
as a live artistic performance, televised events and
artistic programming produced explicitly for television
offer valuable cultural experiences in themselves. The
Rockefeller Report urged that teachers take advantage of
their students' immense interest in television. "For
example, television programs could be discussed and
evaluated for artistic and value content and compared
with other more traditional arts media; arts performances presented on television could be assigned for
homework and used as a base for developing critical
skills."[34]   Indeed, public television may not only
transform the way in which cultural experiences are
acquired and developed; it may also shape a new
constituency to give political support for public
culture.

   There are dangers involved in following an approach
that is too political. Increasing budgetary allocations
for public arts agencies do not necessarily denote
successful public cultural policies (although decreasing
budgets make successful cultural policies virtually
impossible). Cultural policy must be judged relative to
some standards of artistic excellence. The seeming
absence of such criteria has brought public culture
under attack from some of its one-time supporters.
Ronald Berman, former chairman of the National Endowment
for the Humanities, attacked the NEA as "an agency that
donates entertainment."

> Its principles are to spread money as far as
> it will go; to imitate the workings of HEW and
> other domestic agencies; to insist upon forms
> of equity like age, color, and sex which are
> moral and political rather than artistic
> . . . to encourage political and quasi-
> political groups to support the administration
> by conveying funds to them, regardless of
> artistic effect, function, or capability, to
> identify art as hobbies, crafts, individual
> pursuits, group modes of "participation,"
> regional fairs, clambakes, or assertions of
> consciousness; and to suggest, above all, that
> the distribution of funds from a pork-barrel
> is the same thing that Van Eyck understood as
> patronage.[35]

Joseph Ziegler, writing in the same vein as Berman
decries the "crisis of the arts." He believes that the
shift from private to public funding has resulted in a
loss of the "freedom to concentrate on the exceptional."

The criteria for judgment of a public agency must necessarily be qualitative rather than quantitative.

> In short, public money is political money. As such, it tends to promote expansion, decentralization, and re-definition in order to show that the arts are reaching the broadest possible constituency of taxpayers and voters. The arts have become a form of revenue sharing, a way to get the people's money back to them in services.[36]

Public culture is judged tainted because it partakes of the political process: gathering constituency support, making appropriations on regional grounds, seeking broad citizen involvement, establishing principles of equity. But even if we admit that the distribution of public cultural funds has not been beyond reproach, what is the alternative? As Berman and Ziegler are aware, private patronage alone would not suffice, nor is there any tradition in the United States of political deference to the claims of an elite to superior judgment in cultural questions. What may have been true in the fifteenth century for Van Eyck is not true today. Moreover, it is a legitimate goal of a public policy to reach as many potentially concerned people as possible. While by law, the National Endowment for the Arts cannot (indeed, should not) produce art, it can support programs to make art (especially if broadly-defined) more widely available than would be the case under a system of exclusively private patronage.

We would also be gravely mistaken if we assumed that it is public culture alone that has been charged with making programmatic judgments on other than aesthetic grounds. Private arts organizations have also been criticized for subservience to box office proceeds and to the conservative taste of members of boards of trustees. Such considerations can have an authoritativeness equal to any governmental decree. In his study of the administration of the Philadelphia Orchestra, Edward Arian made the following observations about the values of its Board of Trustees:

> Without exception, the Board members interviewed were proud of the business-like way in which the Orchestra is run. To them, considerations of economy and efficiency took undisputed preference over any obligations which they may have felt that Orchestra owed to the community at large. . . . [T]he concept of making the Orchestra available to more people in the community through a variety of activities is personally distasteful to most

Board members and goes against their basic
values as businessmen.[37]

Arian sees a sharp dichotomy between a board's
business ethos and the cultural responsibilities of a
symphonic organization. He is critical, in particular,
of programming policies that refuse to provide an outlet
for new musical talent and that also abandon responsibility for the cultural education of the community.
"The result is that the appreciation and understanding
of symphonic audiences for the most part ends with
Tchaikovsky, Brahms, and Beethoven." Finding such an
aesthetic situation deplorable, Arian (at one time a
member of the Philadelphia Orchestra's string section)
concludes that a solution must be found to keep
orchestras financially solvent and, at the same time,
"socially responsible."[38]

Public subsidy enables cultural institutions to do
what they cannot afford and encourages them to do what
they would not otherwise consider. Public funds, for
example, can make possible low-cost concerts for groups
outside the usual concert-going clientele; allow performances and displays in smaller cities, work places,
shopping centers, health care facilities, and custodial
institutions; commission new works from lesser-known
artists; encourage and develop young talent. Professor
Arian is of the mind that there is more to the programming of an orchestra than to entertain and sell tickets;
it should also involve audience education, developing
aesthetic standards, and the exploration of innovative
music.[39] The realization of such comprehensive goals is
beyond the financial needs of any institution. More
important, such broad-scale determination of cultural
values should not be undertaken without the participation of those affected.

The problem is how to create a public culture that
is not an "official culture": that is, one propagated
by the state that serves its interests and legitimizes
its activities. The solution would seem to rest in
basing public support for the arts on a poicy of
cultural pluralism: not a pluralist policy by default
(because of an inability to define a public interest),
but a pluralism of choice (recognizing that it is not in
the public interest to define the content of culture).
For the government to favor a particular artistic style
or mode of expression is to risk the official establishment of that cultural form. But government support for
programs that encourage "grassroots" artistic activities
or "outreach" efforts by major institutions, while
definitely seeking to enhance their availability to a
larger public, influences only who is sharing in those
cultural activities, not what that culture is. The
public policy goal is procedural, not substantive;

government acts as a regulator to broaden access, to create greater social equality, to stimulate diversity.

This is not to suggest that a policy of cultural pluralism is without problems. One of the most fundamental is the perennial question of group representation. Which publics are to be included in shaping public culture? These are also questions about whether institutions will be diverted from fundraising efforts in the private sector to seek a public subsidy for operating expenses. Also, just how far in advance of community values can publicly supported culture be? Or for that matter, how critical can a cultural activity be of the public or a public agency that provides the funds? There are admittedly "political" issues of a sort that seem to disturb some critics of public culture. But it must be emphasized again that cultural institutions are already "politicized" by their boards of trustees and subscribers. (Box office receipts and contributions are no less influential than subsidies and grants.) And no one is proposing that public funding replace private sources of support. Public funding can partially free these institutions to provide more adventuresome programming, to reach out to new audiences, to keep admissions prices down while surviving financially. In effect, public subsidy allows a degree of experimentation and diversification that would not be possible in the existing artistic marketplace.

Public culture, especially one that is explicitly pluralistic, can seek to guarantee that the broad range of cultural heritages in this country receive support and recognition for the contributions that they have made. Public money joins corporate contributors and private philanthropy as sources of support for artistic activities; government officials join audience members, trustees, arts administators, critics, and artists as members of the cultural world. What public culture might seek is artistic programming that would be sensitive to different ethnic backgrounds, social classes, educational levels, ages, and places of residence. This would be an ambitious undertaking that, not surprisingly, has not yet been translated into a clearly-defined public cultural policy. What has been realized over the past fifteen years is a political commitment to the principle that the survival of cultural institutions, accessibility to cultural activities, and the preservation of endangered cultures (such as those of Cajuns and Native Americans) is a public good meriting government support. We might hope that this hard-won recognition does not fall victim to fiscal austerity.

THE CASE FOR PUBLIC CULTURE: SOME CONCLUSIONS

What can we say to sum up the case for public culture? The most basic argument rests on the belief that culture is good-in-itself: what economists would call a "merit-good" and what political scientists would call a "value." A society has an obligation to ensure that its noblest cultural accomplishments are passed on from one generation to the next; a liberal democratic society seeks to provide opportunities for cultural participation by as large a number of people and in as many different ways as feasible. Public support can work to insure that no one force becomes the arbiter of cultural standards--neither profit margins nor election returns.

In short, we as a nation agree not only that the arts are good for us but also that govern- ment intervention is necessary to assure more and better artistic production and consumption than would result from unaided pursuit of "narrower commercial purposes" by artists and artistic organizations.[40]

There is the danger that such government interven- tion could produce "cultural imperialism"--the offical imposition of aesthetic preferences. When Lord Reith was the head of the British Broadcasting Company, Sunday programming was almost exclusively symphonic. Such "good music" he doubtless believed to be good for the soul; and, that is what one got--like it or not. Since the BBC then had a monopoly on the air waves, the choice that one had was to listen to Lord Reith's judgment about what was good for you or not to listen at all. This is the sort of official tyranny that public culture should avoid; given the plurality of broadcasting licenses in the United States, it is also unlikely to happen. In fact, public broadcasting provides an alter- native to the commercial stations that too often program to the lowest common denominator of taste in pursuit of short-run profitmaking. Public broadcasting broadens the selection of programming available: PBS or the networks; National Public Radio or commercial stations; Masterpiece Theatre or Three's Company; philharmonic performances or Top 40. It offers choices without imposing a choice. Public broadcasting can represent a relatively easy and effective means to broaden the public's cultural horizons while respecting their right to choose from available programming.
Public culture generally, whether sponsoring alter- native broadcasting, community-oriented performances and

exhibitions, or arts-in-schools programs, represents an effort not only to broaden access to certain cultural forms but also to broaden people's cultural awareness. Public culture can offer an alternative to cultural parochialism: a circumscribed world view and cultural underdevelopment that comes from limited exposure to competing aesthetic conceptions. The government can seek to provide cultural alternatives through a variety of policies: fostering regional distribution (to make the arts available to those outside of metropolitan centers); supporting ethnic diversity (to guarantee that various minorities receive exposure to their cultural heritage); programming for the disenfranchised (the elderly, institutionalized, handicapped not served by established institutions).

There is much to what the "cultural populists" say about the rarefied nature and limited appeal of the fine arts. High culture is admittedly difficult, demanding, and complex: it does not seek merely to entertain but to provide insight into ourselves and to challenge our more comfortable assumptions. A real cultural populism would support policies, that would give everyone the choice to engage in such an undertaking. Public support for the arts is thus a profoundly conservative policy as the government seeks to cultivate a society with an awareness of its cultural heritages and values. We support culture because as a people we have collectively decided that it is an integral part of civilized society. We have come to realize that cultural traditions provide continuing representation of a society's accomplishments. Fostering cultural growth helps to provide successive generations of new citizens with an understanding of our social and moral values. Public support for culture thus provides a public service, creates a public good, and contributes to the public welfare.*

*I would like to thank my colleagues Professor James Bolner and Adam Hayward for their advice in thinking about the issues discussed here. The final results, however, are solely my responsibility.

56

NOTES

[1] Dick Netzer, The Subsidized Muse (New York: Cambridge University Press, 1978), p. 29.

[2] Rockefeller Panel Report, The Performing Arts: Problems and Prospects (New York: McGraw-Hill, 1965), p. 2.

[3] Netzer, Subsidized Muse, p. 122.

[4] Ibid., p. 123. Personally, I would have selected the New York City Ballet as our premier cultural organization but his case still stands.

[5] The pioneering statement on the financial plight of arts organizations is William J. Baumol and William G. Bowen, Performing Arts--The Economic Dilemma (New York: The Twentieth Century Fund, 1966).

[6] National Committee for Cultural Resources, The National Report on the Arts (New York: pamphlet issued October, 1975), pp. 3-5.

[7] Rockefeller Panel Report, p. 55.

[8] Ibid., pp. 54-55.

[9] National Report on the Arts, pp. 25-26.

[10] Netzer, Subsidized Muse, p. 123.

[11] Calvin Tompkins, Merchants and Masterpieces: The Story of the Metropolitan Museum of Art (New York: E. B. Dutton, 1973), pp. 16-17.

[12] Statement by Nancy Hanks, Hearings before the Subcommittee on Department of the Interior and Related Agencies of the Committee on Appropriations, United States House of Representatives, April 19, 1975.

[13] Paul Di Maggio, Michael Useem, and Paula Brown, Audience Studies of the Performing Arts and Museums: A Critical Review (Washington, D.C.: National Endowment for the Arts, Research Division Report #9, November 1978).

[14] Ibid., pp. 8-33.

[15] Ibid., p. 3.

[16] Paul Di Maggio and Michael Useem, "Social Class and Arts Consumption," Theory and Society 5 (March 1978): 144.

[17] Ibid., p. 249.

[18] Americans and the Arts: 1975 Highlights (New York: Associated Councils of the Arts, 1976), pp. 11-12.

[19] The data reported in this paragraph are from Americans and the Arts, pp. 19-20.

[20] Ibid., p. 20.

[21] Quoted in Coming to Our Senses: The Significance of the Arts for American Education, A Report by the Panel on Arts, Education, and Americans, David Rockefeller, Jr., Chairman, (New York: McGraw-Hill, 1977), p. 226.

[22] Ibid., p. 3.

[23] Ibid., pp. 52-53.

[24] Ibid., p. 248.

[25] Ralph Adams Cram, The Ministry of Art (Freeport, N.Y.: Books for Libraries, 1967), p. viii.

[26] Ibid., pp. 92-93.

[27] Ichak Adizes, The Cost of Being an Artist, Research Paper No. 25, Graduate School of Management, University of California at Los Angeles, (Los Angeles: September 1974), p. 1.

[28] Herbert Gans, Popular Culture and High Culture (New York: Basic Books, 1974), pp. 20-21.

[29] Ibid., p. 121.

[30] Ibid., p. 128.

[31] Audience Surveys of the Performing Arts and Museums, p. 41.

[32] Ibid.

[33] Di Maggio and Useem, "Social Class and Arts Consumption," p. 151.

[34] Coming to Our Senses, p. 258.

[35] Ronald Berman, "Letter to the Editor," 68 Commentary (March 1980): 12.

[36] Joseph Wesley Zeigler, "Centrality Without Philosophy: The Crisis in the Arts," New York Affairs 4 (1978): 19.

[37] Edward Arian, Bach, Beethoven, and Bureaucracy: The Case of the Philadelphia Orchestra (University, Alabama: University of Alabama Press, 1971), p. 69.

[38] Ibid., p. 111.

[39] Ibid., p. 11.

[40] Netzer, Subsidized Muse, p. 16.

4
Merit Good or Market Failure: Justifying and Analyzing Public Support for the Arts

David Cwi

    The establishment of the National Endowment for the Arts (NEA) and the growth of state and local arts councils led to a rapid increase in governmental support of artists and cultural activities. Various traditional arguments of interest to economists have been used to justify this use of tax dollars. This chapter examines these arguments for their validity and policy content when they are applied to the arts.[1] A review of the arguments suggests that they often reduce to a set of political assertions. Further, even which the arguments established a prima facie case for governmental involvement, they raise questions as to when programs should be supported and by what means. In short, knowing that government support of the arts is in principle correct does not answer the question of how to identify and justify the objectives of public cultural policy.

    The traditional arguments can be summarized as follows: certain activities are viewed as intrinsically valuable and meritorious. To support them is in the public interest. This "merit-good" approach may be mediated by conflicting views of the role of government in support of meritorious activities. Europeans view the support of cultural services as especially meritorious and an essential state function. English-speaking nations may view the arts as another set of special interests that should only be supported if there is "market-failure." In short, the only class of meritorious activities which should receive special treatment by government are those that cannot survive without government assistance. In addition to merit-good and market-failure arguments, proponents of public support for the arts may suggest that tax dollars devoted to the arts make possible benefits to the entire community that otherwise would not occur. Since these extrinsic benefits are valued even by persons who have no desire for the arts themselves, we are justified in using public tax dollars to support the arts.

After reviewing these traditional arguments, we turn to a related and more practical set of questions. Apart from the desirability of government involvement in the arts, there is the need to sell decisionmakers on the desirability of appropriations to public arts agencies. The chapter concludes by focusing on the way that the debate over arts objectives has been shaped by the need to "sell" the general principle of government support for the arts.

THE ARTS AS MERIT GOODS

The proponents of government support are suggesting that the arts are both socially desirable and unable to be financially self-supporting in a free-market economy. The concept of social desirability may equivocally refer to conditions or activities that people ought to desire as opposed to those they in fact desire. When social desirability is the basis for government support, the activity in question can be viewed as a good or service meriting public support. From a practical and operational point of view, the difference between activities that merit government support in the sense that we ought to desire them and those that merit support in the sense that we do desire them is simply that there is sufficient public demand to prompt some level of public sector subsidy and provision.

From this pragmatic point of view, a "merit-good" is an activity that some segment of the population desires, is willing to pay for with tax dollars (someone else's as well as their own), and expects the government to assist by funding either directly or through subsidy. Were public funding to occur, this would reflect either the imposed preferences of a decision-making elite or widely-shared preferences. From this perspective, public support of meritorious activities can be an end in itself. Questions need not be raised about the private market for that activity nor the persons benefiting from subsidy. Were two economists to differ over whether popular culture "merits" government support, they would not be differing as economists and scholars. They would be differing as political actors and advocates.

Elsewhere I have cited data on the subtlety and complexity of public perceptions of the arts.[2] For example, a national study by Louis Harris and Associates reviewed a variety of issues including public attitudes toward arts occupations, the activities people enjoyed in their leisure time, the importance of exposing youth to different kinds of arts activities and attitudes

toward government support of the arts.[3]   There was little support for governmental subsidy of selected artistic activities.   Only eleven percent of respondents favored governmental support for dance and opera companies, twelve percent for noncommercial theatre and sixteen percent for symphonies.   Museums of all types fared much better and public libraries and parks fared best.   This provides a perspective to the finding that sixty-four percent of respondents would be willing to pay an additional five dollars in taxes were funds used to maintain and operate cultural facilities such as theatre, music and arts exhibitions.[4]
   Confirmation of the subtlety and complexity of public perceptions is provided by a recent assessment of available audience studies.   The research identified 270 studies of arts audiences, including ten which acquired information on public attitudes toward government support.   The earliest study was conducted in 1970.   The review suggests "that within certain regions of America, majorities or near majorities endorse the general principle that the government should help finance cultural organizations that are running deficits, with local intervention clearly preferred over federal involvement (emphasis added)."   They also found that the level of public support varied widely by specific type of cultural organizations, "with museums faring far better than specific kinds of performing arts organizations . . .   The rank order of the level of public support for the various art forms closely parallels the degree to which the forms attract a socially elite audience."
   The examined studies indicate that a willingness to pay taxes in support of the arts "is highly correlated with whether the individual is a cultural consumer. . . .   It is also clear that the arts still rank far below other priorities for most of the public.   When a national sample was asked to evaluate the importance of various community services, the arts rated below health, transportation, education, law enforcement, housing, and recreational facilities."[5]   These data help shape perceptions of the extent to which Americans now view the arts as merit goods.

THE AMBIGUITY OF MERIT-GOODS

   All social needs can be approached from either an objective or subjective point of view.   For example, poverty can be defined in terms of socially established income and other standards or explored from the point of view of persons experiencing the specified conditions.

Elsewhere I have referred to what may be termed the ambiguity of the merit-good argument. Some people appear to argue that the merit of artistic activities derives from their ability to prompt aesthetic experiences. It is these experiences that have merit and, derivatively, the objects and activities which are required to produce them.

Ernest van den Haag introduced a similar distinction in a debate with Herbert Gans on the differences between "popular culture" and "high culture" that justify public support for the latter. Van den Haag argued that having merit can be distinguished from being popular and that popular culture provides entertainment rather than the gratifications provided by genuine art. High culture "reveals and changes one's experience of reality and possibility" while popular culture provides entertainment which "diverts the tired businessman or worker from reality." The key difference appears to be that high culture produces an aesthetic experience and popular culture does not, or so it is claimed. He went on to suggest that popular culture, although it utilizes "high culture elements," is simply a "reduction and misuse" of these elements. "The relationship between popular culture and high culture is about the same as between Popular Mechanics and physics."[6]

Van den Haag's approach ties the value of art to the unique experience that it alone can prompt through the "correct" use of "elements." A dancer, for example, may derive nonaesthetic satisfactions akin to those of a gymnast or other athlete. Other satisfactions may be associated with group processes and the individual creative process, whether the result is a play or a new machine. Audiences may be "gratified" in the same nonaesthetic ways by a baseball game as by a symphony. In fact, the gratifications provided by "high culture" may include a heavy dose of the nonaesthetic. The marketing of the arts is premised on this. These types of gratification should not be disparaged even if some are nonaesthetic. Van den Haag's analysis seems to suggest, however, that the arts are meritorious solely because they prompt aesthetic gratification. He could have argued instead that art activities can provide multidimensional gratifications whether participants are trained or not. Popular culture may be popular simply because it provides a greater variety of gratifications than high culture. And there may be no market failure and equivalent benefits to the general public.

Van den Haag's analysis also suggests that an aesthetic experience can only be prompted by certain kinds of activities and that persons must be suitably trained. Thus, the sole merit value of art to a consumer is its ability to prompt authentic aesthetic experiences. These require a person to be suitably

trained. If true, this would have important implications for cultural policy. For example, are certain
persons no matter how trained incapable of appreciating
"serious art?" How widely distributed in the population
is this ability? If the ability is not widespread, then
a total focus on serious art may deprive portions of the
population from whatever level of satisfaction their
current sensibilities are able to provide. If the
requisite ability is not widespread, this would also
affect our views of the appropriate size of the "arts
industry," including the live performing arts, the
sector for which there has been the most concern
expressed respecting market failure.

Equally important, when art objects and activities
are viewed not as meritorious in themselves but only as
means to the production of intrinsically valuable
aesthetic experiences, it becomes possible to examine
more efficient ways to produce these experiences than
through the direct subsidy of arts activities. To the
extent that the ultimate goal of cultural policy is
simply the promotion of aesthetic experiences, then an
emphasis on the most efficient means toward this end
might lead to an emphasis on records or television
rather than "live" attendance at individual arts events.
Perhaps we should be concerned not for whether live
symphony is readily available, but whether people are
buying recorded symphonic music and whether it is
available.

There are those who would object that nothing
duplicates or approximates the live performance or
encounter with art. William Baumol, for example, once
cited an "eminent authority" who likened "the experience
of listening to a recording" to "kissing one's sweet-
heart over the telephone."[7] In the case of the performing arts, this raises the question of whether the live
performance is the essence of the aesthetic experience
or whether commensurate experiences can be prompted now
or in the future by other means including advances in
television and electronic sound production.

In this regard, it would be important to understand
whether live events are fulfilling because they produce
higher quality aesthetic experiences or whether they are
attractive because they also fulfill social and other
needs. If the nonaesthetic "gratifications" provided by
live art--e.g. snob appeal, spending an interesting
evening with friends--can be met by other activities for
which there is a thriving private market, and if the
merit experience can be provided by other means, then we
may adopt a level of subsidy which allowed for only
occasional experiences with the live arts, assuming that
there was indeed market failure. This is a topic to
which we will turn in a moment.

Finally, van den Haag's approach emphasizes the requirement that persons be suitably trained. Public policy might very well choose to distinguish government's educational responsibility to assure that the citizenry receives the basic skill-training required to take satisfaction from "serious art" from any responsibility to intervene through subsidy in the production and propagation of particular art forms and institutional types. A combination of a change in educational policy and appropriate tax policy might lead a suitably-trained populace and the free market to produce a commercially-competitive high culture without public subsidy. In any case, the selection of which activities have merit and deserve an audience would be left to the audience which would be best able to judge.

The foregoing discussion has examined the merit-good argument for its policy content. Its validity rests on the extent to which cultural policy favors the appreciation of activities that are in fact meritorious, a judgment that in van den Haag's terms could only be made by the suitably trained. In this connection, it may be useful to recall Mill's distinction between the quality and quantity of pleasure. He argued that two pleasures could be qualitatively distinguished and weighed only by persons capable of experiencing both. It was presented as an empirical claim that persons capable of experiencing both would make the same choices.

To the extent that public subsidy is justified, there is a presumption that the arts activities receiving subsidy include those that the general public would desire to have supported had they the ability to experience them.[8] If they have not felt a need for the (subsidized) arts, this is treated as a lack of consumer skill. In short, there is an objective function to taste that reflects real differences in arts activities. But it may not be true that there is an objective function to taste even were it true that training is required in order to derive authentically aesthetic experiences from art objects and activities. Consequently, knowing that the arts are meritorious does not tell us how to define the community's specific needs and possibilities for the arts. This suggests concern for the processes by which government defines "arts needs," and chooses among alternative solutions. It would be important to demonstrate that these processes favored the interests of the entire community rather than articulate and influential groups with a valid but incomplete conception of the meritorious in art.

MARKET-FAILURE AND THE U.S. ARTS INDUSTRY

The assumption that the arts are meritorious is an essential element of the case for public support. Assuming the arts are deserving of public support, it is then necessary to show that public support is needed. William Baumol and William Bowen have put the case simply: "if through no fault of their own the arts cannot survive without public support, the necessary support should be provided."[9] This raises two issues. Do the arts need additional support? And to what extent, if any, is their predicament attributable to their own shortcomings as opposed to economic realities from which they cannot escape?

Currently, there is no one source for economic data on the entire range of commercial and non-profit arts activities. Data have been collected by service organizations representing symphony, opera and theatre, while data on commercial activities is available from the Census of Business. The crafts and visual arts industries are little understood and only partial glimpses are available of the museum industry from surveys conducted by the National Endowment for the Arts and the Institute for Museum Services (IMS). Other sources of information include census data by reported occupation as well as surveys conducted by individual state and local arts agencies.[10]

It has proved very difficult to estimate the number of non-profit arts organizations in the United States. Census of Business data pick up organizations only if they pay FICA taxes for their employees. However, it has been estimated that forty-nine percent of all performing arts groups did not pay Social Security for any of their employees.[11] The data that is available suggest that U.S. non-profit arts activities involve organizations with very small budgets and a correspondingly high reliance on volunteer and part-time staff. In recent years the number of non-profit institutions as well as individuals desiring a career in the arts appears to have grown rapidly while it remains true that the vast preponderance of artist employment and available arts activities is provided by the commercial sectors of the industry.

GROWTH IN ACTIVITY

An analysis of available census data by the Research Division of the (NEA) suggests that there were roughly 600,000 persons in the U.S. in 1970 at least sixteen years old reporting that they were artists. This includes actors, architects, dancers, designers, musicians and composers, painters and sculptors, photographers, radio and television announcers and a residual category of artists, writers and entertainers not elsewhere classified. By 1976 the number had increased fifty percent to 900,000, while the number of persons in all professional occupations rose twenty-three percent.[12]

Median income in the 1970-1976 period remained constant at $7,900, while the consumer price index rose 47 percent in the six year period. While salaries are low, artists are reported to be part of households with incomes that compare favorably with other professional households. Their household income rose 40 percent during the six year period. 1970 unemployment rates for all artists were 5.9 percent for those age sixteen to nineteen and 3.8 percent for those thirty and over. Corresponding rates for actors were 28.8 percent and 33.7 percent and for dancers 12.2 percent and 21.4 percent. Less than half of artists aged 16-29 worked 50-52 weeks in 1969 (45.6 percent) while 69.7 percent of artists 30 and over worked 50-52 weeks.

A recent national study by Louis Harris and Associates points to equally rapid growth among non-profit arts organizations. They found that twenty-nine percent of the organizations in their sample came into being after 1969. A 1976 study in New York City found that seventy-five percent of the surveyed groups were founded after 1959 and thirty-five percent after 1969. A 1974 study in Arkansas reports that the number of art groups has doubled since 1965. The IMS survey of 4,609 non-profit museums of all types confirms this picture of rapid growth. The study suggests that half of the U.S. museums were started after 1960 and that new museums were established in that period "at the rate of one every three and one-half days."[13]

FINANCES

These data sources suggest that the vast majority of arts institutions are volunteer-based and small-budget enterprises. The IMS museum study indicated that forty percent of museums had budgets of less than $15,000. Some sixty percent had budgets of less than $50,000; seventy-four percent less than $100,000. Only seven percent had budgets over $500,000. The New York City study indicated that fifty-one percent of surveyed organizations had budgets under $50,000. In a Wisconsin study thirty-four percent of organizations reported revenues of less than $5,000. A 1972 New York State study found that fifty-two percent of museums and two-thirds of music, theatre and dance groups had budgets of less than $50,000. Only seventeen percent of these organizations had budgets over $250,000.[14]

As one would expect, these organizations rely heavily on volunteers and part-time staff. The Louis Harris study estimated that sixty-eight percent of all staff in arts organizations were unpaid. Of paid staff, sixty-seven percent were part time. A study of cultural organizations in the New England region found that full-time hours as a percentage of paid hours of employment ranged from eight percent to thirty-four percent depending on the type of organization. Volunteers were estimated to contribute 168 hours for every hour worked by full and part-time employees.[15]

In 1971 the Ford Foundation collected data from non-profit performing arts organizations operating on a fully-professional basis with annual budgets of $100,000 or more. They estimated that there were 195 repertory theatres, operas, symphonies, ballets, and modern dance companies that met these criteria during the 1969-1970 season. The 166 responding organizations, their budgets, and the percent met by earned income are shown in Table 4.1. Earned income refers to ticket income, income from tuition and service fees, recordings and royalties. It should be noted that the Metropolitan Opera, with operating expenditures of $19.6 million in 1970-71, equalled the total of all other operas at $19.1 million.[16]

The Ford data shown in Table 4.2 suggest the labor-intensive nature of the industry with total personnel costs ranging from fifty percent of expenditures for modern dance to seventy-seven percent for symphonies. The art forms also differ in their ability to depart from this dependence on labor. The study notes that:

> . . . symphonies have the highest ratio of salaries and wages to nonsalary costs, and symphony expenditures for artistic personnel are proportionately higher (61 percent) than those of the other art forms. Theatres, on the other hand, operate under quite opposite conditions. They can mount plays with very few performers, fewer on the average than the other art forms with the possible exception of modern dance, and theaters can have quite high scenery and costuming costs. As a result, they are at the other end of the scale from symphonies with respect to the proportion of expenditures devoted to artistic personnel (33 percent). The remaining art forms are in between. Theaters would also have the highest

TABLE 4.1
Performing Arts Institutions--Percent of Total
Operating Expenditures Met by Earned Income, 1970-71

Type (Number Responding)	Total Expenditures (in thousands)	% Expenditures Met by Earned Income
Theater (27)	$ 19,617	64%
Operas (31)	38,743	51%
Symphony (91)	82,830	46%
Ballet (9)	13,897	53%
Modern Dance (8)	2,270	71%

Source: The Ford Foundation, The Finances of the Performing Arts, Vol. 1, Table 3, p. 41 and Table 21, p.
63.

proportion of nonsalary costs were it not for
the fact that dance companies tour more than
organizations in the other art forms and thus
have relatively heavy transportation expenses
that increase their nonsalary costs.[17]

In addition to earned income, non-profit organizations utilize contributions from individuals, corporations, foundations, and government at all levels. This
"unearned income" constitutes a significant portion of
budgets. The difference between earned income and total
expenditure has been referred to as the "earnings gap."
In 1970-71 the differing art forms evidenced varying
degrees of dependence on government as a source of the
unearned income needed to fill this "gap." Modern dance
received sixty-eight percent of its unearned income from
government while symphony received "only" ten percent.
Sources of private and public support are shown in Table
4.3.
A study initiated by the NEA in 1972 provides
similar information for museums. The study of 1,831
museums found that they derived income from the following sources: contributions from individuals, member-
ships, foundations and corporations (21%); income from
admission, museum shops and ancillary facilities such as
restaurants and parking lots (29%); non-operating
revenues primarily from investments (13%); municipal and

TABLE 4.2
Performing Arts Institutions--Percent Distribution of
Expenditures, 1970-71

	Theater (27)	Opera (31)	Symphony (91)	Ballet (9)	Modern Dance (8)
Performing Artistic Salaries/Fees	21	35	53	31	29
Non-Performing Artistic Salaries Fees	12	10	8	10	12
Non-Artistic Administrative Salaries	16	11	11	10	9
Stage Hands/ Crew/Shop	8	8	1	6	2
Fringe Benefits	5	2	4	5	4
TOTAL PERSONNEL COSTS	62	66	77	62	56
TOTAL NONSALARY COSTS	38	34	23	38	44
TOTAL OPERATING EXPENDITURES	100	100	100	100	100

Source: The Ford Foundation, The Finances of the Performing Arts, Vol. 1, Table 6, p. 46.

county government (18%); local government (7% of which 48% went to municipal-county museums); state government (7% of which 61% went to state museums); federal government (12% of which 78% went to federal museums).[18]

COMMERCIAL VERSUS NON-PROFIT ACTIVITIES

Using 1972 data, Dick Netzer in The Subsidized Muse provided an analysis of "the arts sector as a whole," including both commercial and non-profit activities.

TABLE 4.3
Performing Arts Institutions--Percent Distribution of
Unearned Income, 1970-71

	Theater (27)	Opera (31)	Symphony (91)	Ballet (9)	Modern Dance (8)
Individual Contributions	27	31	13	33	7
Business Contributions	7	7	11	6	0
Combined/United Art Fund Contributions	9	16	11	0	0
Local Foundation Contributions	9	11	8	12	8
Other Local Contributions	7	11	12	7	0
TOTAL LOCAL NON GOVERNMENT CONTRIBUTIONS	59	76	66	58	1
Federal Government Grants	14	8	4	6	14
State Government Grants	10	2	2	9	54
Local Government Grants	2	6	4	4	0
TOTAL GOVERNMENT GRANTS	26	16	10	19	68
NATIONAL FOUNDATION (GRANTS)	15	8	12	23	17
CORPUS EARNINGS USED FOR OPERATIONS	0	0	12	0	0
TOTAL EARNED INCOME	100	100	100	100	100

Source: The Ford Foundation, The Finances of the Performing Arts 1, Table 34, p. 76.

This analysis examined "employment by organizations centrally concerned with the arts," "artistic share of employment by organizations only partially concerned with the arts," and "employment partially concerned with the arts," and "employment of artistic professionals and supporting staff in other fields in which the arts are a peripheral factor." Netzer concludes that the arts sector is:

> . . . overwhelmingly commercial in origin, organization and objective. It is estimated that more than 85 percent of the financing of the arts sector comes from admissions, sales of products and services to customers, and-- for broadcasting and periodical publishing-- advertising revenue. Performing arts activities in this country are dominated by movies, broadcasting, recording, the commercial stage, and other live performances under commercial auspices (ranging from rock festivals to piano bars). Although such activities may strike the reader as largely irrevelant to issues of public policy towards the arts, they employ most of the actors, singers, dancers, and musicians who earn their living as such in this country.
>
> Similarly, the literary arts are dominated by commercial profit-oriented publishing activities, not by non-profit literary ventures. Noncommercial activities are relatively more important for the visual arts, largely because of the high costs that art museums incur and the very low sales earnings of visual artists. No doubt, most visual artists, like most writers, dislike having to worry about selling their output and would welcome public or private patronage that would permit them to ignore commerce and focus on art. In the absence of such patronage, they are and will continue to be in the commercial part of the arts sector.[19]

However, while most of the nation's artistic production and employment is provided by profit-making organizations, public policy has particularly focused on non-profit arts organizations. The question of "market-failure" in this context must be addressed from two points of view, focusing on artistic and cultural activities irrespective of whether they are non-profit and focusing on non-profits in particular.

IS THERE MARKET FAILURE?

In a purely private market, the mix of available goods and services and the utilization of resources is the expression of a vast number of economic decisions by households and firms. Government involvement can be justified when the market fails to provide the goods, services or other opportunities that society values highly. In the case of the arts, market failure would include the potential loss of our cultural legacy to future generations as well as the exclusion of portions of our society from the enjoyment of the arts due to lack of opportunity or high admission costs.

Has the market failed to provide enough arts activities or is there a surplus? It is clear that there are a number of activities that find a thriving private market including films, dinner theatre, Broadway and related touring shows, commercial art galleries, and the record and publishing industries; in fact, most of the nation's artistic production. When market-failure issues are raised it is typically in connection with the non-profit visual and performing arts. Advocates tend also to emphasize the merit of these activities. In fact, it is sometimes difficult to distinguish market-failure from merit-good arguments. For example, we may be told that a museum or performing arts group was unable to expand or had to cut back on services. Advocates consider this market failure. However, the organizations in question may have balanced budgets, and may not be in danger of going out of business. Simply because one would personally like to see more arts activities does not mean more are needed. Because the arts are so market-oriented, it is difficult to imagine how need would not in some way be related to demand.

Those concerned about future generations believe that we have a responsibility to assure continuity and access in future years to the product of current artistic endeavor. It is felt that without subsidy some of that activity will either disappear or be available in only limited quantity, quality, and variety. There is no doubt that the availability of certain activities would be affected by changes in subsidy practices. Activities may not be available to all, or at levels of quality and variety that some may find deficient. Of course, some cultural activities will continue to thrive without subsidy.[20] The argument by appeal to future generations assumes that future generations will, and ought to, share the proponent's cultural interests and that future generations will be unable to revive these interests should this be necessary.

The argument also suggests that artistic resources are like natural resources--once gone, gone forever.

This may be true of art objects such as paintings or
sculpture. But it is not as clearly true of other
artistic traditions. Skills and styles can be
maintained across generations to be relearned later.
One might also argue that with the advent of new
technologies--for example, holography and full-scale
Polaroid prints, new techniques in sound and video
reproduction and recording--one can envision much less
costly ways to maintain an artistic and cultural
heritage. These technologies might also facilitate a
more widespread dissemination by the private market.

More fundamentally, there appears little reason to
believe that our artistic legacy is in jeopardy. Dick
Netzer suggests that:

> Despite long-term projections of financial
> disaster for the arts, most arts organizations
> are in relatively good financial condition,
> with a few exceptions, notably the Metro-
> politan Opera. On balance, therefore, at the
> current level, public subsidy does not seem so
> small as to threaten the preservation of the
> legacy for future generations. In fact--again
> with the notable exception of the Met--the
> overall artistic legacy may well be in better
> financial shape today than it ever has
> been.[21]

Equity considerations emphasizing the quality and
regularity of contact with the arts by all segments of
our population can affect public policy. This approach
to market-failure implies that the poor ought to attend
more often than they can afford to when prices are not
subsidized. If the poor have no desire to attend, then
it would be more difficult to make the case for public
support. In any case, assuming they would like to
attend, the necessity for the public sector to subsidize
prices is supposedly justified on equity grounds, or
because such attendance is meritorious or, as in the
case of education, because of the resulting community
benefits. It may well be objected that this argument
justifies public support of almost anything the poor
cannot afford.

We should note though that acceptance of this
argument creates new complications. There are
perspectives in welfare economics which suggest that
when subsidy is desirable in order to increase use it
should be directed toward the user, not the service-
provider. For example, instead of subsidizing
institutions which may choose to be sold out by
subscription and whose audiences may include large
numbers of persons who could pay increased ticket costs,
strategies might be developed that are aimed at target

audiences, for example through ticket vouchers. Since people appear more likely to view an art activity as a merit-good if they have become a cultural consumer (even an infrequent one), we have an opportunity for equity and advocacy to coincide.

More generally, as Alan Peacock has noted, concern for the poor suggests the need for both long and short term solutions.

> The short-term one requires that support is moved away from the subsidizing of producers of cultural activities toward the subsidizing of individuals. The long-term one is to devise a means of altering the preference functions of future generations so that Baumol's disease may be counteracted through the market as well as through the political mechanism which offers state support.[22]

We will examine "Baumol's disease" shortly.

Dick Netzer suggests another type of market failure in the arts, a "lack of information on the part of potential consumers." He notes that a taste for art-- and therefore a willingness to pay for it--may never be developed if there are no opportunities to sample the product. In addition, it may be economically infeasible for individual arts organizations:

> . . . to overcome the lack of information by heavy advertising expenditure. . . . The only way of overcoming the lack of information may be through subsidized production of more of the arts, so that would-be consumers and producers do have first-hand experience with the arts.[23]

It is indeed true that rural towns and small cities may not have the market or the private philanthropy to support the total array of professional, full-time, resident arts activity typically available in the larger cities. Even larger cities cannot support all the specialized arts activities that hope for a segment of the market although major arts institutions do seem capable of promoting themselves through direct mail and other techniques. At issue is the level and sort of activity required to prompt the development of "taste." It is clear that taste can be acquired from activities that are less than fully professional (or even live). Most, if not all, in-school art programs presuppose this. Most of us have probably developed a taste for the arts from contact with activities that were less than professional--in which case the market may not be failing after all.

THE BAUMOL-BOWEN THESIS

Market failure arguments to this point have
suggested the need for government subsidy to expand
employment or access to arts activities by current
members of our society or future generations. In
Performing Arts: The Economic Dilemma, William Baumol
and William Bowen argue that subsidy is needed to
maintain any given level of output in the performing
arts. They stress that performing arts organizations
cannot expect to earn sufficient income through ticket
sales to pay for the labor and goods they require for
their performances. Consequently, their "earnings gap"
will continue to expand requiring ever increasing
increments of public subsidy to augment increases in
private contributions that are unlikely to be sufficient.

Because the performing arts are labor intensive,
they are particularly troubled by rising wage rates
imposed by the national economy. Wage increases in
other sectors which they must match are supported in the
general economy by increases in productivity. But the
performing arts cannot raise productivity per unit of
labor since the production of artistic output permits no
substitution of new technologies for labor. No matter
how output per unit of labor increases elsewhere in the
economy, it will still take the same number of musicians
to perform a symphony. Therefore, without subsidy,
admission prices will rise substantially over time.
Unless customers are completely insensitive to these
rises, we can expect art institutions to be threatened.

The potential threat to the performing arts was
further illustrated by the Ford Foundation study cited
earlier. The study projected forward to the 1980-81
season trends found in data over six seasons from 1965-
66 through 1970-71. Without inflation, expenditures
were expected to double, producing an earnings gap three
times the 1970-71 level. If the inflation rate averaged
seven percent, expenditures were projected to increase
nearly four-fold while the earnings gap increased over
five-fold. This would require a four-fold increase in
private contributions assuming government sources increased their support.

If Baumol and Bowen are right, there would appear
to be a genuine reason for concern about the long-term
prospects for the live performing arts. Baumol and
Bowen have been interpreted to mean that costs in the
performing arts must go up faster than income from
philanthropy and the box office. This would require
ever increasing real growth in public subsidy simply to
maintain the same level of output. Subsequent studies
suggest that the Baumol-Bowen model, at least in the

case of the United States, is too simple.[24]   On the
income side, it has turned out that private contributions have risen dramatically while consumer demand
appears to be only moderately sensitive to rising ticket
prices. On the expenditure side, there has been considerable and unforeseen scope for "economizing" operations and introducing new technologies. In addition,
some of the costs that prompted real growth in expenditures may have been due to temporary dislocations--
for example, increases in output and justified increases
in artist wage rates relative to other sectors.

     In sum, we now know that public monies implemented
with future (and present) generations in mind could
introduce inefficiency by supplanting pressure to
economize, raise prices, and seek out contributions.
Dick Netzer has concluded that:

> . . . despite cries of alarm about the
> financial conditions of the arts, there is a
> glaring lack of evidence to support the con-
> tention that without massive transfusions of
> public money "we are going to become a land
> without music, without theater, without
> dance." True financial desperation in the
> arts is relatively rare and seems unlikely to
> become universal.[25]

In a recent article reviewing trends through 1979,
Baumol has also concluded that "past evidence suggests
that even in the most difficult periods the arts have
managed, by and large, to find financial resources." He
agrees that "crisis is likely to remain a way of life.
But crisis is not equivalent to disaster."[26]   Netzer
goes so far as to suggest that there might even be
reason for optimism--citing the growth in private
philanthropy in absolute terms and relative to other
claimants, the opportunities for increased earned income
and some abatement of cost pressures.

     The Baumol-Bowen model has simply proved to be an
over-simplified characterization of the real economic
world. In particular, it leaves unexamined the question
of whether arts organizations, consistent with the
constraints under which they are operating, have been
efficient and cost effective in using resources and
maximizing consumer and philanthropic income. Subsidy
is difficult to justify for arts organizations that have
not made the most of such opportunities. This raises
the question of the extent to which their recurring
budget struggles are their own fault as opposed to an
unavoidable consequence of the economics of the arts.

THE ORGANIZATIONAL CLIMATE OF THE NON-PROFIT ARTS

Many have suggested that the recurring problems of arts organizations are to some extent of their own making. Baumol and Bowen have themselves noted:

> . . . that the objectives of the typical non-profit organization are by their very nature designed to keep it constantly on the brink of financial catastrophe, for to such a group the quality of the services which it provides becomes an end in itself.

As more money becomes available it is spent and other projects identified. "It is hardly surprising that such groups feel themselves strapped. It becomes clear that they are simply built that way."[27] It has also been suggested that arts institutions are dominated by dreamers with insufficient attention given to proper planning and feasible development. Lee Kimche, director of the Institute for Museum Services, is quoted as saying that new museums often get into trouble because "people become building happy and the dreamers . . . go out on a limb and spend a lot more money for the building and the original investment than they thought they would."[28]

The more basic point is that arts institutions operate more like service institutions than businesses. Businesses exist to satisfy the customer and to produce a good or service the customer is willing to buy. Service institutions are usually paid out of a budget provided by a legislature or a board. Peter Drucker suggests that the achievement of results "in the budget-based institution means a larger budget."[29] Their success is measured in terms of size of budget and staff so that increased government support .is a mark of success, not failure.

More important, the real constituency which individual arts institutions may exist to serve is not the general public but others from whom institution officers and staff derive prestige. Bruno Frey and Werner Pommerehne in their analysis of museums suggest that "the top echelons of the museum derive utility from . . . meeting the high standards established by the profession of museum directors" as well as donors and trustees, art historians and the directors of other museums. "No important constraints are imposed by the general public, which usually has neither the opportunities nor the incentives to influence museum policy."[30]

Finally, it is clear that arts institutions are small businesses. Their officers and staff may have limited capabilities and time, if not inclination, to plan and manage like a corporation. As economic enterprises they may be built to fail. The potential problems confronting arts organizations are illustrated by a report to the National Endowments by the Taft Corporation. The report examined the management and fund-raising programs of some 173 Challenge Grant applicants and found ten areas of need including the need for more long range planning and financial-management skills, better marketing, and improved working relationships between boards and art organization administrators.[31]

The implications for public policy are clear. Institutions should be evaluated not only in terms of whether they deserve an audience but with respect to deficiencies in their own management and planning. Subsidy policies would also need to be examined in terms of their impact on private sector support and maintenance of effort on the part of recipients. The Challenge Grant programs of the National Endowments are examples of grant approaches developed with these issues in mind. Indeed, a recent evaluation of the NEA's Challenge Grant program suggests that the requirement that the grantees develop a long-range plan was a major benefit and that a recurring problem is the "difficulty motivating the board to assume its full fund-raising responsibilities."[32] The implication of course is that public dollars may at times be substituting for a board's unwillingness to raise funds privately.

In addition to assessing community need, and institutional quality in accordance with appropriate artistic and management standards, it may also be useful to assess the quality of an institution's community commitment and impact. Public policy may want to distinguish organizations that function like private clubs seeking to maximize the utility of the boards and members from activities providing, and committed to, a genuine service role. The reality that arts organizations are competing among themselves for audiences and public and private support has clear implications by itself. Public policies that implicitly sanction and reward the creation of new groups may serve to expand the public agency's constituency but may also have the effect of encouraging the fragmentation of audiences and contributors.

PUBLIC EXTERNALITIES

The final arguments in favor of public support for the arts emphasize the public benefits that accrue.

Some meritorious activities are "public goods," others lead to results that benefit a broad public. "Pure public goods" are typically defined as those that allow neither excludability nor rival consumption. National defense is the classic example. Consumption is nonrival in that provision to you does not affect the quality or amount available to others; and once provided to you, others cannot be excluded should they want to be. It is typically suggested that market mechanisms do not exist to assure an adequate supply of public goods and, therefore, they must be supplied by government.

There are goods provided by the private market that go a long way toward meeting the definition of a public good. Broadcasting is an oft-cited example in that the provision of television transmission is largely public in the requisite sense. This indicates that an activity can be a public good although not provided by government. Further, it is clear that having a public quality is not sufficient to justify government provision. The public good may lack merit. For example, nuclear war is "public" in the requisite sense, but typically not thought to be meritorious.

Many writers have acknowledged that arts activities are not public goods in the requisite sense but that they do have a mixed private and public character since there are public externalities prompted by the private consumption of the arts. It is suggested that these external goods are a basis for public support in that they redound to the acknowledged benefit of the general public; that these goods are generally desired; and that additional benefits can only accrue if the private market is augmented by public support.

Baumol and Bowen, for example, have compared the arts to education. In one sense, education is a private good. "It can be sold to an individual purchaser because it yields benefits specifically to him." However, "education is also a public service because it enriches society as a whole--it not only increases the productivity of the individual, it makes for a better life for everyone in the community."[33] Public benefits cited include: the educated are more productive; have more stable families and better educated children; and education is a prerequisite of responsible participation in the democratic process.

In the case of the arts, various externalities have been cited as a basis for public support. It has been suggested that the arts enhance national or local identity, pride and international prestige. Others have argued that the arts have important direct and indirect economic benefits to cities: a) they are "people magnets" introducing a vitality attractive to business, consumers, and tourists; b) they are labor intensive and able to absorb the full range of job skills; c) their

expenditures as well as those of their employees and
audiences benefit the community through direct and
multiplier effects on local businesses; d) as an
economic enterprise they are ecologically and environ-
mentally sound and do not rely on irreplaceable physical
resources; 3) they are in demand by a class of individuals which may be crucial to the continued vitality of
communities and so may affect the locational decisions
of these individuals.[34]   (Culture and cities are
discussed in greater detail in Chapter 10.)

As has already been noted, it has been claimed that
the arts have an important role in the education of
children and adults. In addition to the reasons already
cited, Alvin Toffler notes that:

> The arts play an important role in integrating
> individuals into subcultures within the larger
> society; they act on value systems that
> accelerate or retard change and they educate
> individuals to new role possibilities and
> style of life.[35]

Art forms are also interdependent. As Dick Netzer
notes, "all the musical art forms--opera, dance,
concert, 'serious' music, jazz and the 'popular' music
forms--tend to support one another," in that they draw
materials from one another and provide training and
employment opportunities for professionals.[36] So, if
you enjoy one of the art forms, you will benefit from
support to the others.

It should be noted that not all of these
externalities are "public" in the classic sense. The
benefits cited may not accrue to the entire community.
This leads to a somewhat weaker statement of the
argument that public support may prompt benefits that
taken singly or in combination are desired by
significant numbers of the population. Therefore, such
support is a (relatively) efficient way of promoting the
general good and at the same time supporting a merit-
good.   These arguments are essentially appeals to
rational self-interest. We are being told that if we
spend a portion of our tax dollars on the arts--an
activity we may not desire--things will happen which we
do desire.

It has been objected that these arguments justify
public support of any activity in as much as every
public expenditure has (collective) externalities in the
strong or weak sense noted.   Even accepting the
argument, we would need (as C.D. Throsby has noted) to
identify whether the external benefits "may in fact be
produced in sufficient quantities without the need for
further support."[37] Matters are perhaps even stickier
than that. If the basis for the public expenditure is

simply the externalities, then we would want to know who
benefited, at what cost in terms of their tax dollars,
and whether an expenditure on another class of activities might bring the same benefits at less cost or
greater benefits at the same cost. A host of interesting empirical questions arise for which it is difficult
to obtain answers. Matters become even more complicated
when we ask about the negative consequences of public
investment, or introduce merit considerations. More
generally, optimal expenditure from the standpoint of
externalities may not provide what some would consider
sufficient quality, quantity, or variety. For example,
in recent years arts advocates have emphasized the "economic impact" of the arts. If this impact were the sole
or primary justification for public subsidy or provision, it could lead to funding levels insufficient to
support an institution's artistic aspirations. Given
community taste and preference orderings, a point is
likely to be reached when further investments in quality
cannot be justified by the returns to the community.
Equally interesting, an emphasis on economic impact
could lead to differential funding among organizations.[38] Finally, an emphasis on who benefits will
affect our sense of the proper role of each level of
government. If the benefits are largely local or state-
wide, there may be little justification on externality
grounds for federal involvement. Even within a single
metropolitan area made up of multiple jurisdictions, an
emphasis on benefits can affect our view of each
jurisdiction's fair share of local governmental
support.[39]

CONCLUDING POLICY OBSERVATIONS

        Government involvement from the point of view of an
economist becomes justified when the market fails to
provide the goods, services or other outcomes that
society values highly. Decisions as to desired outcomes
and desired levels of goods and services are made in the
political arena and through community, state and federal
planning processes. Consequently, individuals committed
to the development of a national cultural policy will
find little of value in the merit-good and market-
failure arguments we have examined. It is clear that
they can be used by advocates to support policies that
presume all the important matters of interest. The
arguments focus on the principle of public support for
the arts. By themselves, they justify no particular
piece of spending.
        To develop policy it is necessary to have some

notion of the optimal level of public support by each
level of government given the realities of budget
constraints.   Merit-good notions by themselves simply
boil down to "spend money on the arts because the arts
are important."   The addition of market-failure notions
constitutes an advance only if we already agree on how
much consumption and production ought to be provided by
the private market--of what quality, when, where, and
how often.   These are value judgments not based on
economics.

Further, when arts advocates claim that arts
activities merit governmental support, they are often
content to speak in generalities.   Crafts, individual
performing and visual arts institutions, artist
residencies, festivals, shows and art centers are among
the activities that are lumped together as "the arts."
Knowing that the arts in general are meritorious does
not tell us how to choose the activities that deserve an
audience as well as meet standards of organizational
performance and public accountability.   The means by
which to best promote artist employment and increased
public benefit are not addressed, nor is the fundamental
issue of how to most authentically define a community's
needs and possibilities for both commercial and non-
profit activities.   The arguments, in short, cannot be
used as a substitute for policy analysis addressing our
responsibility to be specific about realistic objectives
and the differing responsibilities of each level of
government.

It is not enough to argue that "X per cent of
Americans think that art is important" leading to the
support of an equally broad social goal expressed as "no
American should be deprived of the arts."   Such goal
statements have limited usefulness in individual policy
and program decisions.   They are analogous to "America
is a nice country" and "no foreigner should be deprived
of a visit."   In fact, the statements about art may be
worse.   At least we know what is meant by America.   When
people say that arts are important, what do they mean by
art? And in what respect is it important? And for whom?
And how often?   And at what cost?   And where?   Are
certain activities more important than others?   If you
could not have both, would you prefer a fully professional symphony or two ballet companies and a museum?
Almost anything you could propose would help ensure that
some Americans--somewhere, some way, sometime--got
exposure to something that someone called art, thereby
helping to ensure they were not deprived of it.

American public support for the arts began with a
basic vision: the arts are too important to be left to
private philanthropy and the commercial market place;
there is no substitute for live visual and performing
arts activity; and, Americans deserve access to high

quality artistic production. At all levels of government there was also the sense that our national, state
and community image demanded evidence of a commitment
to, and support of, artistic excellence. At the same
time, professional-level artistic activity requires
markets not universally available as well as ongoing
levels of private philanthropy that have not appeared
able to increase at rates appropriate for our artistic
aspirations.

The little public money that was made available was
often distributed through (matching) grants intended to
stimulate the flow of dollars from other levels of
government and the private sector. The bulk of this
money remains devoted to institutions and not individual
artists. Government agencies have functioned as foundations, with resource allocations made by staff and
boards on a project by project basis. These decisions
have been substantially insulated from both political
and market processes.[40] As Netzer has noted, this
insulation--and the grant approach--was a deliberate
policy decision. "The use of intermediaries for decision making frees the political processes from what
would be an intolerable load; Congress cannot vote in
any sensible way on annual lists of several thousand
proposed grants." Netzer goes on to note that the
political decisionmaking process does not lend itself to
the use of expertise and to the sort of review required
to evaluate grant proposals and that, in any case, the
"dangers of favoritism and political retaliation are
very great."[41]

Nevertheless, because agencies have functioned as
foundations, their vision has extended little beyond the
merits of individual proposals and applicants. Program
evaluation and community needs assessment have, on the
whole, not taken place, and little effort has been
expended at developing the data base necessary to
develop policy intelligently. Consequently, agencies
have been unable to use the grant process to encourage
or discourage trends or activities identified as in the
public interest.

At the one extreme, "these efforts entail explicit
definition of objectives, spelling out priorities,
matching proposed grants to these objectives and
priorities and paying careful attention to the specific
forms of subsidy." The alternative extreme is "an
apparently aimless dispensation of funds on the basis of
nothing more concrete than noble intentions."[42] In the
absence of a well-grounded policy framework, we run
the risk of providing subsidies that are not needed to
groups that benefit no one and have no serious develop-
mental prospects. Subsidies may also address a concern
that could have been dealt with in other (better) ways
or serve to increase incomes and lower prices without

changing quality, quantity, or use; or otherwise encourage inefficiency and expensive practices, supplant private philanthropy; or, perhaps unwarrantedly, encourage people to believe that they should strive to make their (sole) living in the arts. As the public dollars available to the arts have grown, it is now legitimate to expect the development of policies by which the public can account for their use.

The politically aware know that specific policy targets divide while broad goals unite. Consequently, they prefer arguments to the effect that "no American should be deprived of the beauty of the arts," a goal so broad as to support spending for almost anything described as artistic. These broad political statements designed to generate political support for legislative appropriations can become so opaque as to complicate rather than expedite policy development. While early statements of our cultural policy goals were deliberately intended to embrace all the arts and every possible good intention, "the arts" are now being used even more generally to denote everything that affects community well-being.

In a November 4, 1977 letter to Patricia Harris, Secretary of the Department of Housing and Urban Development, Atlanta Mayor Maynard Jackson spoke eloquently on behalf of the United States Conference of Mayors Task Force on the Arts, for the "essential role the arts must play in achieving a meaningful national urban objective." He argued further that a national urban policy must be built "on the foundation of concerns for which the words 'the arts' have become a synonym." A May 5, 1978 statement by Mayor Jackson claimed that "the arts" "embraces the issues of urban design and amenities," and that they can be "a key determinant in the equation governing the economic vitality of a city." This conception of the arts is a far cry from that found in the arguments we have examined.

We can expect that in the future the arguments for increased appropriations for the arts will prompt a closer look at the claimed community benefits. People will want some hard answers as to how they benefit when their taxes are used to support activities they do not desire. Consequently, we can expect continued efforts to change public perceptions, as well as attempts to merge arts policy with policy in other areas. More fundamentally, as legislative actions call for more authentic approaches to policy development, we can expect an increasing effort to address seriously the issues raised by the merit-good and market-failure arguments.

NOTES

[1] This chapter incorporates material for an article by the author that appeared as part of a Symposium on Subsidization of Cultural Activities. See David Cwi, "Public Support of the Arts: Three Arguments Examined," The Journal of Behavioral Economics 8 (Summer 1979). This article has been reprinted in the Journal of Cultural Economics 4 (December 1980).

[2] See Cwi, "Public Support of the Arts."

[3] Louis Harris and Associates, Americans and the Arts (New York: The Associated Councils of the Arts, 1975), p. 106. The study found that respondents had more respect for bus drivers and professional baseball players than art critics, poets, ballet dancers and professional actors (p. 18). No more than seven percent cited attending concerts or going to theatre, opera or dance performances as the leisure activity that gave them the most creative or artistic satisfaction. Thirty-eight percent cited reading followed by gardening (twenty-seven percent) and handiwork (twenty percent) (p. 12).

[4] We should note that a willingness to pay an extra five dollars in taxes has little policy relevance unless it has already been determined that increased taxes are needed and equal to five dollars per taxpayer. Every family on my block might be willing to pay an additional five dollars in taxes to provide another fire alarm box. But this might generate vastly more money than is needed to provide the fire alarm, should an additional alarm be needed.

[5] Paul DiMaggio, Michael Useem and Paula Brown, The American Arts Audience: Its Study and Character (Cambridge, Mass: Center for the Study of Public Policy, 1977), p. 89 and p. 91. This study is now available as Audience Studies of the Performing Arts and Museums: A Critical Review, National Endowment for the Arts, Research Division Report no. 9 (New York: The Publishing Center for Cultural Resources, 1978).

[6] Ernest van den Haag, "Should We Subsidize Popular Arts? No--An Elitist View," New York Times, February 9, 1975, sec. 2, pp. 1, 17.

[7] William J. Baumol, "Performing Arts: The Permanent Crises," Business Horizons 10, no. 3, pp. 47-50.

[8] The implications of this discussion for the identification of arts needs and the researcher's role in developing cultural policy are discussed in David Cwi, "Toward an Ideology of Cultural Policy Research: Concluding Observations," in William Hendon, James Shanahan, and Alice MacDonald, eds., Economic Policy for the Arts (Cambridge, MA: ABT Books, 1980).

[9] William J. Baumol and William G. Bowen, Performing Arts--The Economic Dilemma (New York: The Twentieth

Century Fund, 1966), p. 369.

[10] The Research Division of the National Endowment for the Arts has commissioned several studies intended to design procedures for collecting better data and assess what is already known from census data as well as studies sponsored by arts institutions, their associations and other private and public agencies.

[11] Louis Harris and Associates, The Status of Non-Profit Arts and Museum Institutions in the United States in 1976 (New York: Louis Harris and Associates, 1979).

[12] National Endowment for the Arts, Artists Compared by Age, Sex, and Earnings in 1970 and 1976, Research Division Report no. 12, (New York: The Publishing Center for Cultural Resources, 1980), pp. 9-12.

[13] Louis Harris and Associates, Artists, p. 23; Growth in New York City Arts and Culture: Who Pays? (New York: Cultural Assistance Center, Inc., 1976), p. 13-16; The Arts Are For Everyone (The Office of Arkansas State Arts and Humanities, 1976), p. 14; The Institute for Museum Services, cited by Lee Kimche in "American Museums: The Vital Statistics," Museum News, October 1980, p. 54.

[14] Lee Kimche, "American Museums"; Cultural Assistance Center, Growth; Wisconsin Arts: Highlighting the Economics of Not-for-Profit Arts, The Wisconsin Arts Council; Louis Harris and Associates, A Study of the Cultural Industry of New York State, 1972, p. 183; The Institute for Museum Services study of 4,609 non-profit musuems included the following types: history (50%), science (18%) art (14%) general (18%) specialized (5%), park and visitor center (4%), children's/junior (1%).

[15] Louis Harris and Associates, A Study of the Cultural Industry, p. 35; The Arts and the New England Economy (Cambridge, MA: New England Foundation for the Arts, 1980), p. 39.

[16] The Ford Foundation, The Finances of the Performing Arts, 2 vols. (New York: The Ford Foundation, 1974), 1:41,63.

[17] Ibid., p. 47.

[18] Louis Harris and Associates, Museums U.S.A. (Washington, DC: The National Endowment for the Arts, 1972).

[19] Dick Netzer, The Subsidized Muse (New York: Cambridge University Press, 1978), p. 12.

[20] Netzer suggests that the products which ought to particularly concern us are those produced by individuals or organizations striving for a long-term impact. He notes that this may "justify a subsidy policy that distinguishes between high art culture and popular art culture," "since the latter is intended to be evanescent and its immediate consumers can be reasonably asked to pay for it through charges" (p. 23). An artist's intentions may be irrelevant to society's

responsibilities to future generations. Similarly, pure merit-good considerations may make irrelevant any consideration of the current market for certain products and activities. Much of what we now esteem was intended to be evanescent and had a thriving market.

[21]Netzer, The Subsidized Muse, p. 159.

[22]Alvin Peacock, "Welfare Economics and Public Subsidies to the Arts," The Economics of the Arts, Mark Blaug, ed., (Boulder, CO: Westview Press, 1976), p. 333. With respect to the subsidization of individuals, Peacock finds two problems with ticket vouchers: 1) it may be difficult to identify appropriate groups not only respecting level of poverty but "actual and potential" interest in the arts; 2) recipients of the vouchers might resell them to those who could afford commercial prices. Peacock suggests that "one might be able to circumvent the problem of voucher resale by a block-booking system of subsidized seats, so that no voucher was assignable to a particular individual."

[23]Netzer, The Subsidized Muse, p. 82.

[24]See David Cwi, ed., Research in the Arts: A Conference on Policy Related Studies of the National Endowment for the Arts (Washington, DC: The National Endowment for the Arts and the Walters Art Gallery, Baltimore, 1978).

[25]Netzer, The Subsidized Muse, p. 180.

[26]Hilda Baumol and William J. Baumol, "On Finances of the Performing Arts During Stagflation: Some Recent Data," The Journal of Cultural Economics 4 (December 1980): 12-14.

[27]William Baumol and William Bowen, "On the Performing Arts: The Anatomy of their Economic Problems," American Economic Review (May 1956) and reprinted in Blaug, ed., Economics of the Arts, p. 218.

[28]Quoted in The Sun (Baltimore), November 23, 1980, sec. B, p. 27.

[29]Peter Drucker, "Managing the Public Service Institution," The Public Interest 33 (1973); reprinted in Managing Nonprofit Organizations (New York: AMACOM, 1977), p. 22.

[30]Bruno Frey and Werner Pommerehne, "An Economic Analysis of the Museum," in Hendon, et. al., eds., Economic Policy for the Arts, pp. 250-251.

[31]Taft Corporation, Background Papers for Working Discussions, a report prepared for the National Council, June 1977.

[32]Diane J. Gingold, The Challenge Grant Experience (Washington, DC: National Endowment for the Arts, 1980), p. 90.

[33]Bowen and Baumol, Performing Arts p. 381.

[34]The role of the arts in urban economic development is examined in David Cwi, The Role of the Arts in Urban Economic Development, Urban Consortium

monograph, the Commerce Department, Economic Development Administration, Washington, D.C., 1980 and in "Models of the Role of the Arts in Economic Development", in Hendon, et. al., eds., Economic Policy for the Arts. A six-city study for the Research Division of the National Endowment for the Arts is also forthcoming: David Cwi, Economic Impact of Arts and Cultural Institutions (New York: Publishing Center for Cultural Resources) as Research Division Report No. 15. An overview of the economic effects of musuems can be found in Museum News (May-June 1981) and an overview of the author's research and policy framework as "The Arts as a Business and a Strategic Tool: Two Perspectives for Analyzing Their Impact," in the Proceedings of A Conference on the Economic Impact of the Arts, Cornell University, May 27-28, 1981.

[35]Alvin Toffler, "The Art of Measuring the Arts," in Bertram Gross, ed., Social Intelligence for America's Future Explorations in Societal Problems (Boston: Allyn and Bacon, 1969), p. 263.

[36]Netzer, The Subsidized Muse, p. 23.

[37]C.D. Throsby, "The Economics of Melodrama," Current Affairs Bulletin (Australia), September 1977, p. 8.

[38]Some policy implications of narrowly circumscribed "return on investment" criteria in the development of public policy are reviewed in Cwi, Economics of Arts and Cultural Institutions, forthcoming.

[39]The author has reviewed alternative approaches to fair share funding among local jursidictions in "Regional Cost Sharing of Artistic and Cultural Activities," Northeast Regional Science Review 8 (1979).

[40]Ironically, while the initial vision may have included the belief that "art" was too important to be left to private philanthropy and the commercial sector, the grant approach leaves the arts in nonprofit abd commercial hands. Grants are made availabe to subsidize artistic production for its own sake while the boards of recipient institutions may represent the public interest.

Equally intriguing, while there may be great interest in insulating institutions from government "interference," arts institutions themselves have been effective in taking their case directly to state and local legislative bodies, bypassing the public arts agencies ostensibly charged with developing public arts policy. Major arts institutions have been effective in securing capital funds. The implications of current practices for the development of new institutions and for public accountability are barely touched in this paper. For an interesting example of arts politics in practice, see Charles Mark, "Q: How Do I get an Arts Subsidy? A: Become a Symphony Orchestra," <u>The New York Times</u>, November 3, 1974, sec. 2, p. 1, 10.

[41]Netzer, <u>The Subsidized Muse</u>, p. 35.   Those familiar with Netzer's work will recognize his influence on the discussion that follows.

[42]Dick Netzer, "Large-Scale Public Support for the Arts," <u>New York Affairs</u> 1, no. 1, p. 87.

5
The Private Muse
in the Public World

Derral Cheatwood

THE PARADOX OF THE ARTIST IN THE PUBLIC WORLD

Beginning with the early Renaissance and emerging in full form during the Romantic era, society has created and maintained an image of the artist as a private soul isolated in a visibly public world. It does not matter how accurate this image was, it has become its own reality. Now artists and the public accept this vague stereotype as somehow related to being an artist and producing art; a fact which has led some theorists to regard the "artist" as a unique personality on the continuum of personality types. In addition, the pervasiveness of the stereotype has led persons with particular personality characteristics to turn to art as a career. For all of those individuals in the profession, the stereotype of the eccentric artist, the avant-garde individualist, and the enfant terrible has provided the dominant role model for emulation. "An essential part of the Romantic revolution was," as Anthony Alvarez notes, "to make literature [and all art] not so much an accessory of life . . . but a way of life in itself."[1]

For the public sector concerned with the production of art, it has created a paradox wherein art, in one sense the most shared or public of all creations, depends for its creation upon the most private of personalities. Political bodies and the agencies of social policy are, by their very nature, public. They are recognized as properly and necessarily so within a democratic ideology. Art and the agents of art, on the other hand, have no such clear delineation. The artist is envisioned as both the anonymous representative of his or her culture and as the isolated genius and antagonist of that culture. It is this irreconcilable conflict which underlies all discussions of public policy and the arts in modern society.

91

This is not a dilemma new to our age. The paradox has, however, been accented by two major trends in art in the United States over the past fifty years. The first is an increased public involvement in the arts: from the Works Progress Administration and Treasury Arts programs of the Depression to the formation and growth of the National Endowment for the Arts. The second is the concomitant increased emphasis on the artist as the central feature of art and, as a logical derivative of this, the focus on personality and process rather than product as the final reality of art. The impact of this change in orientation--in short, the rise of the artist to preeminence in art rather than any product of art-- can scarcely be overstated for those who must make and enact policy. It alters all prior conceptions of ownership of art objects, and changes substantially the relationships among art, artist, audience, sponsor, and critic.

Although the existence of art seems to be a constant across time in relatively stable societies, the nature of the relationship of the society and the art produced has changed dramatically. The fundamental questions asked of this relationship, no matter how they were phrased, dealt with the content of the art, the process of its production, and its ownership upon completion. At certain times and places the artist, the nature of the process of production, and the product itself were seen as commodities owned by the sponsor who provided the time and materials for such production. However, as public agencies have become increasingly involved and as the images of the artist and of art have changed over the past two centuries, the conception of art as a physical commodity has changed. As a result, the question has become less of ownership and more of accountability. At the simplest level of the modern model, art belongs to the people, but the artist belongs to no one and he or she alone is the only true determinant of the proper process for art. Even here the paradox is apparent. If the artist has become the measure of art, then how can "art" belong to the people and the "artist" belong to no one?

Yet to the degree that the production of art is supported by any agent or individual external to the artist, one may reasonably expect some accountability for the resources expended in that sponsorship. In one sense, that is what this book is about. The real difficulty, however, is in understanding the relationship of the artist as the private muse to the larger agencies and institutions which shape public policy and thus determine the very structure of art in our society.

Neither this book nor this chapter will provide an answer to the question of the relationship of the artist to public policy. There is no such answer. There is no actual structure or "accurate" model upon which to base such an answer. In understanding art in its relationship to other social forms it is crucial to understand the constantly changing nature of the artistic process. This is not process as simply the action of the artist; rather, it is the overlaying series of activities in which artists, sponsors, critics, and audiences engage in the social and political arena. With the growth of the modern stereotypes of art and artist it is crucial to understand the ongoing negotiation of reality which must constantly take place between the public policy maker, the agent of that policy, and the individual artist.

Policy made and enacted in the public sphere demands accountability, and this means that there must be closure: some point at which an account can be made. Yet the principle of modern art denies the existence of closure, and most social science models of art and society support such a denial. To deal with the individual artist in public structures one must maintain a sense of art as a fluid process. Further, with the advent of the post-Romantic image of the artist as the ultimate measure of art, one must be aware of the range of models of accountability which can exist and which may exist simultaneously among the various participants in the structures of art production. Final policy decisions are predetermined by the selection of a specific model of accountability. That choice restricts the questions which can and will be asked, the resources which can and will be used to answer these questions, and the answers which can and will be obtained. Finally, only by understanding the simultaneous existence of contradictory models of accountability by individuals within one framework of interaction can any successful program be initiated, enacted, and completed.

ART AS PLEASANT REBELLION

Art, with religion and science, is one leg of the great triad of primary symbol-producing agencies in society.[2] The artist creates public symbols of suffering out of the pain of his or her private trials (or so it is popularly believed). For most of its existence art survived in service to other structures and institutions. There is nothing unusual about that. When survival is an immediate concern, then all forms of human endeavor serve the religious, political, military, and economic systems which rise to ensure existence. As

John Dewey observed: "The collective life that was manifested in war, worship, the forum, knew no divisions between what was characteristic of these places and operations, and the arts that brought color, grace and dignity into them."[3]

So long as art served some other institution, it was the artistic product and the content of that product which was important. As art was released from servitude to systems other than itself, however, it was the producer of art and the process of production which became primary. In a very real sense art became a system generating its own internal values only with this change. For "in all periods of Western art--despite their immense variety--works of art were created, until the beginning of modern art (about 1850), primarily, if not exclusively, with reference to their meaning."[4] Meaning was determined by the systems and institutions of the society which existed outside of "art" or the production of art. Even to this day art is a social institution with roles and rules, and which relates to other institutions in the social system.[5] The critical change, however, remains the movement from the primacy of the finished work of art as an agent of some other institution to the modern stress on the production of art by the individual artist.

As this image of the artist evolved it gathered miscellaneous baggage. It began with the attachment (or re-attachment) of beauty to art as its primary reason for being. The corollary for the artist was obviously a sensitivity to this beauty and, as art changed from being an accessory to being a way of life, this demanded a general sensitivity of personality. Living in an imperfect and particularly insensitive society, the artist was required to be in opposition to the very forms he or she had previously served. The artist was doomed to suffer and, through that suffering, to express the pain of existence to an audience of individuals who could not identify the cause or express the depth of their own private suffering. "Out of their private tribulations the best modern artists have invented a public language which can comfort [human] guinea pigs who do not know the cause of their death."[6] From the equation of art and beauty as absolutes finally evolved the conception of the tortured, sensitive, creative genius. Indeed, "the creation of the myth of the 'inevitable' rejection of genius has created a perfect situation for the 'extreme' artist, who seeks refusal perhaps even more eagerly than he seeks acceptance."[7] Or, as Hanna Deinhard notes, "The present-day concept of genius is primarily characterized by the fact that it opposes the genius to the mass."[8] Suffering and rejection are embodied not only in metaphysical and social mythologies, but in the more pragmatic realities

of success on an economic level as well. The psychi-
atrist Otto Rank concluded that: "Success is therefore
a stimulus to creativity only so long as it is not
attained."[9]

Since the artist is engaged in the creation of a
new language which is unknown to most people and in
opposition to the status quo institutions of the
society, only the artist and the sensitive few within
the artistic institution can understand what he or she
is doing. As the role of "artist" becomes a totally
inclusive definition for an individual and a pivotal
category of self-definition, the action of the artist
becomes more important as a consideration in art than
the artistic product. Because of the unique and
sensitive nature of the artist, all activities in which
he or she engages can be considered art. By the middle
of the twentieth century this had turned full circle and
art became, as Andy Warhol said, anything done by an
artist.[10] Increasingly, the central core of art
continues to shift from the product to the personality
and on to the process. The commodity of art is
disappearing as a product or as a person. Tom Wolfe
summarized this development as follows:

> It's not permanence and materials, all that
> Winsor & Newton paint and other crap, that are
> at the heart of art, but two things only:
> Genius and the process of creation! Later the
> Conceptualists decided that Genius might as
> well take a walk, too.[11]

Yet even process exists or is made concrete through
the activity of persons whom we come to identify as
artists and, within the social structure which allocates
rewards, there remains a demand for accountability for
the commitment of resources. The artist and society
remain locked in a reciprocal determination of roles and
rewards which shapes the structure of art in the public
sphere. As always, "the concept of art and of the work
of art were and are dependent to the highest degree on
the social value that is attributed to the position and
the work of the artist."[12]

MODELS OF ACCOUNTABILITY

In modern Western societies there are at least five
major models of accountability which can be employed to
describe the complex relationship of artist and sponsor.
The first is the most traditional and commonsensical:
the artist is responsible to the sponsoring agent or

agency, the source of materials and financial support
necessary for the artist to produce. Traditionally, the
sponsor and the final critical audience were the same.
In democratic societies, however, the sponsor is assumed
to be an agent or representative of the larger, more
democratic audience for the work. The implied assumption is that the National Endowment for the Arts (NEA),
for example, is merely a channel for the public funds
into the proper artistic vessel. The ideology of the
structure holds that only through such a professional
agency can the needs and desires of the public constituting the audience for art be best met.[13] There is
also a demand not only for some accountability for the
scarce resources allocated, but also for some system by
which the most intelligent decisions can be made by the
sponsoring agency as to whom these resources should be
allocated. Both of these requirements--for a system for
determination of the best allocation of resources and a
system of accountability for the resources allocated--
stand in direct contrast to the open, non-accountable
personality of the artist.

If art becomes synonymous with the personality of
the artist, the only criterion for allocation of
resources and accountability for those resources is that
personality. Yet such a model inevitably favors maintenance of a status quo, since the past record of the
artist is the most convenient measure of worth. Moreover, it tends to equate the role of sponsor and critic
within the governmental bureaucracy. In any case, the
new artist, the unknown artist, or the artist lying
outside of the structure of accepted criticism is in a
hopeless situation. It is important to realize that
there is nothing new in this, such artists have been in
hopeless situations for at least the past two hundred
years. It is also part of the post-Romantic creed.

In such a model, the relationships among the
sponsor, the artist, and the mass audience tend to be
unspecified and unclear, and no one group has the trust
of the others. Hanna Deinhard sums up this situation:

> The typically modern attitude, as passionless
> as it is ambivalent, can be characterized
> roughly as follows: on the one hand, every
> layman who is interested in art is inclined to
> honor the artist as a sort of higher being,
> and he willingly submits to the spell that
> surrounds all genuine creativity. On the other
> hand, he has, at the same time and especially
> toward living artists a feeling bordering on
> conviction that they are not to be taken
> seriously, viewing them as arrogant unreli-
> able, frivolous, with all the cliches of
> bohemian life. . . .[14]

The negative stereotypes are not purely one-sided against the artist, however. The mass audience, the public, the "common man" gets short shrift from the artists and the critics. Frank Lloyd Wright called him "the enemy of culture." "Culture is not made for him-- but in spite of him."[15] Adolph Gottlieb is less generous. "The average man is enraged by . . . an abstraction . . . because it makes him feel inferior. And he is inferior."[16] Joachim Fest's discussion of art in the Third Reich is no less accusatory. "What took the place of the banned works . . . was nothing more than the artistic prejudices of the . . . man in the street, who now saw his intellectual backwardness and cultural narrow-mindedness sanctioned by the state itself as healthy common sense."[17] The traditional arguments of the "high art" versus "low art" proponents are merely variations on this theme. No matter which position a scholar, artist, or policymaker may take, it is naive to overlook the reality of the suspicion and outright hostility of both groups--artist and public-- toward each other.

Further, when the government is identified totally with "the public," the result must be control not only of the production of art, but of critical and related structures of art as well.[18] Anthony Alvarez has clearly stated the artist's responsibility in such cases.

> When the artist is valued . . . only to the extent to which he serves the policies of the state, then his art is reduced to propaganda . . .In these circumstances, the price of art in the traditional sense and with its tradi- tional values is suicide--or silence, which amounts to the same thing.[19]

It is crucial for the policy agent in a democratic society to understand clearly the advantages and disadvantages of the model of sponsorship accountability and of its implications for art sponsorship and the artist. It has the advantage of solidifying the criteria for responsible and accountable art and of making clear and concrete the relationship of the work of art, the artist, the sponsor, and the audience. Such an advantage is not to be scoffed at when one considers the reality of limited governmental funding and the attractive nature of such a package when one seeks continuance of governmental support. The disadvantages and dangers can not be ignored, however. Under such a model it is easier to deal with the arts organization or the arts manager rather than the artist. In most such models "art", with no more than a passing nod to acknowledge that it is being done, becomes synonymous with arts organizations and arts managers and directors.

The 1977 Conference on Policy Related Studies of the National Endowment for the Arts is illuminative in this respect. Of two major sections on research at the conference, one dealt with "Artistic and Cultural Institutions," the other with "American Artists and Craftsmen." The first section was dominated by economic analyses and econometric models of the arts, and those subjects studied consisted solely of orchestras, theatres, museums and galleries, and opera and ballet companies.[20] The second section, however, discussed the assessment by the National Center for Educational Statistics on the educational progress in the arts, "by which is meant the visual arts of painting, sculpture, and photography," none of which were even mentioned in the previous section.[21] Three of the remaining reports discussed actors, orchestra musicians, and young conductors or musical directors, all of which have some relevance to the earlier section, but a fourth study examined craft artists engaged in "woodworking, pottery, ceramics or other crafts."[22] The situation is one where scholars working in the same area met for the sole purpose of discussing their common topic, and found themselves talking about two different things. Such a schism of language does nothing to assuage the more prevalent disadvantage and danger: the equation of the government with sponsor, critic, and audience. Such an equation heightens the suspicion artists have toward all these groups, and the suspicion the various groups have toward each other.

Closely related to the model of sponsorship accountability is the traditional formulation of the artist being ultimately responsible to the "artistic" structures of society. Ironically, although this second model tends to raise the status of the artist to that of a prophet or messiah, it does so only as he or she is a representative of the "proper" role of artist. The artist is accountable not to the agency which sponsors his or her work nor to the broad audience for that work, but only to the informed and elite structure of art within the society. Since structures are abstracts which are made concrete only through actual persons, it is obvious that the artist becomes responsible to those informed individuals who compose that structure. Closely allied with the modern image of the suffering artist, this elite argues that since the artist is doomed to be misunderstood by the broad public for whom his or her work is too advanced, only the educated and sensitive few are truly capable of evaluating any work at the time it is produced. "Pure art is becoming more and more the possession of an elite in this age of democracy," Catalle Mendes wrote, "the possession of a bizarre, morbid, and charming aristocracy. It is right that its level should be upheld and that it should be surrounded by a secret."[23] Success for the artist-- Calvinist desire for assurance that one's work is part of the truly preordained substance of lasting art--can come only from the critical structures of art within the society.

Yet, there are as many critical structures as publishers willing to publish them, schools willing to teach them, and artists willing to adhere to them. Since there are still agents for sponsorship which exist independent of any given critical structure, these systems confront each other; critical models conflict; and, one--or more--winners are declared.[24] But the responsibility and accountability of the artist is not to himself or herself, nor to the works of art except as these are interpreted by the critical structure. The artist as an individual is lost in the requirements of representativeness of school, time or critique.[25] Since there is never any single "truth" for critical art, public policy and public sponsorship devolves to a question of who the current winner is within any given sponsoring-agency. This is not to suggest that this is radically different from what has happened before. It is merely to point out that it exists and, if the model of accountability to critical structures of art is adopted, then certain ramifications will follow for the artist within the public sphere. Predominant among these is the influence of some particular critical establishment within the sponsoring agency.

The peer-review system of the National Endowment for the Arts is a prime example of the difficulty of determining this audience and the problems inherent when a sponsor becomes involved in such a determination. Michael Straight pointed out that: "The identification of excellence [of grant applicants] rested between 1970 and 1978 on the Endowment's ability to recruit the best professional advisors and to insulate them against all external pressures."[26] However, he also notes the pressures which were brought to bear on this design over time. In 1973 Congress "added that the panels [of experts] should have 'broad geographic representation,'" and in 1976 that "they should give 'the broadest possible representation of viewpoint . . . so that all styles and forms of representation which involve quality in the arts . . . may be treated equitably.'"[27] However, special interest groups on sexual, racial, geographic, and employment issues applied pressure so that the Endowment often found that it had "established formal balance on a panel of women and men, blacks and whites, southerners and midwesterners, traditionalists and iconoclasts, only to lose the creative core that could think profoundly and imaginatively about government action in relation to the arts."[28]

Contrary to the rhetoric of this elite (but in keeping with our understanding of the reality of social life), even the identification of the artistic critical structure involves a negotiation of power. Recognition of this by the Endowment was in all probability a contributing factor to a restructuring of the panel system into policy and grant panels.[29] This organization allowed for "a separate judgement on priorities and directions on the one hand and grant review on the other," thus avoiding structurally some of the difficulties discussed.[30] Throughout, however, it remains clear that "the peer review system is at the heart of the work of the Arts Endowment."[31] Increasingly, the possibility of being funded or supported may rest upon one's accessibility to limited critical structures--the Salon of the time if you will. Under this model it is easier to establish clear criteria for selection, performance, and accountability, as well as clear procedures for fiscal and managerial responsibility. Again, however, it is the individual artist who slips between those cracks which the forms can not cover and the computer cannot program. The history of art consists in part of a liturgy of condemnations of such models of control.

There are at least two models of accountability which are more strikingly individualistic and which place the responsibility of the artist outside of any specific social institution. These models are obviously much less pragmatic for the structures of sponsorship and critical evaluation and are much less popular within these institutions for obvious reasons. Yet, given the paradox underlying this chapter, they are more popular with the individual artist for those same reasons.

First, it is possible to conceive of art as a totally self-contained universe in which art is responsible only to art (l'art pour l'art). Second, one may hold the artist responsible only to his or her personal self-concept. In a sense, these models represent end points on a continuum from a metaphysical "essentialist" view of life to a personal, existentialist philosophy.[32] The ultimate adherents to the l'art pour l'art philosophy would seem to argue for a metaphysical notion of the artist as merely a carrier of some ultimate intangible. Adherents to the other extreme would argue that there is nothing outside of the persona of the artist to which he or she is responsible, not in the structure of the society nor in the metaphysical supracultural realm beyond the concrete time and place.

The former view, art accountable to art, can accommodate a number of conceptions of the psychological structure of the artist. However, no matter where they begin in their explanation, all of the arguments must ultimately devolve to a vessel model of the artist's personality. The artist, no matter how tragic or triumphant, is no more than the container moving this amorphous commodity of "art" one generation forward. Sponsors, critics, and audiences of art are merely the appendages whose primary responsibility is not so much to help as it is to avoid harming. If art exists beyond the artist and beyond the structure, and has an existence which is independent of those agencies, then sponsors and critics must be careful simply to try to avoid placing obstacles in the way of this irreversible force. In some cases they may be able to help by sponsoring the right artist or the right work, or by improving the climate for such workers and such works, but their actual contribution is incidental and indirect. The artist is not accountable in the public realm. Rather, the public realm--the sponsor and the critic--is responsible to the ultimate truth, or beauty, of art. The model of public accountability is reversed, and the judge becomes history as it will be written in the future.

Such a model, although comforting initially to the artist by placing him or her in a larger, almost religious, pattern of meaning, is less than useless to the sponsor, critic, or public policymaker. In fact, it threatens their reason for being, their criteria for selection under any other model, and their authority. As such a threat to the sponsor, it is also ultimately a threat to the artist. If art will move on regardless of the eddies of particular times and places, it is irrelevant in the broad scope whether any particular artist is in the mainstream or is swept into some forgotten bayou. It requires a tremendously selfless artist to accept this logical conclusion, and as a result the art for art's sake model is popular as little more than a conversational piece and pleasant philosophical oddity. It translates into reality in Daniel Fox's observation that: "Artists damn all government patronage when they do not receive the kind they want."[33] Since only the artist knows where art is and where he or she is taking it, patronage or sponsorship can be good only if it comes to them; good sponsorship and good art being more rigidly bound and tautological in this model than in any other. It is a decorative piece for the artist and for the sponsor so long as neither takes it too seriously as a basis for accountability.

Much more useful in the public sphere is an individualistic model of accountability which holds the artist ultimately responsible only to his or her personal construction of self, with the art produced being a reflection of that self. "Painting is self-discovery," Jackson Pollock argued. "Every good artist paints what he is."[34] Such a conception is more compatible with the theories of Sigmund Freud or William James and the psychologists and sociologists who followed them, as well as with the other-directed, autonomous self-structure of modern Western states and the empirical, causal, time-bound model of science in those same states. Arnold Hauser has written that, "one sees how consistently the European outlook on life has developed since 1830. This outlook has one constant, always predominant and ever more profoundly rooted characteristic: the constant of estrangement and loneliness."[35] With slight modifications, specifically by arguing that the core of the artistic self is an understanding of some social, metaphysical, or transcendental reality, the model can accommodate the demands for meaning imposed by a number of other social and political ideologies.

Indeed, this model has been wed to such an unlikely companion as Marxist theory, one author arguing that:

> In the period of the bourgeois democratic revolution (1789-1848) the dissolution of feudal-aristocratic bonds breaks the material and spiritual ties that bind the artist to his . . . patron and makes possible his emergence as a freely creating individual whose source of creative potentiality lies in his own personality and way of perceiving.[36]

The author does hedge, however, writing that: "On the other hand, individual creativity would seem to have no vital social force: the quasi-divine artist is socially impotent."[37]

To the degree that the artist's "self" conforms to a stereotype or role that the structures of sponsorship and evaluation can account for, this personal model of accountability can be allowed to exist in an easy peace with the public model of accountability of the policy institutions. The public sector needs only a concrete form or a clear, specific role for the artist to play--a product or a personality--in order to accommodate the art as self-construct ideal. H. D. Duncan has integrated this awareness into his theory of the role of art and the artist in society, observing that: "In the act of creation the artist addresses himself, but his self-address becomes public once he gives his address form."[38]

Indeed, the very individuality of the self which modern Western society and science adhere to is elevated to the primary characteristic of the role of the artist. The final cooptation of that individuality occurs as it is made the defining characteristic for that role within the system. It becomes the individual counterpart of the structural de-definition of art, and the artist is integrated into the systems of sponsorship and critique as the structural stranger, the tolerated rebel. Duncan himself goes on to note that, "art is a socially sanctioned realm of change, ambiguity, and doubt. . . . Art institutionalizes change in society."[39] Yet increased governmental or public sponsorship means increased bureaucratic involvement in sponsorship and accountability, and the nemesis of bureaucracy is change.

For society generally, the role of artist along with such roles as genius, eccentric, or perhaps even professor, is envisioned as being "outside" of the normal range of social and moral demands of the social order. Yet the avoidance of these demands, an avoidance which would not be tolerated for other roles, is not only allowed for the artist--it is expected and required. If it is the artist who is responsible for removing the layers of time and place to capture the centrality of personal experience, what Ernst Fischer called the "constant features of mankind," the society will interpret actions on his or her part as an attempt to do this.[40] The vocabulary of motive that most persons will attribute to the actions of the artist, and which the society will supply for the artist to employ serves to explain and justify his or her actions on these grounds. Since the artist is supposed to be the individual who strips away the superficial shells of people, this is tantamount to saying that he or she is the individual who can cut through the situational aspects that most persons simply take for granted. In short, the artist is expected to see through the assumed order that the group expresses, the moral order of the normal man, and to express the commonality of personal experiences in the face of this social front. We expect the artist to violate this moral order, for "the power of art . . . lies in its capacity to break down the walls that separate men."[41] As Kenneth Burke has observed, "character, in the social sense, is based upon an integrity, or constancy, which an artist--as artist-- need not have."[42] Illegitimate, bizzare, "immoral" actions are explained away as necessary components of the artistic personality. Such actions are demanded by the now established structural role of the artist and art reaches for the boundaries until it becomes "anything you can get away with."[43]

Although such activities often prove temporarily embarrassing for the sponsor, it is better to have them explained before hand and accepted by the powers-that-be than to have to deal with them item-by-item. If the acceptance of the role of the artist as the oddball and amoral wierdo can be integrated into the general structure of funding agencies, then a model of accountability which focuses on the organization or manager is more secure and more acceptable, and all parties concerned are allowed to negotiate the reality which is most acceptable to each.

The National Endowment for the Arts has achieved this integration by clearly noting that in their fellowship program they fund the artist, and not the art which is produced. The Endowment does not "commission" works nor does it involve itself with the content of works produced. Rather, it makes awards "to individuals of recognized excellence [to] sustain and further develop a high level of quality."[44] In the Endowment's statement of purpose, there is a clear absence of the concept of product in fostering support for "effort by individual artists." On the other hand, in the attempt to "foster creative effort and the development of excellence in the arts in America," the agency avoids mention of individuals when it sets out its proposal to do so "through support of institutions for projects and productions of substantial artistic significance."[45]

Although this accents the preeminence of the individual artist over the artistic product, it provides the necessary defense against the charges of obscenity and absurdity which inevitably occur in a public agency funding the arts. Michael Straight's narrative on his tenure as Deputy Chairman for the NEA is laced with the conflicts between the social moral order and the artistic product; conflicts from President Nixon's reaction to the sculpture Adam to Senator Helms's response to Fear of Flying.[46] It is instructive to note that in each of these cases the artist never became directly involved. This model of accountability provides a survival mechanism for the artist through the protection afforded by the shield of the agencies of sponsorship and critical evaluation. The Endowment is well aware of the political risks involved in support for individual artists.

> Support of individual artists is . . . riskier than institutional support. A politically controversial work or one that proves embarrassing because it was an experiment that misfired is likely to bring greater criticism to the funding agency when an individual fellowship is involved. In the case of an institutional grant gone sour, blame is more likely to be shared with the erring arts institution.[47]

The "integrated outsider" is a role loaded with pitfalls, but one which can allow the individual to stand both in the world of financial support and the world of ultimate personal responsibility.

One final model of accountability should be mentioned. It is often implied in sponsorship or

critical establishment accountability models, and is
quite popular in various forms in academic work, particularly within sociology. This is the concept of the
artist as a product of his or her culture, and thus to
argue that the artist is accountable to that society.
It is a model which, when drawn to its logical conclusion, is also the easiest to employ for the ends of
power by particular groups, sub-cultures, or nation
states. Through the argument that the true artist
reflects the glory of the culture which gave him or her
form, both the artist and the state are raised to a
position of supremacy; both remain supportive and un-
challenged as any art or critical standards which would
do so are consigned to trash, or worse. Although the
tendency is greater in totalitarian societies, the pro-
pensity for such use exists in any model of the artist
as representative, mirror, vessel, or seismograph of his
or her time or place. Almost all states recognize the
importance of a public, supportive art. Even in Western
democratic societies we find the Pulitzer Prize winner,
the Poet laureate, the French Academy.

Variations on these themes underlie most Fascist
and Marxist models of art. There is, however, a
constant intellectual sleight of hand necessary
in both ideologies to define how the properly identified
groups produce the proper artists doing the proper sort
of work and, in revisionist works, how the former
explanations and definitions were in error. In this
regard Robert N. Wilson has pointed out that: "Marxist
interpretations commonly flounder on one of two major
obstacles. The first of these is the protean nature of
the artist: his many-sidedness often leads to 'betrayal'
of his presumed class interests . . . Secondly, a direct
one-to-one correspondence between class and art product
is very difficult to establish because of the congeries
of other influences at work simultaneously."[48]

The problem with this model in the most enlightened
democratic societies is not that it is an improper
explanation, but that the statement of the problem is
taken as the answer. It is obvious that every artist is
the product of his or her culture, bound by the language
he or she is taught, the technical facilities and
resources of the historical time and place, the
structures available for production, and so on. There
were no photographers in ancient Rome, no video-tape
artists in Renaissance France. But the conclusion that
the artist represents or reflects his or her society is
merely the first statement of the problem. John Dewey
has reduced the problem even further in making the same
point.

It should be just a commonplace that esthetic
understanding . . . must start with the soil,

air, and light out of which things estheti-
cally admirable arise. And these conditions
are the conditions that make an ordinary
experience complete. The more we recognize
this fact, the more we shall find ourselves
faced with a problem rather than a final
solution. If artistic and aesthetic quality
is implicit in every normal experience, how
shall we explain how and why it so generally
fails to become explicit?[49]

How does this thing "art" happen within a society?
How bound by the social structures is the artist and,
more specifically, what kinds of particular structures
are more confining to what particular kinds of
personalities? Which components of the culture does the
artist more thoroughly reflect--class, race, sex,
region, or some other? And what is the nature of the
relationship of sponsorship, evaluation, and
accountability to the artistic personality and the
artistic product which is created in a particular time
and place? At present, the model of the artist as
mirror, cultural vessel, or representative of the
society is a handy beginning, perhaps a useful heuristic
metaphor for scholarly work. As an aid to understanding
the relationship of the artist to the public or as a
model for public policy relating to the arts, it is
little more than a rhetorical device.

BALANCE, NOT RESOLUTION

Our pluralistic, individualistic society creates
conditions of inevitable sub-cultural and individual
conflict. In the world of art, this is most obvious in
the increasing divergence of two major movements within
the system of that world.
Among sponsoring or funding agencies, particularly
public agencies, there is a movement toward organization
and management which makes not only the proper determination for allocation of scarce resources more possible,
but makes the accountability of the agency and the
recipient of those resources more public and observable.
On the other hand, the broader critical conception of
"art" has moved from that of a product produced by an
artist to the process itself. In this movement, the
product of art has become the artist, moving increasingly away from the physical productions and products
which have traditionally provided objects of accountability to the persons or organizations which sponsored
them. This divergence of directions, with each

component moving on its own private vector, becomes more critical and more pronounced as the public involvement in art increases. There has been no resolution of this dilemma; there is every reason to suspect that its real impact is just beginning to be felt.

There is no solution to this paradox, no pleasant resolution to the confrontation of the public world with the private muse. There is no way to eliminate the conflict, no model of accountability which can be used to provide a stable solution. For the administrator, sponsor, manager, legislator or scholar there is no closure, and for all of these roles that is one of the most difficult realities to accept.

Any public policy which deals finally with artists, and any administrator charged with the enactment of such a policy, can do no more than take account of the following four conclusions. First, the policy and those individuals charged with its enactment must accept the lack of closure in the process and the dominance of process rather than product in the artists' world compared to the economic, political, and social worlds in which the administrator more commonly works. Second, the acceptance of the dominance of process over product models forces the programs and policies created to prepare and allow for structures within themselves to accept this condition. Rather than the common models of product evaluation and product change, systems must be designed which deal with process evaluation and change without demanding the paper products which create an artificial item as substitute. Third, the individuals involved at every level must personally allow for such ongoing change and lack of specificity. This involves more than simply allowing for ambiguity within the structures of the policies and programs involved, for the enactment of these policies is carried out by particular people in concrete settings. Unfortunately, the individuals most likely to be involved in such programs tend to come from intellectual and academic traditions in which they are taught that closure and evaluation of results are crucial. The individuals dealing with artists in the public sphere must overcome their own training if the goal, rather than the means, is to remain paramount.

Finally, the policy enactors must not guide nor instruct, but balance. They must not lose sight of the fact that they are merely expeditors. They must not come to believe that their work produces art, but must constantly remember that they are there merely to enable others to do that. They must, at every level, balance the demands of other levels above and below their position and recall that in this field, probably more than any other, those demands will be logically contradictory. The analogy is not to the orchestra

conductor leading the instruments in concert, but to the
juggler keeping four, five, or more objects in the air
with two hands. In regard to the arts, more than any
other arena, the demands upon policy and the individuals
charged with the enactment of this policy defy the
traditional models and teachings of organization,
administration, and evaluation.

NOTES

[1] Anthony Alvarez, The Savage God (New York: Random House, 1970), p. 201.

[2] Ernst Fischer, The Necessity of Art (Baltimore: Penguin Books, 1959), p. 36.

[3] John Dewey, Art as Experience (New York: Capricorn, 1934), p. 7.

[4] Hanna Deinhard, Meaning and Expression (Boston: Beacon Press, 1967), p. 15.

[5] Refer to Milton C. Albrecht, "Art as an Institution," American Sociological Review 33 (June 1968); Howard S. Becker, "Art as Collective Action," American Sociological Review 39 (December 1974) and Robert N. Wilson, The Arts in Society (Englewood Cliffs, NJ: Prentice Hall, 1964).

[6] Alvarez, The Savage God, p. 252.

[7] Edward Lucie-Smith, "Current Social Trends in Contemporary Art," in Jean Creedy, ed., The Social Context of Art (New York: Harper & Row, 1970), p. 34.

[8] Deinhard, Meaning and Expression, p. 101.

[9] Otto Rank, Art and Artist (New York: Tudor, 1932), p. 224.

[10] See, for a rather earthy example, the discussion of the excrement of the artist in Michael Straight, Twigs for an Eagle's Nest (New York: Devon Press, 1979), pp. 130-132.

[11] Tom Wolfe, The Painted Word (New York: Bantam, 1975), p. 104.

[12] Deinhard, Meaning and Expression, p. 94.

[13] One is referred to the discussion in Michael Straight, Twigs, pp. 69-99.

[14] Deinhard, Meaning and Expression, p. 91.

[15] Frank Lloyd Wright as quoted in Selden Rodman, Conversations With Artists (New York: Capricorn, 1957), p. 54.

[16] Adolph Gottlieb as quoted in Rodman, Conversations, p. 90.

[17] Joachim C. Fest, The Face of The Third Reich (New York: Ace Books, p. 374.

[18] See David Stewart Hull, Film in the Third Reich (Los Angeles: University of California Press, 1969), pp. 95-96 for a concise example of the need for control to spread beyond the process of production.

[19] Alvarez, The Savage God, p. 238.

[20] The proceedings of the conference are available in David Cwi, Research in the Arts: Proceedings of the Conference on Policy Related Studies of the National Endowment for the Arts (Baltimore: Walters Art Gallery, 1977). The sections discussed appear on pages 40-68.

[21] Frank Barron, "Changes over Time In Artistic Potential and Productivity," in Cwi, Research in the Arts, p. 72.

110

[22] Constance Citro, "Designing a Study of Craft-artists and Their Organizations," in Cwi, _Research in the Arts_, p. 80.

[23] Catalle Mendes as quoted in Arnold Hauser, _The Social History of Art_, 4 Vols. (New York: Random House, 1951), 4: 198-199.

[24] Discussions and examples of this can be found in Harold Rosenberg, _The De-Definition of Art_ (New York: Horizon Press, 1972) and specifically in Wolfe, _The Painted Word_, pp. 73-89.

[25] See, for example, the argument made in Herbert Read, _Art and Alienation_ (New York: Viking, 1967), pp. 18-28.

[26] Straight, _Twigs_, p. 77.

[27] _Ibid._, p. 79. Refer also to _Hearings_ before the House Subcommittee on the Department of the Interior and Related Agencies, Committee on Appropriations, 96th. Cong. 1st. sess., Part II (1980), pp. 487-488 and 493.

[28] _Ibid._

[29] _Ibid._, p. 457.

[30] _Ibid._, p. 480.

[31] _Ibid._, p. 456.

[32] See Wolfe, _The Painted Word_ p. 7.

[33] Daniel Fox, "Artist in the Modern State: The Nineteenth Century Background," in Milton C. Albrecht, and others, eds., _The Sociology of Art and Literature_ (New York: Praeger, 1970), p. 383.

[34] Jackson Pollock as quoted in Rodman, _Conversations_, p. 82.

[35] Hauser, _Social History_, p. 207.

[36] A. S. Crehan, "The Artist as Producer," in Art, Politics and Society Group, _Social Roles for the Artist_ (Liverpool: Art, Politics and Society Group, 1979), p. 47.

[37] _Ibid._, p. 48

[38] H. D. Duncan, _Symbols in Society_ (London: Oxford University Press, 1968), p. 32.

[39] _Ibid._, p. 190.

[40] Fischer, _Necessity of Art_, p. 13.

[41] Duncan, _Symbols in Society_, p. 223.

[42] Kenneth Burke, _Counter-Statement_ (Los Angeles: University of California Press, 1931), p. 183.

[43] Marshall McLuhan and Quenton Fiore, _The Medium is the Message_ (New York: Bantam, 1967), pp. 134-136.

[44] U.S. National Endowment for the Arts, Division of Planning, _General Plan_ (1979), p. 6.

[45] _Ibid._, pp. 4-5.

[46] A number of examples are in Straight, _Twigs_, pp. 26-28, 31-33, 133-148.

[47] National Endowment for the Arts, _General Plan_, pp. 29-30.

[48] Wilson, _Arts in Society_, p. 48.

[49] Dewey, _Art as Experience_, p. 49.

6
Government Patronage: An Historical Overview

Lawrence Mankin

The American national government's support for the arts has a unique character. Unlike ecclesiastical or royal patrons, the government in its role as patron has not only purchased and commissioned works of art but also has tried to develop an atmosphere in which art itself and artists themselves can flourish. This patronage has taken place in a context of limited public participation in cultural affairs and in a climate where art appreciation is not a widespread social value. Despite these formidable obstacles, the U.S. government has persisted in its efforts to foster cultural development. The American government has tried to act as patron by providing support for the arts through rhetoric, symbols, and programs. This chapter will examine each of these forms of patronage provided by the American national government.[1]

RHETORICAL SUPPORT

For most of our history, government support of the arts has been rhetorical rather than monetary. The creation of an atmosphere favorable to artistic production has been the aim of several presidents. Words have been necessary because support for the arts does not seem to flow naturally from our people. Our early puritan background created cautious attitudes regarding the arts.[2] Today we are pragmatists who demand tangible results from our investments. It is difficult to convince people to support art for its own sake; it must be justified as conducive of some further good. At times it is stated that the arts should be the recipient of federal funds because they further some noble cause. For example, the arts are important for good mental health and on this basis the government

111

should support them. Apparently, this "backdoor
approach" to support for the arts is judged to be more
successful in gaining support than arguments that
discuss the intrinsic worth of culture.[3]

Official encouragement of artistic activity began
with our first president. George Washington remarked
that "the arts and sciences are essential to the
prosperity of the state and to the ornament and
happiness of human life."[4] Recent presidents have given
similar endorsements. Dwight Eisenhower stated that "in
the advancement of the various activities which would
make our civilization endure and flourish, the federal
government should do more to give official recognition
to the importance of the arts and other cultural
activities."[5] In 1963, John F. Kennedy expressed the
following hope.

> I see little of more importance to the future
> of our own country and our civilization than
> full recognition of the place of the
> artist. . . . I look forward to an America
> which will award achievement in the arts as we
> reward achievement in business or statecraft.
> I look forward to an America which will
> steadily raise the standards of artistic
> accomplishment and which will steadily enlarge
> cultural opportunities for all our citizens.
> And I look forward to an America which
> commands respect throughout the world not only
> for its strength but for its civilization as
> well.[6]

Six years later Richard Nixon stated that America had
become an international leader in the arts. "America
has moved to the forefront as a place of creative
expression. The excellence of the American product has
won worldwide recognition."[7] Nixon judged the artist to
play an indispensable role within American society:

> Our creative and performing artists give free
> and full expression to the American spirit as
> they illuminate, criticize and celebrate our
> civilization. Like our leaders they are an
> invaluable national resource.[8]

Gerald Ford shared a similar view and described himself
as a convert to public support for the arts and he noted
that "converts are often more ardent advocates than
those who are brought up in it."[9] Congressmen have also
lent their support to artistic encouragement. However,
the essential point is that although words of
governmental support for the arts span centuries, little
has been done until recently in the way of programmatic

support.   Senator Jacob Javits summarizes the thoughts
that have just been expressed.

> Federal concern with the arts goes back a very
> long way--way back to George Washington's
> time. We have not done too much about it.[10]

SYMBOLIC GESTURES

Recent presidents have tried to use their
ceremonial role to communicate to the nation the
importance of culture, as well as to communicate to the
artist the national government's concern for his
welfare.   The Kennedy administration's favorable tone
toward the arts manifested itself early.   A number of
artists were invited to attend his inauguration and
Robert Frost shared the rostrum in order to read a poem.
There was a jubilant response by artists to Kennedy's
attitude. John Steinbeck said, "what a joy . . . that
literacy is no longer prima facie evidence of
treason."[11]   E.B. White was no less enthusiastic in his
response to Kennedy.

> One of the excitements of American citizenship
> is a man's feeling of identity with his elect-
> ed President. I never had this feeling hit me
> so hard as January 20, 1961, when watching on
> television from a Maine farmhouse, I saw first
> the lectern take fire, then so much else--
> thanks to your brave words.   I promise that
> whenever I can manage I'll blow my little
> draft of air on the beloved flame.[12]

Kennedy did not appreciate all of the arts equally but
tried to convey an enthusiasm for each of them.
Theodore Sorensen observed that Kennedy "had no interest
in opera, dozed off at symphony concerts and was bored
by ballet." But Arthur Schlesinger noted that:

> The character of his personal interest was
> less important than his conviction that the
> health of the arts was vitally related to the
> health of society. He saw the arts not as a
> distraction in the life of a nation but as
> something close to the heart of a nation's
> purpose.   Excellence was a public necessity,
> ugliness a national disgrace.   The arts
> therefore were in his view, part of the
> presidential responsibility, and he looked for
> opportunities to demonstrate his concern.[13]

It was the era of "Camelot" and the atmosphere embraced all. Washington was often found with artists performing at the White House. The Presidential Medal of Freedom was awarded to artists during the Kennedy administration and the President and his wife took a personal interest in the parks and architecture of Washington.

Kennedy's personal belief in the worth of the arts seems clear but political motives also contributed to his support for the arts. Sorensen says that:

> His effort, to be sure, had political advantages. It was not the endorsements and entertainment which artistic celebrities could provide in further campaigns. That was never a reason. More important was the fact that liberal Democrats, reformers, wealth contributors and independent Republicans were among the culturally minded. They warmed to an intellectual President who patronized the arts when his position on fiscal and other matters might well have cooled them. The President frequently sought statistics on how many Americans (i.e., voters) played musical instruments, visited art galleries and museums or in some other way participated in cultural life.[14]

Thus, although the motives behind Kennedy's support for the arts were mixed, Lewis Mumford described Kennedy as "the first American President to give art, literature and music a place of dignity and honor in our national life."[15]

While Lyndon Johnson lacked the cultural and intellectual image of John Kennedy, he believed that it was a president's obligation to encourage the arts. One of his symbolic gestures was a White House arts festival which was designed to lend recognition and support to the arts. It turned into a humiliating event for the President. Artistic creations were to be exhibited or performed or read aloud. According to Eric Goldman, thoughts of propaganda or partisan political advantage were absent from the original motives which generated the idea for the festival. The Dominican invasion and increased bombing of North Vietnam intervened between the conception of the festival and its date of occurrence. A number of artists believed that the festival was being used by Johnson as evidence that artists and intellectuals supported his policies. Goldman takes issue with this viewpoint:

> Between the time of his first interest in the festival and the final approval, he had ordered systematic bombing of North Vietnam

and the criticism had flared in intellectual and artistic circles. Perhaps then he started thinking of a tool to quiet opposition to the war. But I doubt this was ever a major consideration; he simply did not mean to take the festival that seriously. Overall LBJ appeared to think of it as a pleasant day, the sort of thing a President ought to do in view of all the interest in art around the country, one that would particularly please the ladies, and that was that.[16]

The day of the festival found the poet Robert Lowell boycotting it and critic Dwight MacDonald circulating a petition on the White House grounds stating the following:

> We should make it clear that in accepting the President's kind invitation to attend the White House arts festival we do not mean to repudiate the courageous position taken by Robert Lowell, or to endorse the administration's foreign policy. We quite share Mr. Lowell's dismay at our country's recent actions in Vietnam and the Dominican Republic.[17]

Mrs. Johnson listened to John Hersey make the following remarks before he read an excerpt from Hiroshima:

> Let these words be a reminder. The steps from one degree of violence to the next is imperceptibly taken and cannot easily be taken back. The end point is horror and oblivion. We cannot for a moment forget the truly terminal dangers in these times, of miscalculating, of arrogance, or accident, of reliance not on moral strength but on mere military power. Wars have a way of getting out of hand.[18]

The festival lasted for thirteen hours and although it was an awkward day for Johnson, Howard Taubman noted that "no President in history, not even John F. Kennedy, has ever played host to so concentrated a demonstration of American achievement in this field."[19]

Richard Nixon continued to share his predecessors' interest in the arts. Artists gave performances in the White House, heard the encouraging words of the President at art conferences, and were recipients of the Medal of Freedom award. The inscription on the Medal of Freedom award presented to Philadelphia Orchestra conductor Eugene Ormandy reads:

He has reminded audiences here in his adopted
country and all over the world that the heart
of music is a human heart and that the glory
of music reflects and sustains the true glory
of the human spirit.[20]

The last forty years has witnessed not only words of
support and symbolic gestures of support for the arts by
government officials but also innovative programs of
support. The next section examines the most significant
of these programs that existed prior to the Kennedy
Administration.

PROGRAMS OF SUPPORT

If one excludes buildings designed to house
governmental offices and various monuments commemorating
important events and individuals, federal programs in
support of the arts have been practically nonexistent
for most of our history. Earlier it was suggested that
the necessary cultural foundations were not laid for
artistic support in America. Robert Myron and Abner
Sundell add that the failure of early governmental arts
projects had a strong negative influence for further
governmental endeavors in this area. Paintings which
were purchased for exhibit in the Capitol building were
ridiculed by artists and a statue of George Washington
that was commissioned by the federal government became
the subject of almost universal scorn.

Horatio Greenough's monumental marble statue
of George Washington was fifteen feet tall,
twenty tons in weight. Greenough labored for
nine years in a Florentine studio to bring
forth a half-nude George Washington, bare to
the waist, seated like Ceasar on an ancient
Roman throne. A drape thrown over one
upraised arm covers the lower half of his
figure, while his other arm grasps a spearlike
scepter. Greenough's intent was to represent
Washington, symbolically, as a man retired
from the military service who has given up the
sword and taken the mantle of the lawgiver.
With uplifted hand he proclaims judgment. The
statue was the perfect image of the
President's face and features blended with the
Roman past, from toga, sandals, and sword down
to the acclivity reproduced Roman throne. But
in 1843 neither the American public nor
Congress was ready to accept the "father of"

our country' as a half-naked Roman. Far ahead of its time in concept and vision, it ended up the butt of countless jokes and an expensive dust collector in the basement of the Smithsonian Institution responsible for the discouragement of government partonage of the arts for almost one hundred years.[21]

Calls for programs of artistic support could occasionally be heard in governmental circles prior to the 1930's but few national programs materialized.[22] Cultural and educational programs were considered to be the responsibility of state and local governments.[23] The notable exception to this inactivity was a governmental provision for copyright protection. Artists were granted a monopoly over the use of their works for an initial period of twenty-eight years. Some criticized this legislation as inadequate as an artist could lose control over his work in the latter part of his lifetime; a period in which earning capacity tends to decline. The Rockefeller Panel Report, following this rationale, recommended expanding copyright protection,[24]

> . . . to a term compared to that prevailing in England and most of Europe, which is the author's lifetime plus fifty years. At present, many elderly artists are in the curious position of outliving the royalties in their early works at a time when the income may be most valuable to them.[25]

Congress finally accepted this rationale and since January 1, 1978 artists have been granted the protection recommended by the Rockefeller Panel.

NEW DEAL PROGRAMS: THE SUPPORT

The national government's attitude toward the arts changed in the 1930s as a reflection of a broader conception held by many of the government's proper role in society. The twenties, the era of the flapper, illicit alcohol, and a free spirit gave way to the somber mood of an economically depressed nation. Hope was the most valuable possession of many. Some reached out in desperation to groups which promised deliverance to better times. Arthur Schlesinger has labeled the politics of this period "The Politics of Upheavel."[26] A sense of emergency pervaded the new Roosevelt Administration. Old formulas had failed to bring

economic recovery and experimental programs were
initiated. There was not time for sound planning,
action had to be taken. This is the atmosphere in which
the New Deal's cultural programs were launched.

Thousands of artists were among the multitude of
the unemployed. Twenty thousand theatrical people alone
were out of work.[27] Employment was the number one
priority of the Roosevelt Administration. Out of the
need to put people to work the government became
involved with the arts as it never had been before.
Relief administrator Olin Dows states that:

> Human economic relief was the motive behind
> all the New Deal's art programs. That is why
> they were so easily accepted by the public and
> the politicians. If it had not been for the
> great depression, it is unlikely that our
> government would have sponsored more art than
> it had in the past.[28]

Dows exaggerates the ease with which these programs were
accepted. Administration critics waited for the proper
opportunity to launch their attack against these
programs but more will be said about this below.
Historian Jerre Mangione suggests that a fear of
revolution played a part in the development of these
programs.

> To what extent the possibility of revolution
> influenced the actions of the Roosevelt
> Administration is, of course, a matter of
> speculation. However, it must have acted as
> something of a prod for New Dealers to
> initiate programs like the Federal Writers
> Project, which in any other era would have
> been rendered too radical for government
> sponsorship.[29]

The Public Works Art Project (P.W.A.P.) was the
first cultural program to be initiated in the New Deal.
Operated under the auspices of the Treasury Department,
it was better run than the other New Deal art projects
which would follow it. Historically, it marked "the
first time the government had subsidized an art project
of national dimension."[30] Funds for this project were
supplied by the Civil Works Administration to employ
painters and sculptors to create works for public
buildings.

> The P.W.A.P. employed about 3,750 artists at
> low daily wages. They provided over 15,600
> works of art. . . . The total cost was

approximately $1,312,000, which makes the cost per artist $350.[31]

This program expired after seven months of operation in June, 1934 and was succeeded in the Treasury by what was eventually to be known as the Section on Fine Arts. Sculpture works and murals were created for buildings throughout the nation. Local panels were employed by the Section to recommend the commissioning of artists for projects in their areas. This program was quite successful and only ended in 1943 because of the economic constraints imposed by World War II.

> During those nine years of activity the Section awarded 1,124 mural contracts for which it paid $1,472,199 and 289 contracts for sculpture costing $563,529 . . . 1,205 individual artists placed their work in federal buildings. The average price for the mural commission was $1,356 and for sculpture $1,935. Administrative costs were $393,516.[32]

A number of reasons accounted for the program's success. Edward Bruce, who designed the program, combined the skills of artistic ability and appreciation with those of a pragmatic administrator. Olin Dows observes that:

> Being a lawyer, businessman and economist and knowing most of the important politicians and administrators informally, Bruce would talk to them in their own language, and so inspired their confidence in what he was trying to do.[33]

His relations with members of both political parties were good and he was the chief architect of strategies to cope with political questions such as congressional relations.[34]

Cordiality characterized the relationship between the Section and the local judging panels. No local panel's selection of an artist to be commissioned to do a mural or sculpture was revised by the Section.[35] This type of relationship avoided internecine warfare which can consume both the resources and energy of an agency and sabotage its goals. The WPA Arts Projects (discussed below) were not as successful in avoiding this danger.

Contributing to the success of the Section was the enthusiastic support of President and Mrs. Roosevelt and Secretary of Treasury Henry Morgenthau and his wife.

The Section of Fine Arts was stronger than was
warranted by its subordinate position in the
Treasury department table of organization.
Many officials knew that President and Mrs.
Roosevelt and Secretary and Mrs. Morgenthau
were interested. The latter especially kept
in close touch with our activities. Her wise,
sympathetic and intelligent advice was a great
asset. Although she helped to solve a few
difficult administrative matters, there was
never any question of professional interference or pressure.[36]

For the most part, the Section on Fine Arts shunned
projects which might result in controversy but it was
not entirely successful in escaping from criticism.
Both the P.W.A.P. and the Section on Fine Arts
commissioned projects by artists who were not usually
unemployed or destitute. According to Mangione, the
P.W.A.P.:

. . . employed artists on the basis of
recognized competence rather than economic
need, its critics attacked it for paying
salaries to affluent artists who were not in
need of work.[37]

The Treasury Arts Relief Project, created in July
1935 as the third cultural program which the Treasury
Department administered, was not subject to the above
criticism. Funding for this program was provided by the
Works Progress Administration and Arts Relief Project
under its administrative guidelines. For most of the
Project's existence, seventy-five percent of the people
employed by it came from the relief rolls[38] and like
the other Treasury programs, it commissioned artists to
provide murals and paintings for federal buildings. The
program, which employed approximately 330 persons,
existed for four years at a total cost of $735,700.[39]
Federal expenditures were pumped into the economy to
acquire the services of artists whose finished projects
demonstrated artistic competence. Controversial
projects which might result in attacks upon the program
were avoided. The Works Progress Administration (WPA)
Art Projects, on the other hand, were constantly
surrounded by controversy and its operations were
dramatically affected by it.
Experimental, idealistic, political and frustrating
are all terms which aptly describe the WPA art projects.
Never had the government engaged in such a program, nor
has it since. Under favorable conditions it would have
been difficult to determine whether the program would
have flourished but given the conditions under which it

was conceived and operated only a constant struggle for survival could ensue. Persued by the need to alleviate the economic plight of thousands of artists and lobbied by cultural organizations, the government proposed the WPA Arts Projects as a solution. The Emergency Relief Act of 1935 was the authorizing legislation for the creation of the WPA. Mangione states that:

> An inconspicuous but significant clause in the act authorized assistance to educational, professional and clerical persons; a nation-wide program for useful employment of artists, musicians, actors, entertainers, writers . . . and others in these cultural fields.[40]

The WPA, an agency mainly concerned with construction work, was created by an executive order on May 6, 1935 and the arts projects were begun on September 12, 1935. The following five projects constituted the arts programs of the WPA: (1) Theater Project, (2) Writers' Project, (3) Art Project, (4) Music Project, and (5) Historical Survey. (The Historical Survey, as a special case, is not discussed in this study.) Although their priorities at times became blurred, the goals set for the art projects were clear. The President and Harry Hopkins (the Administrator of the WPA) envisioned the program to be primarily one of economic relief with secondary emphasis on artistic competence and achievement.[41] At times the administrators of the various projects, who were artists themselves, tended to forget this ordering of priorities but all were in agreement that the projects should instill an appreciation of the arts in people. It was hoped that support from the people would obviate further national government underwriting of the arts.

The day the WPA came into existence was the first day it confronted its enemies. Congress at best was passive in its support of the new agency. William F. O'Donald states that:

> At no time can it be said that Congress, as a whole, truly and generally supported the principle of work relief. Congress merely permitted its use, because in 1935 it was afraid to do otherwise and, having started the WPA, was after 1935, afraid to stop it.[42]

McDonald summarizes the sentiments upon which arguments and opposition to the arts have long been based.

> Music, drama, literary activities, painting and sculpture were in the layman's mind avocations that existed either for the

delecation of those who could pay for them or
for the self-satisfaction of those engaged in
them. If the idea that they properly entered
into popular culture, or were of importance in
the life of the common man, ever suggested
itself to men of affairs, it failed to lead to
action. Private individuals, to be sure, out
of largess of spirit, might make contributions
and bequests that made the arts accessible to
the many; but the thought that there existed a
public responsibility on the part of the state
to encourage art and the enjoyment of the
aesthetic experience occurred only to those
whose general philosophy, political culture,
was regarded in better circles as, if not
radical, at least unsound.[43]

The press was unsympathetic and even hostile in its
attitude toward the WPA and its Arts Projects.[44] Jane
DeHart Mathews says of the Director of the Federal
Theater Project that:

In nearly every batch of press clippings that
poured in from across the country, Hallie
Flanagan found references to the government's
ill-advised venture into show business.[45]

When the Dies committee investigated the Arts Projects,
it found a sympathetic press willing to publicize its
activities. It is estimated that the committee was
"able to win the support of three quarters of the
newspaper reading public, a distinction seldom achieved
of any congressional committee."[46]

The Arts Projects also faced the problem of
incorporating creative people within the confines of a
governmental bureaucracy. Creativity requires freedom
and to the artist rules and regulations can be like
ropes tied around a pair of creative hands. Paper work,
wage and hour regulations frustrated working
relationships and delayed the completion of projects.
McDonald notes that:

Within a given project unit, workers in
different categories worked a different number
of hours a month; even workers in the same
category (e.g., professional and technical)
did not work the same number of hours a week
if the prevailing hourly rate for each group
were not the same. This made it difficult,
and at times impossible, to synchronize hours
of work of workers on a given project. Thus
both quality and continuity of supervision
suffered, and the proper proportion of skilled

to unskilled workers, necessary for efficient operation, was not as readily maintained. Furthermore, the morale that comes from regularity of hours with a working group was lacking, and workers with higher hourly wages and correspondingly shorter hours not infrequently accepted private employment in their leisure time--a practice that aroused the jealousy both of fellow project workers and of those in private employ who saw in the practice a threat to their own security.[47]

If all of the above presented enough obstacles to hinder the success of the Arts Projects, the organizational design in which the Arts Projects operated was an additional burden. In the early months of their existence the Arts Projects were officially given a great amount of autonomy which unfortunately led to a high degree of intra-organizational conflict. Each WPA state administrator had on his staff a director for each of the Arts Projects but this was only a formality. In fact, the state directors were controlled by the Arts Project national office and state directors in turn controlled district supervisors. The state directors and district supervisors of the WPA provided services for the state and district directors of the Arts Projects rather than the reverse. Mathews states that for "reasons of economy" the Arts Projects were placed in the administrative framework of district and state WPA offices."[48] This decision reflected a lack of awareness of the possible political consequences of such an organizational design. McDonald's description below demonstrates the early autonomy of the Arts Projects.

> In the initiation and operation of a project unit of Federal One, the district art supervisors were responsible for: (1) the determination of eligibility of available personnel; (2) the classification of eligibility within the wage group; (3) the kind of project to be operated in the locality; (4) the predesignation of desired personnel for employment; and (5) the immediate supervision of the project unit. The federal arts director, or their field representative, was responsible for: (1) the final approval of the project application; and (2) the overall technical supervision of the project units. The federal WPA administrator, acting on the advice of the federal director of professional and service projects, was responsible for: (1) the allocation of funds to the states for the project units; (2) the

conditions attached to the spending of the money; and (3) the decision to discontinue any project unit. Indeed, the only privilege left with the state and district WPA officials was that of protest.[49]

Thus, controls over the finances and personnel of the Arts Projects were in the hands of its own officials.

Tension between the Arts Projects and its host agency was also heightened by differences in loyalties and perspectives of state WPA administrators and state arts directors. The appointment of state administrators required senatorial confirmation and thus they were subject to the practice of senatorial courtesy. Most state administrators owed their appointment to a senator from their state. Although Harry Hopkins had formal control over WPA state administrators, he confronted political limitations which constricted his authority. McDonald discusses these limitations:

> In the first place, the WPA did not exist by virtue of a substantive law but merely by virtue of appropriations acts previously noted. Congress, and especially the House, could at any time either refuse money or, as indeed it did, progressively reduce appropriations. The state administrators, who for the most part held their appointments because of senatorial connections were in a position to make their point of view powerful in Congress. Harry Hopkins could resent, at times fight, this power but never defy it. In the second place, the philosophy of the state governments expressed itself naturally through pressures upon their senators and representatives, who, in turn, brought this philosophy to bear upon national issues.[50]

In addition to these strains, many states were opposed to the concept of work relief and resented the federal controls which came with the welfare funds.[51] The state directors exercised effective control over their staffs but tension between arts personnel and the non-arts personnel in the WPA characterized their relationship throughout the existence of the Arts Projects.

President Roosevelt was personally involved in trying to shape the policies of Federal One as the Arts Projects were known.[52] His judgment alerted him to the political sensibilities that would be affected by the creation of an arts project and, therefore, the need to have a broad base of support. Roosevelt believed that in order to insure public support the art project had to be (1) part of a larger relief project and (2) felt

appreciated by the common man across the nation.[53]   The
Arts Projects were designed as a relief project and
levels of competence varied within and between projects.
Nevertheless, the Federal Art Project was able to
maintain a fairly high level of staff competence.

> From the beginning, however, the federal
> director emphasized considerations of
> professional competence in the selection of
> project personnel.   Even in the early months,
> when the pressure was to employ as many as
> possible as quickly as possible, Cahill (the
> director of the Federal Art Project) tempered
> his exhortations with cautions against lack of
> discrimination in choosing personnel.[54]

This was not the case with the Federal Writers'
Project.

> White collar workers who could not be fitted
> into any other WPA agency were likely to wind
> up in the Writers' Project.   This was
> especially true in the early months of the
> project, when field officers were required to
> hire personnel on short notice.[55]

The intra-organizational tensions that resulted
prevented effective cooperation between the arts
personnel and the non-arts personnel in the WPA
bureaucracy.   Even so, state WPA officials attempted to
sabotage the arts programs.   Mangione reports one such
attempt that occurred on the Federal Writers' Project.

> In Idaho the Project Director's job was
> complicated when one of his enemies on the WPA
> administrative staff "tried" to pack the
> Project's staff wtih former inmates of mental
> institutions.[56]

Plans to spread theater across the nation encountered
difficulties which prevented their fulfillment.   Theater
personnel could be loaned or transferred from one state
to another but in the Midwest this practice was hindered
by WPA state administrators.

> Anyone who thinks a state boundary line is an
> imaginary affair, or states rights an
> expression out of history books, should have
> tried to move companies or even individuals
> across the former or to make plans which,
> seemed in the minds of state administrators,
> to conflict with the latter.   Midwest state
> administrators for the most part, refused to

allow people from our talent sources, Chicago and New York, to be brought into their state, even when expenses, plus return fare, were guaranteed out of state funds. Illinois state officials on the other hand did not like the idea of personnel or equipment, paid for with "Illinois money," being sent to other states.[57]

During the period of struggle for power within the WPA bureaucracy, the state administrators gradually received concessions from the Washington WPA office which resulted in increased control over the Arts Projects. McDonald cites 1937 as the year which marks the establishment of predominant control by the state administrators over the Arts Projects for it was in that year that state administrators received authority (with permission of the Washington office) to close state arts projects. The discomfort and friction which existed between the arts personnel and the non-arts personnel of the WPA continued until the end of the arts program.

WPA ART PROGRAMS: THE ATTACK

The WPA Arts projects began at a time of high popularity for the Roosevelt administration and although critics denounced the program, they lacked the power to damage it. The Federal Theater Project, in particular, incited opponents of the arts program because they judged it to be a propaganda vehicle of the Roosevelt administration. Statements by Harry Hopkins to the effect that some of the Living Newspaper reproductions were propaganda only served to fire critical tempers.[58] 1938 marked the year when critical voices became serious threats to the Federal Theater Project. Roosevelt, who then appeared to be a lame-duck president, had suffered serious setbacks in the congressional elections and his own attention was changing from concerns with domestic policy to the ominous signs posed by events in Europe. For Roosevelt's detractors there was no better program to challenge than one that symbolized his domestic welfare programs. The more extreme critics saw the opportunity to strike out at a program that they believed had been captured by radicals and leftists who would use the art projects for their own purposes.

The plain fact was that Communists were exceedingly active in the WPA Theater and Writers' Projects; they did all they could to

get their own people into it and to turn the
whole enterprise into an agitprop machine.[59]

But such activity could not sustain a charge of
Communist domination of the projects. Motives ran
deeper than the mere exposure of Communist infiltration
of the arts program. Historian Robert Vaughn concludes
that the Dies Committee, which became the focal point
for charges of communist infiltration of the Theater and
Writers' Projects, was used as an instrument to
discredit the policies of the Roosevelt
administration.[60]

Those who directed and staffed the Federal Theater
Project were professional theater people unfamiliar with
the political machinations needed to operate in
Washington. Dedicated to the principle that the theater
was both a vehicle for entertainment and a means of
social enlightenment, they concentrated their energies
on program content. Their dream was that the nation
would adopt the theater to its breast but their
conception of theater was considered dangerous by other
political actors. Like crusaders before them, Federal
Theater bureaucrats viewed the world through blinders
and Anthony Downs's description of the administrative
"zealot" best characterizes the Federal Theater
official.

> The peculiarities of zealots' behavior spring
> from two characteristics; the narrowness of
> their sacred policies, and the implacable
> energy they focus solely upon promoting those
> policies. The narrowness of their interests
> causes zealots to be poor general
> administrators. They tend to concentrate
> their energies and resources on their sacred
> policies regardless of the breadth of their
> formal responsibilities, thereby ignoring
> important bureau functions. Moreover, they
> antagonize other officials by their refusal to
> be impartial and their willingness to trample
> all obstacles.[61]

Administrative survival, and the consequent need to
develop political sophistication, was an important
bureaucratic function that was largely ignored. Hallie
Flanagan, director of the Federal Theater Project, came
from the world of stage and academe. She rather naively
accepted Hopkins's promise that the Federal Theater
Project would be uncensored and thereby illustrated the
politically fictitious world in which the Project
operated.[62]

After several controversies concerning Theater
Project productions, a centralized board was established

with responsibility for approving plays before they were performed. This did little to still the voices of criticism. Productions appeared to be as controversial as ever and political wisdom dictated the need to place some shackles on the politically unanointed. An administration in the midst of an emergency program to overcome a depression could not afford inviting further antagonism from a hostile Congress, and this is exactly what some of the productions brought. On several occasions the WPA intervened to modify the content of a play or to prevent its performance. While plays whose themes were anathema to some congressmen might be tolerated, the limits of toleration were passed when congressmen were portrayed as enemies of the people. Congressional criticism brought modifications in the production. At an Appropriations Committee meeting Senator Richard Russell (D - Ga.) said:

> Some very dangerous precedents were being set, when public figures were "exalted" or "minimized" with funds from the public treasury. Senators Townsend (R-Del.) and Byrnes (D-S.C.) agreed. When taxpayers' money was involved argued Townsend, plays should be very carefully censored, so as not to hold anyone up to ridicule.[63]

Theater operates in the world of ideas and therefore will never be the sole property of those who are theater professionals. Political sensitivities of audience members can be offended by ideas expressed in the theater and demands for censorship can result. Robert Friedman suggests the following relationship between group prestige and political effectiveness:

> A professional group with high self-esteem and substantial prestige can play a major part and exert great influence over public policy within areas closely associated with its own expertise. The influence can transcend the technical findings of the group so long as the style of the group does not lead it to encroach upon policy matters that are redistributive, regulatory or highly salient to society. The influence of the group will diminish but remain greater for those groups that have "high" professional standing than those that have "low" professional standing.[64]

Professional standing refers to the "prestige of the professional group within society."[65] Since the artist's professional standing has been quite low historically, the bureaucracy operated by theater professionals and ideas expressed in the Theater Project were vulnerable to attack. As one of the major cultural conveyors of the thirties, the Federal Theater Project was more vulnerable to attack than it would have been in the era of television. As Vaughn remarks:

> With the exception of the cinema, the cultural atmosphere of the thirties may indeed have been influenced by the Federal Theater Project in the sense that more people saw plays than any other form of entertainment.[66]

Given the important communications dimensions which the Federal Theater Project had and the low social prestige of those engaged in theatrical work, the political awareness of those on the Project should have been keener. Plays which were critical of congressmen could have only resulted in attacks upon the Project. As Vaughn states:

> Mrs. Flanagan's decision to use federal subsidies to produce plays condemning her subsidizers is another example of an impolitic decision that might have been avoided by less idealism or more political pragmatism.[67]

But such pragmatism was lacking and, instead of courting the approval of Congress, the Project was alienating it. Wider support from Congress might have been coming if, as said earlier, the presentations had been less controversial or if the Theater Project had been a truly national one. Bound by rules and regulations, the Theater Project was not given the opportunity to function in most congressional districts and from there to develop grass roots support which might have been converted into congressional support. Jane DeHart Mathews notes that there was a critical difference between the controversial Federal Theater Project and the nearly as controversial Federal Writers' Project. The Theater Project was:

> . . . restricted initially to those areas where twenty-five qualified professionals could be formed into a local company, forced subsequently to disband these small and often artistically inferior units.
> As such it could count on the active support of congressmen from New York, California, Illinois and a few other states which local projects had served loyally and well. But the backing of 56 out of 192 members of the House was simply not enough.

The more geographically dispersed Writers'
Writers' Project, on the other hand, could
present every congressman in Washington with a
guidebook to his particular state.[68]

Devices were needed to enlist the funding agency's
support but none were forthcoming. While the Dies
committee listened to charges by witnesses of large
scale Communist inflitration of the Theater Project, WPA
officials and Theater Project personnel remained
quiet.[69] Some did not even consider the Committee's
investigations to be a serious threat. Finally, when
the Dies committee was willing to hear a defense of the
art projects, such a defense was lacking. Ellen
Woodward, Director of the related Women's and
Professional Project, attempted to defend the Theater
Project but she was too distant from its everyday
operations to make a convincing case.[70] Hallie Flanagan
next tried valiantly to parry the onslaught of charges
the Dies Committee unleashed at her. Determined to find
the Project subversive, the Committee spewed out a
variety of questions ranging from her alleged Communist
sympathies to whether she approved of profanity in
plays.[71] Her answers were direct but lacked political
tact. Chairman Dies in a series of questions was
successful in having Mrs. Flanagan admit that in some
cases the Federal Theater Project did serve
propagandistic purposes. She too could not adequately
defend the Theater Project. Jane De Hart Mathews
comments:

> Even if her testimony had been accurately
> reported in its entirety, the more discerning
> reader would have been forced to conclude that
> Hallie Flanagan could not, as she claimed,
> positively refute "every charge" made against
> the project. She could demonstrate that
> Federal Theater plays were not advocating
> overthrow of the government, that its
> audiences included a variety of thoroughly
> American groups, and that its Director had
> consistently forbidden the distribution of
> communist literature on the Project time by
> Project personnel. She could not, however,
> effectively deny the distribution of such
> literature had taken place--albiet illegally--
> that members of the Workers Alliance, the CPC
> or the Supervisors Council had exerted the
> subtle pressure of which they were accused.[72]

Further investigation by the Dies committee, a
special committee to investigate the WPA, and a House
Appropriations subcommittee inquiry continued to haunt

the Federal Theater Project and signaled its imminent
demise. Changes in the political climate, both
domestically and internationally, in the brief period
since the establishment of the Federal Theater Project
meant trouble for the Roosevelt administration's social
programs in general. When the House Appropriations
Committee failed to provide funds for the continuation
of the Federal Theater Project in 1939, there was little
the administration could do, or would do, to save it.
Administration officials would not put its entire relief
program in jeopardy to save the Federal Theater Project.
Hallie Flanagan recounted that:

> WPA officials were in a difficult situation.
> They had to push through a tremendous
> appropriation or else millions of people on
> July 1 would be thrown out of work. How could
> they placate the opponents of WPA enough to
> get the largest possible appropriation
> through. These opponents were out to hang the
> New Deal. Perhaps a hanging in effigy would
> do. Federal Theater was ideal for the
> purpose; although small, it was potent enough
> to allow the opponents of WPA to trumpet a
> victory through the press. I do not mean to
> say that the abandonment of Federal Theater by
> the WPA was discussed in just those terms, it
> didn't need to be.[73]

From its inception the Federal Theater Project was a
political program--something which its zealous
administrators failed to realize. It ended not because
of its failure as a professional project but rather
because of its failure as a political project.

> For many that raucous, rancorous session, the
> ban on the Theater, like the embargo in the
> Neutrality Act and provisions in the tax and
> farm bills provided another opportunity to
> take a slap at the administration.[74]

And as Flanagan came to realize:

> It was ended because Congress, in spite of
> protests from its own members, treated the
> Federal Theater not as a human issue or
> cultural issue, but as a political one.[75]

The Emergency Relief Act of 1939 radically changed
the character of the Arts Projects. An abrupt end was
brought to the Federal Theater Project and state
sponsors were required to provide support for the other
projects. Mangione states that:

Inevitably, the new state of affairs gave the
sponsors more power than was healthy for the
general welfare of the Writers' Project. More
and more the sponsors tended to use the
writing staffs for their own purpose--programs
that had little or no relationship to what the
Writers' Project had set out to do. In
Washington, as well as in the states,
supervisors found it expedient to pay close
attention to the demands of the sponsors.
Survival rather than quality of work became
the chief consideration, and they were unhappy
about that.[76]

The extinction of the programs were grimly awaited by
the personnel who remained with projects until they
finally ended in 1943.

ACCOMPLISHMENTS OF WPA ARTS PROJECTS

Internal and external organizational pressures
interfered with the complete attainment of the goals of
the Arts Projects. But given the context in which they
operated, it is amazing how much was accomplished.
Artistically gifted individuals were saved from pursuits
in which their talents would have been wasted. The
Projects were more than busy work. The total investment
of $5 million in the Arts Projects produced a body of
"unofficial art" now conservatively valued around
$450 million.[77] The Living Newspaper, a dramatization
of controversial current events, was a new form of
theater. These productions did have a definite slant
and one which was often less than subtle. The following
speech by Harry Hopkins before the cast of Power, a play
about the electrical industry, gives one an idea of the
nature of these productions.

People will say its propaganda. Well, I say
what of it? It's propaganda to educate the
consumer who's paying for power. It's about
time someone had some propaganda for him. The
companies have spent millions on propaganda
for utilities. It's about time the consumers
had a mouthpiece. I say more plays like Power
and more power to you.[78]

The Federal Art Project was fairly well received by
the nation. Well known for the murals that were executed
under its direction, art historian E. P. Richardson says
of them:

> In general the mural paintings done at this
> time amount to rather unsuccessful
> illustrations pasted on the wall with little
> understanding of the architectural
> effect. . . . Regionalism in mural painting
> became identified with sentimental hometown
> subject matter presented in a horrid melange
> of ill-digested modernism.[79]

While the murals may not have been universally
acclaimed, the Project made a technological breakthrough
with the development of the silk screen process.

Art education centers were established throughout
the nation. Local citizens could pursue their interest
in art by attending classes taught by members of the
Arts Project. Approximately eight million people took
advantage of the opportunities presented by the
program.[80] Richardson concludes:

> There is no question in my mind that these
> played a part in getting people all over the
> United States looking in some medium--paint,
> wood, textile, clay--not as a livelihood, but
> as a pleasant part of their daily lives.[81]

A research division, the Index of American Design,
collected information on various art forms practiced
throughout the history of America. Although only about
ten percent of the Art Projects personnel were employed
on the Index, it became the most popular part of the
Project.[82] The Art Project, like the other WPA art
programs, never received the popular acclaim it deserved
for its original contributions to the art world.

The Federal Music Project was the least
controversial of the Art Projects although pressure to
ease its hiring standards was exerted by the American
Federation of Musicians.[83] The Project conducted a
number of different programs. Musicians were employed
in newly-formed symphonic orchestras. "By March, 1938
thirty-four symphony orchestras under the Federal Music
Project were employing 2,533 musicians."[84] Some of
these orchestras stayed in existence even after the
Federal Music Project ceased to exist. Although a
number of operas were sponsored by the Project, actual
productions were limited because of their cost. If a
panel of judges approved, a composer could hear his work
performed by an orchestra. A nationwide program of
music education, both appreciation and practice, was a
large part of the Project. "A summary compiled at the
end of the fiscal year June 30, 1939 listed 1,197,936
classes held by project leaders with aggregate pupil
attendance of 13,849,919."[85] The Music Project like the
Art Project and the Writers' Project became involved in

historical research and the preservation of art forms. The Index of American composers, an unfinished project, attempted to list all major American composers, their works and critical reactions to them.[86] A collection of folk music from throughout the United States was gathered by the Music Project as a part of a WPA folks arts project. Members of the project were sent on the road to obtain recordings of Southern folk music. The state music projects cooperated by researching and collecting folk music in their respective states and making this material available to the national project.[87]

The Federal Writers' Project shared the spotlight of controversy with the Federal Theater Project. Although it was fortunate to have in its employ writers such as Nelson Algren, Richard Wright and Saul Bellow, many others who claimed to be writers were frankly incompetent. There were also ideological tensions dividing staff members of Trotskyist and Stalinist beliefs.[88]

The composition of the staff of the Writers' Project and sensitivities to the political climate of the time dictated that its programs be non-fictional. Most of the Project's writers lacked creative writing ability and it was felt "that if writers were allowed to work on their own subjective efforts Congress and public opinion would soon put the Project out of business."[89] The American Guide series was the Projects major work. Each state program was supposed to compose a geographical, descriptive and historical account of their respective states and important localities within them. Yet, what seemed to be a needed and politically-safe project was not free from controversey. Emphases on certain events, as well as their interpretations, were questioned. It was claimed that the Massachusetts guidebook placed too much emphasis on the Sacco and Vanzetti case and:

> As it was discovered on close scrutiny that the Massachusetts Guide contained a number of passages written from a pro-labor and anti-establishment point of view, particularly on such matters as Child Labor, the Boston Police Strike, and the historic 1912 strike of textile workers in Lawrence. Several mayors throughout the state decided to ban the book. Governor Hurley ordered the state legislature to examine the book for all objectionable passages and asked the writer responsible for them to be identified and dismissed.[90]

However, the Massachusetts case was not the typical reaction to the guidebooks. For the most part, they were well-received.

A folklore study, conducted by the Writers' Project, sought to catalog popular customs, beliefs and legends. The study not only explored the past but also delved into contemporary American views and attitudes. Reflections and life-perspectives were recorded by interviewers. A related program, the Social-Ethnic Studies program, recorded the ways in which various groups helped to mold their local communities and the nation itself.

> Social-Ethnic studies fell into three classes: (1) intensive studies of single groups (nationalities or occupations); (2) cross-sectional studies of whole communities; and (3) extensive studies of larger areas (regions).[91]

There were several other programs that the project conducted. Mangione sums up the contibutions of the Writers' Project by stating the following:

> In less than four years the Project had produced some three hundred twenty publications, of which almost one hundred were full sized books. Besides state, city, small town and highway guides, the list included works on subjects as diverse as ethnic studies, place names, folklore and zoology. More than six hundred other books were in various stages of completion. It made quite an impressive record, especially when one considers the difficulties of conducting a project made up largely of workers with little or no writing experience, most of whom had to qualify as paupers before they could be employed.[92]

The above account of the four Arts Projects is not meant to be an exhaustive list of the programs they conducted but rather to indicate that under very trying circumstances they made an original contribution to the American culture. Ideologies, partisan political loyalties, intra-organizational conflicts and lack of traditional popular support for the arts were all detrimental to the operation of the Projects. What could have been if there had been more cooperation and less tension can only be surmised. The Project not only made an original contribution to American culture and provided emergency relief for the artist but, more important, offered a model for future governmental support for the arts. Though this support would take a different form, the precedent for wide-scale public support for the arts had been set with the WPA.

CONCLUSION

There is little to note in the way of programmatic support for the arts from the end of the New Deal until the establishment of the National Endowment for the Arts. President Eisenhower appointed an advisor on the arts but there were not any notable changes in government support for the practicing artist. Those governmental efforts that led up to the Endowment's enabling legislation in 1965 are discussed in the next chapter.

Prior to the 1930's, government encouraged the development of the arts but at little expense. The WPA years represented the highest point of government support for the arts but the support emanated from a need for economic recovery rather than from any deeply held societal value in support of the arts. The WPA programs demonstrated that the American government could nourish the arts as is the case with a number of European countries. The New Deal Arts Projects also demonstrated that the government can harass and retard the arts. Public support for the arts must continue to be examined to determine government's proper relationship to culture. Certainly, the question must be raised whether government can be a neutral patron of the arts. Our early experience with government as patron has revealed its uneven temperament.

NOTES

[1] Some of the material contained within this chapter has been drawn with the permission of the University of Illinois Press from the author's previously published articles "Public Policy Making and the Arts," (January, 1978) and "A Policy Pastiche: The National Government and the Arts," (October, 1980) in the Journal of Aesthetic Education.

[2] Lloyd Goodrich, "Government and Art," College Art Journal (Spring 1949): 171.

[3] Ralph Smith, Professor of Aesthetic Education, mentioned this particular reason in a private interview in Urbana, Illinois, March, 1973. For brief discussions on the various reasons given for supporting the arts, see W. McNeil Lowry, "The Past Twenty Years," in The Performing Arts and American Society (Englewood Cliffs, NJ: Prentice-Hall, Inc., 1978), p. 5; and, T. Moore, "Reasons for Subsidizing American Theater" in The Economics of the Arts (Boulder, CO: Westview Press, 1976), pp. 25-41.

[4] Rockefeller Panel Report on the Future of Theater, Dance, and Music in America, The Performing Arts (New York: McGraw-Hill Book Company, 1965), p. 130.

[5] "Text of President Eisenhower's Message to Congress on the State of the Union," New York Times January 7, 1955, p. 111.

[6] Address delivered by President Kennedy at Amherst College on October 26, 1963, cited by Patrick Haves, "The Arts in America-Our New National Product," The Annals 405 (January 1973): 136.

[7] New York Times, December 11, 1969, p. 66.

[8] Ibid.

[9] "Ford, A 'Convert' Pays Tribute to Arts Council and Sees Play," New York Times, September 5, 1974, p. 46.

[10] U. S. Congress, Senate Committee on Labor and Public Welfare and House Committee on Education and Labor, On Bills to Establish Foundations on the Arts and Humanities Joint-Hearings before the Special Subcommittee on Arts and Humanities of the Committee on Labor and Public Welfare, United States Senate and the Special Subcommittee on Labor of the Committee on Education and Labor, 89th Cong., 1st sess., 1965, p. 5.

[11] Arthur M. Schlesinger, Jr., A Thousand Days (New York: Fawcett Crest Book, 1967), p. 671.

[12] Ibid., p. 617.

[13] Ibid., pp. 670-671.

[14] Theodore C. Sorenson, Kennedy (New York: Harper and Row, 1965), p. 88.

[15] Schlesinger, A Thousand Days, p. 677.

[16] Eric F. Goldman, The Tragedy of Lyndon Johnson (New York: Alfred A. Knopf, 1968), p. 42.

138

[17]Ibid., p. 471.

[18]Ibid., p. 465-466.

[19]Howard Taubman, "Salute to the Fine and Lively Arts," New York Times, June 15, 1965, p. 48.

[20]U.S. President, Weekly Compilation of Presidential Documents, Vol. 6, No. 4 (Washington, DC: Office of the Federal Register, National Archives and Records Service, January 26, 1970), p. 67.

[21]Robert Myron and Abner Sundell, Art in America (New York: Crowell-Collier Press, 1968), pp. 67-68.

[22]For a short period there was a National Art Commission supported by President Buchanan. See Ralph Purcell, Government and Art (Washington, D. C.: Public Affairs Press, 1956), pp. 19-20. In 1917, the Commission on Fine Arts was established which had a similar function of artistic review as the earlier short lived commission. Both commissions served to aid government in its purchase of art.

[23]Goodrich, "Government and Art," p. 171.

[24]Although this chapter focuses upon aid to practicing artists, it should be noted that non-profit art organizations benefited from tax exemptions. However, as Dick Netzer notes "Tax exemption has its disadvantages too. It is of no value to organizations that rarely have positive net income." Dick Netzer, The Subsidized Muse (New York: Cambridge University Press, 1978), p. 44.

[25]Rockefeller Panel Report, The Performing Arts, p. 141.

[26]The term is the title of Arthur M. Schlesinger's, The Politics of Upheavel (Boston: Houghton Mifflin Company, 1960).

[27]Jane DeHart Mathews, The Federal Theater 1935-1939 (Princeton, NJ: Princeton University Press, 1967), p. 27.

[28]Olin Dows, "The New Deal's Treasury Art Programs," Arts in Society 2 (Spring-Summer 1963): 52.

[29]Jerre Magione, The Dream and the Deal (Boston: Little, Brown and Company, 1972), p. 30.

[30]Ibid., p. 34.

[31]Dows, "The New Deal's Treasury Art Program," p. 56.

[32]Ibid., p. 58.

[33]Ibid., p. 55.

[34]Ibid., pp. 72-73.

[35]Ibid., p. 83.

[36]Ibid., p. 72.

[37]Mangione, The Dream and the Deal, p. 33.

[38]Dows, "The New Deal's Treasury Art Program, "p. 52.

[39]Ibid.

[40]Mangione, The Dream and the Deal, p. 39.

[41]William F. McDonald, Federal Relief Administration

and the Arts (Columbus, OH: Ohio State University Press, 1968), pp. 187, 238; and Mangione, The Dream and the Deal, p. 39.

[42] McDonald, Federal Relief Administration and the Arts, p. 112.

[43] Ibid., p. 113.

[44] Ibid.

[45] Mathews, The Federal Theater, p. 54.

[46] Mangione, The Dream and the Deal, p. 294.

[47] McDonald, Federal Relief Administration and the Arts, p. 177.

[48] Mathews, The Federal Theater, p. 41.

[49] McDonald, Federal Relief Administration and the Arts, p. 145.

[50] Ibid., p. 111.

[51] Ibid.

[52] Ibid., pp. 208, 237, 238, 240.

[53] Ibid., pp. 185, 238.

[54] Ibid., p. 402. Although Cahill urged the exercise of care in the selection of artists for the Federal Art Project, Robert McKinzie notes that ". . . most states took a high percentage of mediocre if not incompetent artists." Richard McKinzie, The New Deal for Artists (Princeton, NJ: Princeton University Press, 1973), p. 87.

[55] Mangione, The Dream and the Deal, p. 107.

[56] Ibid., p. 79.

[57] Hallie Flanagan, Arena (New York: Benjamin Blom, 1940), pp. 132-133.

[58] Mathews, The Federal Theater, p. 115.

[59] Walter Goodman, The Committee (New York: Farrar, Strauss and Giroux, 1968), p. 44.

[60] Robert Vaughn, Only Victims (New York: Putnam, 1972), p. 50.

[61] Anthony Downs, Inside Bureaucracy (Boston: Little, Brown, 1966), pp. 109-110.

[62] Flanagan, Arena, p. 28.

[63] Mathews, The Federal Theater, p. 177.

[64] Robert S. Friedman, Professionalism: Expertise and Policy Making (New York: General Learning Press, 1971), pp. 13-14.

[65] Ibid., p. 4.

[66] Vaughn, Only Victims, p. 40.

[67] Ibid., p. 72.

[68] Mathews, The Federal Theater, p. 311.

[69] U.S. House of Representatives, Special Committee on Un-American Activities, Investigation of Un-American Activities in the United States Hearings, on H. Res. 282, Vols. 1, 4, 75th Cong., 3rd Session, 1938.

[70] Ibid., pp. 2729-2830.

[71] Ibid., pp. 2838-2885.

[72] Mathews, The Federal Theater, p. 224.

[73] Flanagan, Arena, p. 353.

[74] Mathews, The Federal Theater, pp. 308-309.

[75] Flanagan, Arena, pp. 334-335.

[76] Mangione, The Dream and the Deal, pp. 344-345.

[77] Roger L. Stevens, "The State of the Arts: A 1966 Balance Sheet," Saturday Review, March 12, 1966, p. 25.

[78] Mathews, The Federal Theater, p. 115.

[79] E. P. Richardson, A Short History of Painting in America (New York: Thomas Crowell Company, 1963), p. 300.

[80] Dows, "The New Deal's Treasury Art Program," p. 85.

[81] Richardson, A Short History of Painting in America, pp. 298-299.

[82] McDonald, Federal Relief Administration and the Arts, pp. 422, 453.

[83] Ibid., pp. 609-610.

[84] Ibid., p. 619.

[85] Ibid., p. 630.

[86] Ibid., p. 643.

[87] Ibid., pp. 637-642.

[88] Mangione, The Dream and the Deal, pp. 136-137.

[89] Ibid., p. 244.

[90] Ibid., pp. 217-218.

[91] McDonald, Federal Relief Administration and the Arts, p. 727.

[92] Mangione, The Dream and the Deal, p. 8.

7

To Change a Nation's Cultural Policy: The Kennedy Administration and the Arts in the United States, 1961–1963

Milton C. Cummings, Jr.

PROLOGUE

Policies of the United States government have had an impact on the nation's literature and other forms of art almost since the founding of the republic. Yet until the 1960s, at least, the indirect effects of policies designed primarily for other purposes were often more important for the arts world than were government actions that were consciously designed for their impact on the arts.

American copyright law had a major influence on the development of American literature in the nineteenth century. Before 1891, only an American author could copyright his work in the United States. This rankled Charles Dickens; but it also had the curious effect of hurting American writers who had to compete with royalty-free editions of the works of established British authors such as Scott, Dickens, and Thackeary. The establishment of the second-class postal rate in 1879 was another policy decision that was profoundly important for American literature. The second-class postal rate was a major cause of the subsequent rapid growth of American magazines which provided, among other things, a commercial outlet for the short story. Had Edgar Allan Poe lived forty years later, he might not have starved.

In the 1930's, under President Franklin D. Roosevelt, the United States government briefly conducted one of the largest arts patronage programs in the history of the world. The primary objective then, however, was not to advance the arts, but rather to combat the high unemployment among artists. And American tax laws--by making contributions to many arts groups tax deductible--have long represented the single most important policy decision by government that affects the arts. (According to one estimate, the 1974 cash value of the tax deductibility of contributions to arts groups was at least 400 million dollars; and it may have been as high as 700 million dollars.[1])

Most of the massive New Deal arts programs were cut back sharply in a political backlash in 1939, stimulated in part by congressional anger over what many congressmen regarded as radical plays presented by the Federal Theatre Project. But many American artists themselves were also leery of a greater role in the arts for the federal government before 1960. In the early 1950's, widely publicized congressional investigations of arts figures for alledged subversive activities also widened the gulf between government and the arts.

As a result of these other factors, artistic activities in the United States in the 1950's were supported primarily at the box office, and by a truly remarkable (and tax deductible) system of private patronage. This private patronage was provided mainly by individual donors, but also by private foundations (especially after World War Two). However, there was no large-scale and continuous tradition of direct subsidy by the government, such as was common in Europe.

Even so, by the 1950's there were four broad types of arts activities in which the federal government had a continuing interest: international cultural exchanges (discussed more fully in chapter 12); the design and decoration of public buildings; government collections such as the National Gallery of Art; and the design of coins and stamps. During the 1950's the role of the national government in several of these spheres increased. Part of this growth came from an increasing use of art as an instrument of United States foreign policy in the "Cold War." Under International Cultural Exchange legislation passed in 1954 and 1956, 111 attractions--ranging from Dizzy Gillespie to the New York Philharmonic--were sent to 89 countries in the program's first four years. And in 1954, the Office of Foreign Buildings of the Department of State launched a ten-year $200 million program to build new embassies and consulates on four continents. Using an advisory committee of three leading architects appointed on a rotating basis, the State Department tried with considerable success to ensure that the new embassies abroad would be distinguished buildings.

Initiatives were also taken which would have a direct impact on the arts at home. In March, 1958, a bill to save the Patent Office Building in Washington for an art museum became law. The Patent Office Building had been designed by Robert Mills (who also designed the Washington Monument) during the administration of Andrew Jackson. The bill to save it was backed by Representative Frank Thompson of New Jersey and Senators Hubert Humphrey of Minnesota and

Clinton P. Anderson of New Mexico. And in September, 1958, Congress authorized the building of a National Cultural Center on the banks of the Potomac River in Washington. Under the act, co-sponsored by Senator J. William Fulbright of Arkansas and Congressman Thompson, the federal government was to donate the land if private funds could be raised to build the Center within five years.[2] There was still no equivalent of the Arts Council of Great Britain in the United States and the arts legislation that was passed by the federal government was often cautious and tentative. But by the end of the 1950's the network of relationships between government and the arts had clearly expanded, and some political leaders (such as New York Senator Jacob Javits) were advocating a greater federal role.

This was the general status of federal government policy concerning the arts as the 1960 presidential campaign between Richard M. Nixon and John F. Kennedy got under way. During the campaign, both candidates took cautious positions on national cultural policy--without committing themselves to specific programs. Nixon placed special emphasis on private initiative, but recognized the need for federal government to play an indirect role through "scholarships and exchange programs, encouragement rather than subsidy."[3] Kennedy pointed to the already existing role of the federal government as art patron which had developed gradually over the years. And like Nixon, Kennedy advocated that a new presidential advisory agency should be created to develop future plans.[4]

There was, therefore, not very much distance between the positions that the two candidates took--with one exception. In an article that appeared in Equity Magazine (the official publication of Actors' Equity) shortly before the election, Kennedy was quoted as follows: "I am in full sympathy with the proposal for federally-supported foundation to provide encouragement and opportunity to nonprofit, private and civic groups in the performing arts. When so many other nations officially recognize and support the performing arts as a part of their national cultural heritage, it seems to me unfortunate that the United States has been so slow in coming to a similar recognition."[5]

The Equity Magazine article followed an interview format and was based on a series of questions that were sent to both Kennedy and Nixon by Dick Moore, the magazine's editor. The Kennedy statement on an arts foundation was probably hastily drafted by one Kennedy staff member and approved by another staff member during the heat of the campaign. There is no indication that Kennedy himself either focused on that campaign commitment or emphasized it during his three years as president. But it did give supporters of new federal arts legislation who were in the Kennedy administration something to point to. As one of them said later, "I don't think . . . he came to power committed in any way to establish a National Arts Foundation. Later on, however, I did feel that having it on the record, we could emphasize that more strongly."[6]

THE BEGINNING

In early November, 1960, John F. Kennedy was elected president by a very narrow margin over Richard Nixon. Attention among Kennedy's advisors soon focused on the problems of staffing the new administration--and on plans for the inauguration. One of the President-elect's friends and Georgetown neighbors, Miss Kay Halle, suggested that a group of leaders in the nation's cultural life should be invited to the Inaugural ceremonies as the special guests of the President and Mrs. Kennedy. The proposal was approved, and telegrams of invitation were sent to 168 "creative Americans in the Arts, Sciences and Humanities." Fifty-eight attended--among them Arthur Miller, Robert Lowell, Mark Rothko, Franz Kline, and John Steinbeck. A special tea was held for the "Eminent Group" by the Walter Lippmanns the afternoon before the inauguration.

That afternoon the weather was terrible. (A foot of snow fell on Washington on January 19th.) Nevertheless, according to Miss Halle's own report, John Steinbeck was "so astonished and thrilled to have been invited that he was quite willing to mush to every event."[7] And the comments of many of those who attended, and of many who could not, "revealed delight that President and Mrs. Kennedy were moved to consider them the equals of the politicians."[8]

Inauguration Day was sunny and crisp. In the ceremonies, Robert Frost forecast "the glory of a next Augustan age . . . a golden age of poetry and power, of which this noonday's the beginning hour." Several months later, two albums filled with letters from artists, writers, and scientists invited to the inauguration were given to President and Mrs. Kennedy. A gracious note of thanks was sent to each contributor by the President, to which he added: "Mrs. Kennedy and I would be particularly interested in any suggestions you may have in the future about the possible contribution the national government might make to the arts and scholarship in America."[9]

But most important for future presidential interest in the arts, the special invitations to the nation's artists to attend the Kennedy inauguration received much favorable publicity. The <u>New York Times</u> first reported the invitations on January 15.[10] Several days after the inauguration, it ran a special story reporting that they had been widely "hailed in the arts world."[11] In her report on the undertaking, Miss Halle stressed the many news stories it has prompted "here and abroad."[12] And she could not resist noting with a touch of national pride "General de Gaulle's recent invitation to a reception at the Elysee Place for the creative French leaders in their Arts, Sciences and Humanities." De Gaulle, she added, "is reported to have said that he had 'taken a leaf out of Mr. Kennedy's book.'"[13]

In truth, the inaugural ceremonies did set a tone for the relations between government and the arts in the Kennedy administration. The gesture was direct and personal, involving all the majesty of the presidency in a bow of recognition to the arts. And it was quite economical. President Kennedy was always worried about things that might be costly in the arts policy area.

The events of Inauguration Day also created an air of expectation in the arts world which White House Staff members who wanted to see the development of a national cultural policy could point to in discussions with the President. As one of them, who later came to Washington to develop a Kennedy arts program, said of the president:

> "I don't think he had any idea of the stir it would cause in the country. I don't think he had any idea of the reverberations or the expectations that it would create in the mind of the artistic community itself. They all said, now the president has done this, what is he going to do next? And I felt later on that really I had been called down to Washington in large part to see that the expectations evoked on that first day were not let run out in the shallows of frustration, that it would not look, in the end, like an empty gesture but would look like a real beginning of something important.[14]

GROPING FOR A POLICY

In the days and weeks following the inauguration, the energies of the individuals who had joined the new Kennedy administration--like those of the President himself--were absorbed in a wide variety of activities, challenges, and crises. Plans for the Alliance for Progress were launched. There was a major fight in the

House of Representatives over the power of the Committee
on Rules--rightly regarded as hostile to much of the
Kennedy legislative program. In April came the failure
of the Cuban invasion. In June the Berlin crisis
began.

Yet there were, in the White House staff and elsewhere in the administration, a number of individuals
with a strong interest in seeing the federal government
play a more active role in assisting the arts. Their
cause was aided by the favorable public reaction to
indications of Mrs. Kennedy's interest in the arts, and
to the announcement in February that the First Lady was
starting a project to decorate the White House with
furniture of the period when the White House was constructed.[15] First among these arts advocates in the
administration was Arthur Schlesinger, Jr. Schlesinger
was Special Assistant to the President and the staff
member charged with special responsibilities for maintaining a liaison between the administration and the
intellectual community. Pierre S. Salinger, the
President's Press Secretary, also had interests in the
arts, as did Frederick G. Dutton, another White House
staff member.

Outside the White House, Philip Coombs, the Assistant Secretary of State for Educational and Cultural
Affairs had an obvious concern for arts policy; and
Secretary of Labor Arthur Goldberg, and his Assistant
Secretary, Daniel Patrick Moynihan, also had strong
interests in the arts. (It was Goldberg's remarks to
Kennedy as they drove to the Capitol for the Inauguration, about how tawdry parts of Pennsylvania Avenue
looked, that stimulated a presidential interest in
improving the architecture on the north side of the
avenue.)

During the first spring and summer of the Kennedy's
tenure, members of the administration with a concern for
the arts held a number of informal and formal meetings
to discuss possible steps the administration might take.
Several of these meetings were organized by Schlesinger
or Salinger. Before one of them, set for July 20, 1961,
Philip Coombs circulated a memorandum prepared by his
associate, Max Isenberg. Called "A Strategy for
Cultural Advancement," the memorandum proposed a plan of
action for the Kennedy administration:

> In his Inaugural Address, following upon
> Robert Frost's prophecy of "a next Augustan
> age," the President called for encouragement
> of the arts and for a global alliance to
> "assure a more fruitful life for all mankind."
> By this, and other declarations this
> administration has committed itself, before
> the country and the world, to cultural

advancement as a major national aim. It must
now address itself to fulfilling this
commitment.[16]

Such a commitment, Isenberg argued, would have
benefits both in domestic and international affairs.

> At the least . . . a serious effort to improve
> the quality of American cultural life would be
> a boost to national morale. It would
> inevitably be more. It would confirm that in
> the endless striving for peace and material
> well-being, we have not lost sight of why we
> want them. . . .
>
> In our international relations, establishment
> of cultural advancement as a major aim of the
> United States could not fail to make us more
> effective. Among nations of like heritage and
> development, it would make the less developed
> nations think better of us as a model; and to
> the nations of the Soviet bloc, it would show
> devotion on our part to a humanism transcend-
> ing political differences, a demonstration
> which holds more promise than any other
> approach tried thus far of bringing forth
> affirmative, even conciliatory, response from
> their side. Arts, letters, and learning are
> the only goods for which a world common market
> exists.[17]

In developing a "program of cultural advancement,"
Isenberg declared, "the President and Mrs. Kennedy,
whose personal identification with arts, letters, and
learning is universally known and respected, are ideally
suited for leadership in this field."[18] And to develop
a program for which they could lead, Isenberg suggested
the establishment of a steering committee, composed of
representatives of the White House, the State
Department, the Library of Congress, the Smithsonian
Institution, and other agencies with a special interest
in a cultural program of the national government. "The
task of the steering committee should be twofold: (1)
to develop a theory . . . of the place of cultural
advancement in national and international policy; and
(2) to work out and set in motion a plan of action to
achieve agreed goals."[19]

The discussion on July 20th did not lead
immediately to the establishment of a formal steering
committee. But in September about a dozen different
individuals from different parts of the government met
to make plans for the next step. Arthur Schlesinger was
unable to attend the meeting. But most of those who

were there recommended that the White House staff should have a full-time Special Assistant for Cultural Affairs, charged with the task of putting together a national cultural policy.

When Schlesinger heard of this main recommendation, he objected strenously in a memo to Salinger. "I do not think," he argued, "that the appointment of a Special Assistant for Culture would be a good idea at this stage; nor do I think that any existing Special Assistant could get free enough from more urgent jobs to do the cultural assignment justice." Instead, Schlesinger recommended that a person be "brought in from the outside as a White House consultant on a part-time basis . . . charged with conducting discussions around the government on all issues connected with culture . . . and instructed to come up . . . with a general program."[20] In addition, Schlesinger told Salinger, he had a man in mind for the job--August Heckscher, Director of the Twentieth Century Fund. "If occasion arises at Newport, you may want to raise this possibility with the President."[21]

DEFEAT IN THE HOUSE OF REPRESENTATIVES

Meanwhile, on September 21st, supporters of new steps to assist the arts received a forceable reminder of how weak support for their cause was in Congress. In July a bill had been reported out of the House Committee on Education and Labor to establish a Federal Advisory Council on the Arts. The council would have been authorized to recommend ways to increase the nation's "cultural resources" to propose methods for encouraging private initiative in the arts, and to act as a coordinating group between private and governmental activities in the arts.[22] The bill was sponsored by Democratic Representative Frank Thompson of New Jersey and Republican Representatives John Lindsay of New York and Carroll Kearns of Pennsylvania. However, the House Committee on Rules, sometimes called the "traffic cop" of the House, refused to grant a rule for the measure to be debated and voted on by the full House. The bill's sponsors then tried to bring the bill to a vote by a suspension-of-the-rules procedure--a move which required a two-thirds affirmative vote in the house to be successful. It did not even come close--166 supported the motion, 173 voted nay.[23]

Opponents focused their fire on the question of whether it was really possible to define what the arts were. Congressman Howard W. Smith of Virginia, Chairman of the Rules Committee, was a leader in the opposition to the bill. In a sally which evoked chuckles from some of his colleagues on the floor of the House, he declared:

> Well, I hate to ask this question. I always hesitate to display my ignorance, of which I have a plenty. But, this bill has been pending up in the Committee on Rules for about three or four weeks, and there is no interest up there in it. We sort of put it away in the cooler, waiting until it got more enthusiastic endorsement. But, the thing that troubles me is--and since it was brought to the floor this afternoon I have asked everybody that seemed to know anything about this bill--what are the arts? And, here is where I display my ignorance. I do not know. What does it include? What is is about? I suppose fiddle players would be in the arts and the painting of pictures would be in the arts. It was suggested that poker plying is an artful occupation. Is this going to subsidize poker players that get in trouble?[24]

The defeat of the Advisory Council bill showed how much weaker support for the arts was in Congress than in the executive branch. It could not help but make Kennedy more cautious, for Kennedy was already having difficulty getting support in the House for major items in his New Frontier legislative program. And the vote showed how much work still remained for the arts supporters to do. As Arthur Schlesinger noted in a letter to Congressman Kearns:

> I fear that the Federal Advisory Council on the Arts bill ran into traffic difficulty this year; but we anticipate passage in the next session. A motion to suspend the rules requires, of course, a two-thirds vote. I gather that this motion was supported by 135 Democrats and 31 Republicans and opposed by 70 Democrats and 103 Republicans. I hope both sides will do better next time![25]

A SPECIAL CONSULTANT TO THE PRESIDENT FOR THE ARTS

Despite this weakness in Congress, several developments in 1961 increased the public's identification of the presidency with the arts. Beginning early in the administration, the President and Mrs. Kennedy, some-

times just one of them, sometimes together, began
attending cultural events. These signs of presidential
interest drew extensive coverage in the news media. And
behind these presidential visits there often lay persistent suggestions and proddings by White House staff
members. Just one week after the president was
inaugurated Fred Dutton sent a memo to the keeper of
the President's schedule, Kenneth O'Donnell:

> If the President is looking for any relaxa-
> tion this evening . . . you might consider
> his going to the African Ballets at the
> National Theater here. . . .
>
> Just the mere going would indicate the energy
> which the public so likes in their presidents
> and which shows so much in this one. The
> African aspect would be widely reported in
> that critical and sensitive area, and it would
> also point up here at home the personal
> interest the President has in Africa. This
> particular ballet would also constitute a very
> fresh way of implicitly re-emphasizing the
> cultural interest which the President wants to
> bring more fully to American life.
>
> A couple of notes of warning: the show
> tonight does not begin until 9:30 p.m. At
> least one number has bare bosomed women--
> highly respectable, the reviews said![26]

A second set of events that involved the President
with the arts was triggered by the announcement on
August 7th that the 1961-1962 season of the Metropolitan
Opera was to be cancelled. The cancellation took place
because the Metropolitan Opera Association and the
American Federation of Musicians union had been unable
to agree on the musicians' wages. The distinguished
American mezzo-soprano, Rise Stevens, appealed publicly
to President Kennedy to intervene to save the Met's
season.[27] A few days later, Kennedy designated Secretary
of Labor Arthur Goldberg to arbitrate the dispute.[28]
After ten days of intense negotiations, Goldberg's
efforts were successful. The association and the
musicians agreed to submit the issue to "final and
binding" arbitration; and the Met opened its season on
October 23.[29] When the terms of the arbitration award
were announced in December, Goldberg issued a set of
accompanying remarks, in which he argued that the
performing arts, in order to survive economically, would
require a mixed partnership of patronage--involving
business, private philantrophy, and the government.[30]
The Goldberg statement was remarkably prophetic of the

course that future arts policy was to take in the United States.

A third development emphasizing presidential interest in the arts was a series of glittering state dinners that were held at the White House. These were planned with Mrs. Kennedy's personal involvement and supervision; and several of them gave artists and members of the intellectual community a place of honor. One of the most notable of these evenings featured a concert at the White House by Pablo Casals on November 13, 1961. It was the first time Casals had played at the White House since 1904 during the administration of President Theodore Roosevelt.[31]

The enormously favorable public reaction to the Casals evening persuaded Arthur Schlesinger that the time was ripe to try to persuade the President to take another step forward in developing a federal government cultural policy. On November 22nd, he wrote Kennedy a two-page memorandum on "Moving Ahead on the Cultural Front."

> The Casals evening has had an extraordinary effect in the artistic world. On the next day, when the advisory council for the National Cultural Center met, a number of people said to me in the most heartfelt way how much the Administration's evident desire to recognize artistic and intellectual distinction meant to the whole intellectual community. You probably saw John Crosby's column this morning ("President Kennedy is the best friend culture . . . has had in the White House since Jefferson").
>
> All this is of obvious importance, not only in attaching a potent opinion-making group to the Administration, but in transforming the world's impression of the United States as a nation of money-grubbing materialists. And it is notable that all this has taken place without any criticism, so far as I am aware. Contrary to the expectations reported by Crosby, no editorial writer has used the Casals dinner to accuse you of fiddling while Berlin burns.
>
> I wonder whether this might not be an appropriate time to carry the matter a step further. You will recall that Pierre Salinger and I gathered together a group of people around government concerned with areas where public policy has impact on cultural matters. The group recommended that the White House

should have a Special Assistant for Culture.
Pierre and I thought that anything like this
would be premature. We would recommend
instead bringing in someone from the outside
as a part-time White House consultant to
survey areas of actual or possible government
impact on culture (from airport construction
to tax policies to honors lists to direct
government sponsorship or subsidy) and to come
up at the end of six months with a report and,
hopefully a program.

The mere existence of this White House inquiry
would do a good deal to generate concern
through the bureaucracy for the government's
cultural responsibilities. At the end, we
would have a much better idea of the resources, possibilities and problems in the
area.

My first thought as the man to do the job is
August Heckscher of the 20th Century Fund.
Heckscher wrote the essay on "The Quality of
American Culture" for the Eisenhower
commission on National Goals. He is a man of
intelligence, and cultivation; he understands
that government can at best play only a
marginal role; and he is deeply committed to
the subject. He used to be editor of the New
York Hearld Tribune editorial page but re-
signed because he could not face the thought
of writing editorials in favor of Nixon. He
supported you in the campaign. . . .

Can we go ahead and get a man down to carry
out this assignment?[32]

This time Schlesinger's proposal fell on receptive
ears, and on December 5th the president sent a letter,
the first draft of which had been written by
Schlesinger, to August Heckscher. The day after the
Kennedy letter went out, Schlesinger sent a copy to
Pierre Salinger with a covering memorandum. The memo
contained only one word--"Enfin!"[33] The new initiative
in the arts was tentative; it was cautious; it was only
a "modest scheme."[34] But the plan for which a small
group of White House staff members had been pressing for
several months was under way.

THE JOB OF THE SPECIAL CONSULTANT

After obtaining approval from the trustees of the
Twentieth Century Fund, August Heckscher made plans to
take on the assignment as Special Consultant to the
President for the Arts. But before the White House
formally announced the appointment, the New York Times
broke the news with a front page story in February,
1962. The reaction in the press and among arts groups
was generally highly favorable--so that, when Heckscher
had his first meeting with the President, it went well.
Although initially Kennedy had said he wanted "a quiet
inquiry, without fanfare," the president was obviously
pleased by the favorable reaction which news of the
assignment had received.[35]
     Heckscher then went to work. The very looseness
with which his job responsibilities were defined gave
him considerable latitude to decide what he would
emphasize in his assignment. Considering himself a
temporary consultant, Heckscher hoped to achieve three
main goals during his stay in Washington: (1)
contribute to the establishment of a Federal Advisory
Council on the Arts; (2) prepare a report, to include
policy recommendations for the future, on the arts and
the national government; and, (3) obtain a permanent
successor, thereby institutionalizing the role of a
Special Assistant to the President for the Arts.[36] In
addition, Kennedy, who was always concerned with
achieving practical, tangible results, was strongly
interested in seeing the National Cultural Center built
in Washington during his administration.[37] Primary
responsibility for that, however, fell on Roger Stevens.
Stevens--a successful theater producer, real estate
investor and a former Democratic campaign finance
manager for Adlai Stevenson--had been appointed by
Kennedy to serve as head of the Board of Trustees for
the Cultural Center in September, 1961.
     Heckscher's job inevitably took on other aspects as
well. There were speeches to make, as Heckscher
increasingly became the administration's spokesman for
the arts. There was the job of getting the President to
make statements on arts matters. There was the need to
be alert to what other government agencies were doing,
and to raise the interests of the arts in other parts of
the government. (Heckscher called this "day-to-day
surveillance.")[38] There was the task of defining what
the arts were, for the government:

>   "I think that one of the useful things that I
>   did . . . was to enlarge the definition of
>   'The Arts.' I was always careful to maintain
>   that they weren't simply painting, the ballet,

the opera, and the theater, but that they included the whole enviornmental condition of the nation's life and that architecture and city planning and so on were very important. . . . At that time government was doing nothing in the field of the performing arts, but spending billions of dollars on architecture. So here was a good place to begin. . . .[39]

There were also continuing efforts to use the White House as a stage for official recognition of the arts, often with the active cooperation of Mrs. Kennedy. One of the most publicized of these efforts was a state dinner on April 29, 1962 at which 49 Nobel Prize winners from the Western Hemisphere were brought together "the most extraordinary collection of talent, of human knowledge, that has ever been gathered together at the White House, with the possible exception of when Thomas Jefferson dined alone."[40]

Not every effort to stimulate symobolic leadership for the arts was successful. As Heckscher later recalled, "We were always trying to get Mrs. Kennedy to do things which she wouldn't do."[41] And although Mrs. Kennedy was both genuinely interested in the arts and enormously helpful to Heckscher, she was also "a somewhat ambivalent figure in all this."[42] "Mr. Hechscher, I will do anything for the arts you want," she said. "But, of course, I can't be away too much from the children and I can't be present at too many cultural events. After all, I'm not Mrs. Roosevelt."[43]

Heckscher also undertook an extensive survey of the things various agencies of the government were already doing that affected the arts. The president, quite correctly, felt the government was doing more to assist the arts than was generally realized. At first he wanted Heckscher to get a dollar figure for the tax deductibility of contributions to arts organizations. This, Kennedy reasoned, amounted to a very substantial sum, and constituted an indirect subsidy of the arts by the government. However, when it was pointed out to the president that by that line of reasoning the federal government was also subsidizing the Catholic Church, he quickly dropped the point. The "religious issue" had been a major problem for Kennedy, the first Roman Catholic to win the presidency, in the 1960 presidential campaign.

By early 1963, Heckscher had completed a draft of his report on The Arts and the National Government.[44] Taken as a whole, it was a remarkable document--one which presaged much that was actually done in arts policymaking during the decade that followed. The report surveyed existing federal programs that had an impact on the arts. It urged that the many existing government agencies should keep the interests of the arts in mind while formulating and administering their policies. It recommended the establishment of a Federal Advisory Council on the Arts and the appointment of a permanent arts adviser to the President. And it proposed the creation of a Federal Arts Foundation to make grants for the arts. After being approved by the President, the report was formally released on May 28, 1963.

THE ADVISORY COUNCIL ON THE ARTS

Meanwhile, progress toward actually establishing getting a Federal Advisory Council on the Arts established had been much slower. After the embarrasing defeat in September 1961, the House sponsors of the legislation, again led by Congressman Frank Thompson, tried once more to move the measure to the floor for a vote during the 1962 session of Congress. Kennedy himself asked for legislation to create the Advisory Council in a special message to Congress on aid to education.[45] But on May 17th it was blocked again by the House Committee on Rules.[46]

At this point, some of Kennedy's advisers urged the President to establish an Advisory Council by executive order, thereby getting by executive action what was proving so difficult to get through the legislature. The negotiations which followed were long and tortuous. In the Senate, there were powerful potential sponsors of legislation to establish an Advisory Council, including Senators Jacob Javits, Claiborne Pell, and Hubert Humphrey. These men felt, almost certainly correctly, that the necessary votes could be obtained in the Senate.

In the House, which on arts legislation as on many other parts of the Kennedy program was much more resistant, supporters of an Advisory Council were not as sure that they had the votes they needed. However, they were prepared to try again to get a favorable vote in the Rules Committee after the May, 1962 setback. For a while, Congressman Lindsay, in particular, was quite optimistic that the necessary switch of votes in the committee could be obtained from some of his Republican colleagues.

The President, again characteristically cautious, for many months preferred to rely on the legislative route to create the Council. As late as February, 1963, Heckscher reported that "the President still feels that this would have greater permanency and prestige if accomplished through legislation."[47] Moreover, Kennedy and his legislative advisors were concerned that members of Congress might feel that "executive action had been taken to bypass Congress," if the president went ahead alone.[48]

By early 1963, however, the pressures on Kennedy from his own staff to establish an Advisory Council began to grow. On January 13th, Heckscher summarized his position on the issue in a memorandum to Arthur Schlesinger:

> A direct move in regard to the establishment of an advisory Council on the Arts now seems urgent.
>
> 1. The Congress is being restrained only with difficulty from putting in bills for this purpose. Such bills almost surely would remain, as heretofore, bottled up in the House.
>
> 2. Senator Humphrey is, in particular, urging us very strongly to go ahead.
>
> 3. Major elements in the arts constituency have been assured that the President is going forward on this, and our failure to do so will be judged adversely.

Shortly thereafter, Schlesinger urged the president to make a statement "as soon as possible announcing your intention to set up the Council and saying that the order and the names will follow. Heckscher has prepared a draft statement."[50]

> If we don't do this, various congressmen will put in bills for this purpose. Then we will have to decide whether or not to make a fight for them; and failure to do so will be judged adversely. The executive order approach could bypass this; and, since the legislators involved are interested in the result rather than the method, they say that they would not regard the executive order as an invasion of legislative prerogative.[51]

The President listened to this advice, but evidently wanted to be sure that understandings had been reached with the congressmen most concerned. After Thompson and Lindsay both agreed that the President should go ahead (and Lindsay, a Republican, promised not to criticize the President if he did so), plans got under way to issue the executive order. In June, 1963, it was formally released. It now remained, or so Heckscher thought, only to prepare a list of names of persons to be appointed to the Council.

THE ROLE OF THE ARTS CONSTITUENCY

Through all of these efforts to establish an Advisory Council on the Arts, supporters of the measure were hampered by weaknesses in the political support which arts groups were able to exert for it. Many individual artists and arts institutions were neither accustomed to, nor organized for, political action. Most had had little experience in exerting political pressure for such legislation. And on the basic issue of whether there should be federal government subsidies for the arts--as on other issues, there were sharp differences among the arts groups themselves.

Some arts groups were active politically in 1962 and 1963. Actors' Equity, the union of professional actors, had a lobbyist, Jack Golodner, working for the administration's arts proposals.[52] The American Federation of Musicians urged its members to write to their congressmen on the measure.[53] But many other elements of what could have been a political constituency for the arts were still unorganized. In the field of dance, for example, a national organization (the American Association of Dance Companies) was not established until 1967. In addition, within one of the potentially most powerful arts lobbies --symphony orchestras--there was at best lukewarm support for, and some outright opposition to, an expanded federal role. The symphony orchestras were one field in the arts which was relatively well-organized. The American Symphony Orchestra League had been established in 1942. The boards of trustees of symphony orchestras included many of the economic and social elite of their community. And the orchestras constituted the largest, best established, and most geographically-dispersed arts institutions in the country.

One of the first systematic surveys of the attitudes of symphony orchestra board members toward the role of the federal government in the arts was taken by the League in 1953. As the League's Executive Director reported, "The responses came in quickly from the boards, and the opinions were decisive. . . . 91% of the governing boards responding to the survey . . . were unalterably opposed to any governmental program in the arts which would relate to local performing organizations, and under no circumstances did they want any form of federal subsidy of the arts."[54]

During the years following 1953, major changes began to take place in the music world which increased the cost of maintaining a symphony orchestra and enlarged the amount of money that had to be raised to supplement income from the box office. Although the weekly earnings of orchestra musicians remained low, they were increasing, and pressures were brought by the musicians' unions to lengthen the season, as well as the number of weeks during which musicians would be paid. After a new survey in 1962, Executive Director Helen Thompson reported that there had been a "tremendous change during the last nine years in the attitudes of community and civic leaders (from whose ranks symphony orchestra boards are drawn) toward the role of the federal government in the arts."[55] There was also "an increasing awareness that symphony orchestras and the arts generally have become a matter of national concern."[56] Mrs. Thompson added: "Apparently, the increased receptivity to the concept that the federal government might assume a more active role . . . stems largely from increased awareness that greater economic stability must be developed for the performing musicians."[57]

Even so, opinion on the symphony boards was still sharply divided. As Mrs. Thompson noted, "In many instances in which a board filed a definite report it was stated that the action represented merely a slim majority opinion."[58]

> There is no clearcut mandate from the orchestras for support of any of the arts legislation.
>
> Neither is there a clearcut mandate from the orchestras for opposition to any of the proposed legislation.[59]

There were also differences of opinion that were related to the size of different symphony orchestras. The smaller, community orchestras were more strongly in favor of an expanded federal role in the arts than were the larger, more prestigious orchestras.[60] And the ambivalence of the symphony orchestras was also reflected in a survey which the New York Times conducted in September, 1962 that focused on attitudes among twenty-four major and thirteen lesser United States orchestras. Most of them, the Times reported, opposed subsidies by the federal government for symphony orchestras and instead favored cash gifts or subsidies on the local level.[61] On the basic issue of pushing beyond an Advisory Council to establish a Federal Arts Foundation (and even on less ambitious government arts proposals), the arts world in 1962 was divided.

THE FINAL MONTHS

Once his report had been released and the executive order establishing a Federal Advisory Council on the Arts had been issued, August Heckscher, thinking his job nearly over, cut back on his time in Washington. His third objective, securing a permanent successor, appeared to be achieved when it was agreed that Richard Goodwin should take the post of Special Assistnt for the Arts. In the summer of 1963, Goodwin was working at the Peace Corps and he had played an active role as a speech writer in Kennedy's presidential campaign. Kennedy, however, asked Heckscher to remain until Goodwin's appointment could be formally made.

As he prepared to leave his job in Washington, Heckscher felt a sense of satisfaction.

> I felt that the time I spent there had been tremendously worthwhile. When I'd finished, I had done a report for the President which had been well-received by him and well-treated by the press. It looked as if this report was not going to be one of those that just lay on the shelf because the President had agreed to the thirty names which would make up the Advisory Council. The Advisory Council was to be appointed in the very near future, and would take up this report as their first order of business, to say how it could be implemented and what portion should be given priority. The President had, at the same time which was crucial to me, agreed to name a full-time successor in my place, which was the one thing which I had asked. So I could feel that . . . the things I had asked for had all been accomplished. Maybe I'd put my sights too low but I had gotten the Advisory Council on the Arts, I'd gotten the report, and I'd gotten a permanent successor. From the first day, I said to the people in my office-- Barbara Donald, Nancy Newhouse, 'When you make up the files you must realize that we are not just putting up files; we are really starting something--an office which I hope will continue here in the White House forever![62]

, During the summer, however, Heckscher was away from Washington for several weeks, and "things . . . began to slip very badly."[63] The names of the persons to be appointed to the Advisory Council had not been formally approved. Kenneth O'Donnell, a member of the "Irish Mafia" and one of Kennedy's closest aides whom Heckshcer

regarded as "rather hostile" to the arts work, had held
up the routine security investigations.[64] In addition,
Goodwin's appointment was being delayed until he
completed the work in which he was involved at the Peace
Corps.

Once Heckscher was back in Washington, he and
Schlesinger were able to get action started again on
clearing the names for the Advisory Council. And in
mid-November Kennedy told Frank Thompson, in what was to
be the president's last telephone conversation with the
congressman, that he planned to announce the
appointments to the Advisory Council "as soon as I get
back" from a planned trip with Mrs. Kennedy to Texas.[65]
On November 21st, the President and Mrs. Kennedy began a
two-day tour of Texas. On the morning of November 22nd,
the New York Times announced that Richard Goodwin would
be appointed as a full-time Special Assistant to the
President for the Arts and ran a profile of Goodwin.
Early that afternoon, John F. Kennedy was assassinated
in Dallas.

EPILOGUE

The specific list of names John F. Kennedy approved
for what would have been the first Federal Advisory
Council on the Arts was not acted upon. But in the
twenty-two months that followed, under President Lyndon
B. Johnson, federal action and legislation to assist
the arts moved forward at a rate that would have seemed
unthinkable in the early Kennedy years.

In the immediate aftermath of Kennedy's death,
there was apprehension in the arts world that Johnson
might not give the arts the same emphasis that Kennedy
had. On November 29, 1963, Arthur Schlesinger wrote
Johnson a two-page memorandum entitled the "Future of
the Arts Program." After detailing what had happened
since Heckscher was appointed in March, 1962,
Schlesinger said: "The question is whether you will
want to go ahead with this effort. I hope very much
that you will. . . ."[66] After indicating what the
program could do that would be of benefit to the arts,
Schlesinger also added a practical political argument:
"It can strengthen the connections between the
Administration and the intellectual and artistic
community--something not to be dismissed when victory or
defeat next fall will probably depend on who carried New
York, Pennsylvania, California, Illinois, and
Michigan."[67]

Very soon after the assassination, Johnson
supported legislation renaming the National Cultural

Center the John F. Kennedy Center for the Performing Arts and providing up to $15 million in federal matching-grant funds for its construction. Then for a while the Johnson administration, faced with the staggering task of taking over the reins of power and with the presidential election less than a year away, did little on the arts front. But in May, 1964, Roger Stevens was appointed as a Special Assistant to the President for the Arts and later that summer, in part because of skillful lobbying by Stevens, legislation creating a Federal Advisory Council on the Arts was finally passed by Congress.

In June, 1964, another event which was eventually to be of importance for the arts took place. A special nongovernmental commission of scholars in the humanities released a report on the status of the humanities in American life. The commission had been created by the American Council of Graduate Schools with Dr. Barnaby Keeney, the president of Brown University, as its chairman. In its report, the commission called for the establishment of a National Foundation for the Humanities with broad similarities to the National Science Foundation. In September, while on a tumultous campaign tour of Rhode Island, President Johnson spoke at Brown University and declared that he looked "with the greatest of favor" on the Keeney commission's proposal for a National Foundation for the Humanities.[68]

In November, Johnson was elected to a four-year presidential term by an enormous majority over Barry Goldwater. At the same time there was a Democratic landslide for Congress which decisively altered the balance of power in the House of Representatives. Many congressmen who had opposed federal arts legislation were defeated. In early 1965, a political compromise was worked out whereby the supporters of arts legislation and supporters of humanities legislation joined forces to work for passage of legislation creating a National Foundation on the Arts and Humanities. The Foundation was to have a separate National Endowment for each field. This alliance added to the forces working for the arts much of higher education's political constituency--which then had nearly five million students, several hundred thousand faculty members, and colleges, universities, or junior colleges in every congressional district in the country. On March 10, 1965, the administration submitted its legislative proposal to create the National Foundation. And in September, after a spirited floor fight in the House of Representatives, the bill was passed. Thus began the National Endowment for the Arts for which Congress has since appropriated more than a billion dollars and which is discussed in Chapter 7.

JOHN F. KENNEDY AND THE ARTS -- AN ASSESSMENT

Once when August Heckscher and John F. Kennedy were having a meeting to talk about the arts, the discussion turned to a more general evaluation of the record of previous presidents. Heckshcer had written a book on Woodrow Wilson and much admired him. He was therefore disappointed to find that Kennedy rated Wilson fairly low. Wilson, Kennedy said in effort, had not won his greatest battle--the League of Nations. He had articulated goals for the nation, but he had been unable to achieve them.[69]

It is one of the ironies of John Kennedy's brief presidency that in the development of public policy for the arts--as in many other policy areas--he was better able to articulate the goals than he was to persuade Congress to pass legislation to help implement those goals. When Kennedy died, legislation to establish an Advisory Council on the Arts had not been passed. The creation of a National Foundation on the Arts had not become a formal presidential proposal. And even the membership of an Advisory Council created by executive order had not been appointed--though if Kennedy had had a little more time, it would have been.

The record of the president's interest in the arts is one of gradual evolution and growth. At the beginning he had no over-all plan. As Heckscher later recalled:

> Everything that was done in this field of the arts--everything President Kennedy did in regard to it--was a trial step. President Kennedy would do something; he would be surprised by the reverberation it caused, then he would go on and do something else. I don't think he ever had any grandiose--he would have hated the word 'grandiose'--any larger plan from the beginning.[70]

> He said, 'Of course, you're going to need legislation,' I mean he was very clear that we would have an arts bill of some magnitude sometime. But he was never anxious--and I think he was right in this--to get out and fight a lonely battle for culture in advance of an interest which had already been shown by the public at large.[71]

In retrospect, it seems clear that the President was both leading and riding a tide that made it almost inevitable that a larger federal role for the arts would evolve. A number of social and political trends seemed to be coming together in the early 1960's.

(1) While the notion of a "cultural explosion" in the United States in this period could be (and was) greatly exaggerated, participation and interest in some forms of cultural activities was expanding at the time when Kennedy came to power. Museum attendance was up. New artistic organizations were being formed, sometimes in communities which previously had not had them. And audiences for some of the performing arts, notably dance, were increasing. Perhaps more important than any actual increases in cultural activities during this period, it was widely believed that interest in the arts was expanding. As a result, the news media were giving greater attention to the role of the arts in American society.

(2) Economic and social trends were raising the costs of artistic activities. They were also increasing the pressures on artists and arts organizations to seek new sources of funding.

(3) The American national government itself began to seem a less forbidding institution for the arts world to embrace. The congressional investigations of artists for alledged subversive activities in the early days of the "Cold War" were receding from memory. A government headed by the administration of John Kennedy seemed much more attractive to many members of the artistic community.

(4) During the 1950's there had developed in Congress a number of key legislators who were genuinely committed to push for arts legislation. Congressmen like Frank Thompson and John Lindsay, and Senators such as Jacob Javits, J. William Fulbright, and Hubert Humphrey were willing to do the hard legislative work that was necessary. And in 1960 a man who was to be one of the strongest advocates of new government programs for the arts, Claiborne Pell of Rhode Island, was first elected to the Senate.

(5) Kennedy appointed a number of men who had a strong interest in the arts to powerful positions in his administration. The White House staff members, Arthur Schlesinger, Jr. and Pierre Salinger, were of crucial importance in launching the administration's cultural program. And men such as Arthur Goldberg and Daniel Patrick Moynihan in other parts of the administration played a major role.

(6) The generally favorable public reaction to the initiatives that the President and Mrs. Kennedy took for the arts did much to keep the program going and to expand it. At a time when many of the President's major programs such as aid-to-education and medicare were going nowhere in Congress, Kennedy--shrewd politician that he was--recognized that his epxressed interest in the arts was a political asset. As Heckshcer said of

some of the other members of the White House staff, "I think they were always rather . . . pleased by the degree of good will that came to the Administration and amused by the fact that it cost so little money. . . ."[72]

(7) There were also other political considerations that made it desirable for the President to be associated with the arts. One of his closest advisers, Theodore Sorensen, felt that Kennedy's arts concern won him some good will among board members of artistic organizations--often well-to-do members of the business community and frequently Republicans. As Sorensen later wrote, "They warmed to an intellectual president who patronized the arts when his position on fiscal and other matters might well have cooled them."[73] And in New York State, Republican Governor Nelson Rockefeller, was also making a record in the arts world by establishing the Arts Council of New York. Rockefeller had been seriously considered as a possible presidential candidate in 1960 and it was thought that he might be Kennedy's opponent in 1964. It was better to lead than to lag behind.

(8) Finally, the individuals and institutions involved in the arts were reevaluateing their own attitudes toward the role of the federal government in the arts. They were also beginning to acquire some practical experience in testifying before Congress and exerting pressure in the executive and legislative branches of government on behalf of government actions that they favored. This growth in the political sophistication of the arts world still had a long way to develop. But it had begun.

The Kennedy administration was only a beginning in the efforts to encourage the national government to give greater assistance to the arts. Little that was firm or institutionalized was completed by 1963. Yet many of the seeds of future federal government policy toward the arts were planted during the first three years: the idea of one or more White House staff members with a continuing interest in the arts; the idea of a separate spokesman for the arts in the goverment, now embodied in the Chairman of the National Endowment for the Arts; the idea of a representative body for the arts, now reflected in the existence of a National Council on the Arts; the idea of a National Foundation on the Arts, now given concrete expression through the National Endowment; the idea of a broad definition of the arts, including architecture, now reflected in many of the government's arts policies; and the idea that a mixed system of patronage would be most appropriate to help support the arts in the United States--a system relying heavily on business corporations, individual donors, private foundations, and the states and localities, as well as on the federal government. This too is what has developed substantially since 1963.

These concepts, and their successful launching, were to prove to be solid accomplishments. But Kennedy had an impact on the nation's arts policy in another way --even though it was a way that he himself professed to consider of secondary importance. The American presidency is both a highly visible theater from which to dramatize new ideas, and a bully pulpit. During his three years in office, Kennedy articulated the vision of an expanded relationship between government and the arts in a way that few American presidents before him had ever done. And the voicing of that vision helped set in motion forces which would change the nation's cultural policy, in the administration of later presidents if not his own. As Kennedy once said in words that now stand on the wall of the Center for the Performing Arts that bears his name:

> There is a connection, hard to explain logically but easy to feel, between achievement in public life and progress in the arts. The age of Pericles was also the age of Phidias. The age of Lorenzo de Medici was also of Leonardo da Vinci. The age of Elizabeth also the age of Shakespeare. And the New Frontier for which I campaign in public life, can also be a new frontier for American art.

NOTES

[1] See Dick Netzer, The Subsidized Muse (New York: Cambridge University Press, 1978), pp. 44, 241-242.

[2] Most of the principal federal arts activities in the 1950's are summarized in Milton Bracker, "U.S. Role in the Arts Is Found to Have Increased in Decade Since World War II," New York Times, December 8, 1958.

[3] Quoted in William Howard Adams, "National Policy on the Arts: The Candidates' Views," Cultural Affairs 4 (1968): 4.

[4] Ibid.

[5] "The Presidential Candidates: Vice President Nixon and Senator Kennedy Discuss the Theatre's Problems," Equity Magazine 45 (November 1960): 10.

[6] August Heckscher, recorded interview by Wolf von Eckhardt, December 10, 1965, p. 4. Oral History Program, John F. Kennedy Library.

[7] "Report on Inaugural Committee Project Concerning Invitation of President and Mrs. Kennedy to 168 Creative Americans in the Arts, Sciences and Humanities to Attend their January 20, 1961 Inaugural Ceremonies," June, 1961, p. 1. Files of August Heckscher, John F. Kennedy Library.

[8] Ibid.

[9] Letter from President John F. Kennedy to Professor Jacques Barzun, September 13, 1961. White House Central Files, John F. Kennedy Library.

[10] New York Times, January 15, 1961, p. 39.

[11] New York Times, January 31, 1961, p. 30.

[12] "Report on Inaugural Committee Project," p.1.

[13] Ibid., p. 2

[14] August Heckscher, recorded interview, pp.3-4.

[15] New York Times, February 24, 1961, p. 1.

[16] Memorandum, "A Strategy for Cultural Advancement," July 10, 1961, p. 1. Files of August Heckscher, John F. Kennedy Library.

[17] Ibid.

[18] Ibid., p. 2.

[19] Ibid., p. 3.

[20] Memorandum for Pierre Salinger from Arthur Schlesinger, Jr., Subject: "The Cultural Offensive," September 27, 1961, p. 1. Files of August Heckscher, John F. Kennedy Library.

[21] Ibid., p. 2.

[22] 1961 CQ Almanac (Washington: Congressional Quarterly, Inc., 1962), p. 387.

[23] Congressional Record, September 21, 1961, p. 20535.

[24] Ibid., pp. 20499-20500.

[25] Letter from Arthur Schlesinger, Jr. to Congressman Carroll D. Kearns, October 19, 1961. White House Central Files, John F. Kennedy Library.

[26] Memorandum to Kenneth O'Donnell, from Fred Dutton, January 27, 1961. White House Central Files, John F. Kennedy Library.

[27] New York Times, August 8, 1961, p. 31.

[28] New York Times, August 19, 1961, p. 19.

[29] New York Times, October 24, 1961, p. 1.

[30] New York Times, December 15, 1961, p. 1.

[31] New York Times, November 14, 1961, p. 1.

[32] "Memorandum for the President, Subject: "Moving" Ahead on the Cultural Front," Arthur Schlesinger, Jr. to John F. Kennedy, November 22, 1961, White House Central Files, John F. Kennedy Library.

[33] Memorandum for: Pierre Salinger, from Arthur Schlesinger, Jr., December 6, 1961. White House Central Files, John F. Kennedy Library.

[34] August Heckscher, recorded interview, p. 9.

[35] Ibid., p. 13.

[36] Ibid., p. 52.

[37] Roger Stevens, recorded interview by August Heckscher, January 22, 1964, p. 17. Oral History Program, John F. Kennedy Library.

[38] August Heckscher, recorded interview, p. 61.

[39] Ibid., p. 16.

[40] U.S. President, Public Papers of the Presidents of the United States, John F. Kennedy, 1962 (Washington: United States Government Printing Office, 1963), p. 347. The Nobel guests included forty-six United States Citizens; one Canadian, Lester Pearson, a winner of the Nobel Peace Prize; and two Europeans who were then living in the United States. Ibid., p. 348.

[41] August Heckscher, recorded interview, p. 49.

[42] Ibid., p. 48.

[43] Ibid., p. 51.

[44] 88th Congress, 1st Session, Document No. 28: The Arts and the Nation Government, Report to the President, submitted by August Heckscher, Special Consultant on the Arts, May 28, 1963 (Washington: United States Government Printing Office, 1963).

[45] New York Times, February 7, 1962, p. 20.

[46] New York Times, May 18, 1962, p. 33.

[47] Letter, August Heckscher to Senator Hubert H. Humphrey, February 13, 1963. Files of August Heckscher, John F. Kennedy Library.

[48] "Notes on Meeting to Discuss White House Policy on Advisory Committee on the Arts, May 12, 1962," Files of August Heckscher, John F. Kennedy Library.

[49] Memorandum for Mr. Arthur Schlesinger, Jr., from August Heckscher, January 17, 1963. Files of August Heckscher, John F. Kennedy Library.

[50] "Memorandum for the President, Subject: "Federal Advisory Council of the Arts," not dated, Arthur Schlesinger, Jr. to John F. Kennedy. White House Central Files, John F. Kennedy Library.

[51] Ibid.

[52] Memorandum, Barbara Donald to August Heckscher, May 24, 1962. Files August Heckscher, John F. Kennedy Library.

[53] Letter from Hal Leyshon, Director, American Federation of Musicians, to August Heckscher, July 20, 1962. Files of August Heckscher, John F. Kennedy Library.

[54] American Symphony Orchestra League, "Report on Survey of Opinion of Governing Boards of Symphony Orchestras on the Role of the Federal Government in the Arts," June 21, 1962, prepared by Helen M. Thompson, Executive Director, for the League Board of Directors (Charleston, WV: American Symphony Orchestra League, 1962), p. 3. Files of August Heckscher, John F. Kennedy Library.

[55] Ibid.

[56] Ibid.

[57] Ibid.

[58] Ibid.

[59] Ibid., p. 7.

[60] Ibid., p. 8.

[61] New York Times

[62] August Heckscher, recorded interview, pp. 52-53.

[63] Ibid., p.53.

[64] Ibid.

[65] Frank Thompson, recorded interview. Oral History Program, John F. Kennedy Library.

[66] Memorandum for the President, Subject: Future of the Arts Program, Arthur Schlesinger, Jr. to Lyndon B. Johnson, November 29, 1963, p. 1. Files of August Heckscher, John F. Kennedy Library.

[67] Ibid., p. 2.

[68] Lyndon B. Johnson, "Remarks in Providence at the 200th Anniversary Convocation of Brown University," September 28, 1964. U.S. President, Public Papers of the Presidents of the United States, Lyndon B. Johnson, 1963-64. Book 2 (Washington: United States Government Printing Office, 1965), p. 1141.

[69] Address by August Heckscher, "Kennedy: The Man Who Lives On," Larchmont Temple, November 20, 1964. Files of August Heckscher, John F. Kennedy Library.

[70] August Heckscher, recorded interview, p. 3.

[71] Ibid., p. 62.

[72] Ibid., p. 54.

[73] Theodore C. Sorensen, Kennedy (New York: Harper & Row, 1965), p. 388.

8
The National Endowment for the Arts: 1965–1980

C. Richard Swaim

INTRODUCTION

The federal government had previously flirted with the idea of supporting the arts. Early attempts and experiments in the support and promotion of the arts had been piecemeal and indirect. Major milestones included such disparate attempts as support of the Freer Gallery, the Smithson bequest, passage of tax laws to encourage private philanthropy and foundation support of the arts, and the short-lived, innovative projects of the New Deal era. It was not until a protracted congressional struggle in 1965, that the federal government provided direct support for the arts by creating the National Endowment for the Arts (NEA) as part of the National Foundation for the Arts and Humanities (NFAH).[1] In the years since the establishment of the Arts Endowment, a number of developments have contributed significantly to the nature and scope of public support for the arts in the United States. The following pages discuss this patronage effort and the likely effect it may have on the arts.

Patronage affects the art it supports. Michael Straight, former Deputy Chairman of the Arts Endowment, commenting on the relationship between art and patronage, reasoned, "Great art is sustained and strengthened by great patronage. Poor patronage discourages and diminishes art."[2] The question is then a simple one--if patronage affects the character of art, the kind of support structure is important and warrants investigation. The structures and processes of the Arts Endowment which represent that support have implications for the developing patronage system in the United States.

ADMINISTRATIVE STRUCTURE

The Arts Endowment, with a mandate for direct support and promotion of the arts, began in 1965 with a staff of twenty-eight and distributed $2.5 million in support. In 1980, the agency employed 245 employees, several hundred part-time experts, and distributed $154 million of support with claims to have sparked much more from state, local and private sources of patronage.[3] Though still small by Washington standards, in these fifteen years the agency has had impact beyond its size. The Endowment's employment history and budget growth are shown in Tables 8.1 and 8.2.

In supporting, promoting, and encouraging the arts, the NEA provides financial assistance and acts as an advocate for the arts.[4] The Endowment provides three major types of financial assistance: fellowships to artists of exceptional talent, matching grants to non-profit, tax-exempt organizations, and grants to state arts and regional arts groups. These grants or fellowships are provided through a programmatic structure reflecting specific artistic disciplines and interdisciplinary fields. There are also several administrative subdivisions (for example, research and planning) which serve the internal needs of the agency. The agency structure has remained fairly consistent as most changes have been cosmetic and added in response to additional funding categories. The Museum program (created in 1970) and the Opera-Musical Theatre program (created in 1979) are two such examples. Each program area is advised and guided by a panel of experts-- advisory structures which simultaneously make for both delight and consternation.

The advocacy efforts of the Arts Endowment stem from cooperative efforts with other federal agencies, the catalytic role of its grants (especially the Challenge Grant program), and the agency's proclivity to comment on other areas of federal activity which affect the arts and artists. The Endowment's efforts in energy policy and program accessibility exemplify this kind of activity.[5] In the areas of financial assistance and advocacy, the agency's advisory bodies (the National Council on the Arts and the panels for each program) play central procedural and policymaking roles.

The art forms assisted by the NEA are prescribed by enabling legislation; however, the emergence, growth, and variation among programs reflect the dynamics of internal processes and mirror the power configurations of the constitutent groups served by the agency. In fiscal 1966, the Endowment awarded grants among eight programs; by fiscal 1980, the number of programs had expanded to fourteen. The Arts Endowment currently

TABLE 8.1
Employment History--National Foundation For The Arts And
Humanities

Fiscal year	FTP/Other NEA	FTP/Other NEH	FTP/Other SS	FTP/Overall NFAH Total
1966	28	28	19	75/
1967	28	28	19	75/
1968	28	31	23	82/119
1969	28	30	24	82/119
1970	27	30	28	85/119
1971	44	40	41	125/161
1972	57	56	52	165/213
1973	75	73	74	222/346
1974	99	97	94	290/450
1975	130/70	130/55	127/45	387/557
1976	130/	130/	127/	387/557
1977	150/76	154/77	160	464/617
1978	222/85	240/85	---[9]	462/632
1979	218/83	246/84	---[9]	464/631
1980	215/85	245/85	---[9]	460/630

Source: For years 1966 through 1976, Personnel Office,
National Endowment for the Arts; years 1976-80, U.S.
Congress, _Hearings_, Department of Interior and Related
Agencies, before a subcommittee of the Commitee on
Appropriations, House of Representatives, 96th Cong.,
1st Sess., p. 469.
SS= shared staff; FTP= Full Time Person.

[9] Beginning fiscal 1978 the two endowments no longer
shared staff.

awards grants in the following major program areas:
Architecture Planning and Design Arts, Dance, Education,
Expansion Arts, Partnership, Folk Arts, Literature,
Media Arts: Film/Radio, Television, Museums, Music,
Opera-Musical Theatre, Special Projects, Theatre and
Visual Arts. Variation among program areas is
determined by the characteristics of clientele, the
number and size of awards, program share of budgets, and
the geographic distribution of awards. These indices
aid in explaining the character of Arts Endowment
policy.

TABLE 8.2
Budget Growth--National Endowment for the Arts

Fiscal Year	Authorization	Appropriation	% Change in Appropriation
1966	7,250,000	2,534,308	---
1967	10,000,000	7,965,692	214
1968	10,000,000	7,174,291	-1.0
1969	11,375,000	7,756,875	8.1
1970	12,375,000	8,250,000	6.3
1971	20,000,000	15,090,000	82.9
1972	30,000,000	29,750,000	97.1
1973	40,000,000	38,200,000	28.4
1974	72,500,000	60,775,000	59.1
1975	100,000,000	74,750,000	23.0
1976	126,000,000	82,000,000	9.6
1977	119,500,000	94,000,000	9.7
1978*	137,500,000	123,500,000	31.4
1979	Such Sums	149,585,000	21.0
1980	Such Sums	154,500,000	3.2

Source: National Endowment for the Arts, National Council for the Arts, <u>Annual Report</u>, 1979 (Washington, D.C.: U. S. Government Printing Office, 1980).

*Administrative funds were provided to both the Humanities and the Arts Endowments jointly until 1978. These figures for the Arts Endowment after 1978 contain the administrative funds as well as program funds; the pre-1978 figures are program monies only. The authorization figure for 1978 is authorized program monies; "such sums. . ." was designated for the administrative portion that year and for both programmatic and adminstrative monies thereafter.

THE ADVISORY BODIES: THE PANELS AND THE COUNCIL

The Arts Endowment is assisted in its policymaking and grants application processes by two kinds of advisory bodies--the National Council on the Arts and panels in each program area. The National Council is a

presidentially-appointed body which has the statutory
authority to recommend grant awards to the Chairman.
The panels are selected by the Chairman and assist in
the grants process by reviewing applications and making
recommendations to the Council for their final approval.
These bodies play a significant role in the policy
process and their existence and character are crucial
for Arts Endowment policy. In discussing another type
of policymaking, Roger Hilsman made the following
observation about organizational arrangements:

> By making it easier for some people to have
> access than others, by providing for the
> accumulation of one kind of information and
> not another, or by following procedures that
> let some problems rise to the top of the
> government's agenda before others--in all
> these ways some organizational arrangements
> facilitate certain kinds of policy and other
> organizational arrangements facilitate other
> kinds of policy.[6]

What is true in foreign policymaking is equally true in
cultural policymaking. The Council and the panels as
decisionmaking bodies have a decided impact on the NEA's
policies. The members of the Council are appointed on
the basis of "the broad base of their experience in the
arts." "Interested parties"--that is, congressmen and
arts lobbyists--provide suggested names as do staff,
other Council members, and panelists. The 1976
reauthorization of the National Foundation for the Arts
and Humanities provided for Senate approval of the
President's appointments to the Council. But then
Chairman Nancy Hanks offered this view while Congress
debated the provision, "[i]ts no big deal . . . we've
been getting 'okays' on the Hill anyway."[7]
    The selection process for panelists is fairly
consistent across programs. The nomination process
begins with solicited and unsolicited recommendations
from ". . . the Council, staff, current panel members,
national art associations, the general public, and the
White House."[8] Among those characteristics considered
are geography, age, sex, and ethnic/minority considerations. Michael Straight, the Deputy Chairman in 1974,
testified that "above all we try to get the very best
people we can."[9] The process of selection for both the
Council and the panels assure the "relevant" interest
groups of participation and representation in the policy
process. In the grant deliberations and the specific
policy discussions, both the panels and Council set the
tone for the Arts Endowment. By deciding the priorities
among and within programs these panels determine policy
directions and the eventual distribution of programmatic

benefits, that is, the grants. As both the Five Year Plan and discussion during recent appropriations hearings reveal, "[t]he panel system might be considered the foundation in the sturcture of the Endowment."[10] Congressman Sidney Yates (D-Ill.) apologized for spending so much time on this aspect, but allowed:

> The reason we are spending so much time must be understood. The panel system and the grant system are what you (the Arts Endowment) exists for apparently and are the key to the whole process.

> * * *

> I think again the panel system is of such consequence and such importance in the operation of the system, it is this layer in the bureaucracy, if I can call the senior members and the Council members bureaucracy, it is that layer which is the key layer in the operation of the Endowment.[11]

THE APPLICATION PROCESS

Grant applications received by the Endowment are collected by program area in panel books and reviewed by panels, meeting in Washington, D. C., as well as around the country. Panel recommendations are forwarded to the Council for approval or rejection.[12] There are two general areas of panel decisionmaking--considerations of grant applications and policy quesitons. These are difficult to distinguish as policy questions inevitably surface during the application review and in 1978 the Endowment moved to a system of policy and review panels in program areas. Each program creates guidelines spelling out the appropriateness of submitted projects though the panels constantly review and revise such guidelines to retain a necessary flexibility. The guidelines remain flexible to allow new areas of consideration if sufficient interest is expressed either because of the nature of the applications or the recommendations of panelists. The Arts Endowment points to this review system as evidence of its responsiveness to the interests of the cultural community.

There is variation among panels regarding the application process.[13] More established programs, for example, those representing the institutional art forms, conduct formal meetings in a business-like atmosphere. Individually-oriented programs, representing areas such as Folk Arts, conduct panel meetings which are more informal and freewheeling. The guidelines mentioned earlier set general criteria for awarding grants and panel members have considerable freedom within these limits. A common denominator for success seems to be the personal knowledge of the applicant by one or more of the panel members. As one observer remarked, "It is imperative to discuss your project with the panel people, as each and every lengthy discussion on the application's merits was the result of prior contact-- though quality was always the first criterion."[14] If no one knows the applicant, panel members rely exclusively on the file and testimonials. While the process may appear very arbitrary and personalized, it can be noted that, "They (the panel members) know the field--if they don't know them, they are not worth knowing."[15] The panelists are clearly familiar with the applicants. One program director reported to the National Council, that from the 700 applications received and reviewed that year, only three applicants were not known by the panelists. After panel reviews and recommendations, applications are sent to the National Council for the Arts.

The Council meets four to five times a year to consider grant applications, general policy, and budget matters. As with the panels, it is difficult to separate budget and policy from application review. Since 1971, however, the Council has devoted one full meeting to policy considerations alone. This indicates a new role for the Council. It is moving away from considerations of applications alone to more general policy determination. The NEA's growth and the increased volume of applications fairly demand that the Council provide policy direction and evaluation. The enhanced policy role of the Council is witnessed by the committee structure that has evolved: Budget, Policy and Planning, and State Partnership. These committees meet throughout the year and provide some continuity.

The amount of actual involvement and time spent by the Council in both application review and policy planning is arguable.[16] A congressional staff report remarked that very little time was spent in application review and affirmed a widespread belief that the real work was done by the staff and during panel review sessions. The Council acts more as a rubber stamp and, on occasion, as an appellate body. The following exchange between members of the Appropriations subcommittee responsible for the Arts Endowment and the Endowment Chairman and Deputy Chairman summarizes the Council's role in relation to the application process and panel decisionmaking.[17]

> Mr. Yates (Subcommittee Chairman): Approval of the grant is to all intent and purposes the approval of the grant?
>
> Ms. Tighe (Deputy Chairman for Policy): In most cases.
>
> Mr. Yates: In how many cases has it been set aside?
>
> Ms. Tighe: A few, but it has happened.

* * *

> Mr. Yates: The Council is really a board of directors, in a sense, and your basic work is done by the panels and staff.
>
> Mr. Biddle (NEA Chairman): Yes.
>
> Mr. Dicks (NEA Official): It is like the committee system in a sense, because the committee does the work, the panel being the committee, and the House being the Council in the sense they review what the committee has done.

Thus, the effective "final" decision is made in the panel meetings and the Council represents a final, and symbolically important, legitimation of decisions already made. In the few cases of panel decisionmaking being overruled by the Council or the Chairman suggesting "another look," it is nearly always on the basis of new information. The role of policymaker is split among panels, the Council, and the Chairman. The advisory bodies' role is largely as a source of ideas and a legitimation of steps contemplated or already taken.

The Council has always had a policymaking role. It is prescribed in the enabling legislation that established the NEA in 1965. This policy role was reaffirmed in 1972 when Nancy Hanks as Chairman told the House Appropriations subcommittee, "[the role of the Council] is to advise the Chairman of the Arts Endowment on policy directions of the agency in terms of programs, as well as review of submitted applications. . . ."[18] This is most evident when tracing programs to individual Council members, as for example, the Art in Public Places projects and Rene D'Harncourt's sponsorship while on the Council. It now appears that the policymaking role of the Council is replacing its considerations of applications as a primary activity. "The role of the Council has changed from considerations of applications to a fifty-fifty approach for policy and applications."[19]

The manner in which the Chairman uses the Council and the panels also enhances their policy role. For example, Nancy Hanks used both as a source of ideas and a legitimation of agency direction. "It is the Council that she (Chairman Hanks) goes to for advice and decisionmaking. There is an emphasis on the panels as a source of ideas or leads for planning; ideas emerge from panel meetings."[20] The exact nature of the policy role rests with the Chairman. It is very much like the role between a chairman and a board of directors. While the Council (the board) may originate an idea, its adoption depends on the Chairman's decision. This was true for Chairman Hanks and it remains the case with Livingston Biddle. One Arts Endowment staff member saw the relationship between Council and Chairman accordingly:

> I see the Council as a board of directors and the staff as visionairies in the sense that the Council has an overview and specific concerns. The staff has to take those ideas and package them into some plan. Nancy Hanks is the chief executive officer and it is true that Nancy gets what Nancy wants but that is the way it should be. Any good corporation operates like that.[21]

Biddle's conception of the Chairman's role is similar. He characterized the relationship as follows: "I have always thought of the Council, however, as a board of directors and I think the previous Chairman had that feeling as well."[22]

The panels perform similarly. They represent a main source of information from the field because of their membership, the frequency of their meetings and their interaction with the staff. This enhances their ability to function as a source of ideas and identifier of those issues which the Endowment needs to address. The Planning Division monitors both the Council meetings and the panel sessions and uses those meetings and expressions of interest as points of departure for policy and programming ideas for the Endowment.

> We are making increased use of the panels and the Council. When we were smaller, policy was made between Nancy and the Council. Now we generate ideas from the staff, panels, and Council.[23]

When the rhetoric and promises of earlier discussions are eventually translated into dollars, the key document in the process is the budget. While the Council performs a policy role, the budget is primarily the result of the agency's programmatic priorities. While the Council discusses the budget, it is drawn up by the staff. In recent years, however, this secondary role of the Council has been changing.

> The budget process now starts with the National Council on the Arts. There is a budget committee within the Council, a sort of executive committee, four members. They make recommendations regarding the funding of programs.[24]

Because of a lack of time, information, and energies, the real budget process still resides with the "policy centers" in the agency. The Council essentially legitimates staff decisionmaking. Occasionally, however, programs will use the Council as an appeals body. This occurred during the 1973 meeting when Expansion Arts "put on a show" and received more money.[25] Most recently, during the November, 1980 meeting, the Jazz program made a similar appeal. Billy Taylor, a former Council member, spoke for the Jazz program and made a pitch for greater attention. He noted the indigenous nature of the art form as the "center of the American aesthetic" and "most important the rise in applications from 800 to 1400, a 76.5% increase in one year."

The Council and panels both serve a trustee role in their capacity as experts and public servants. They need to be responsive to the overriding criterion of quality, as well as representatives of the public. This is the paradox. While these often emerge as contradictory issues, they need not be such. However, it will continue to be a major policy dilemma for the agency. The responsiveness remains to quality and representing special interests. That this is acceptable in any sense rests on the assumption that all interests are equally equipped to participate in the process of cultural politics. Perhaps more important is the assumption that this is good for patronage and for the arts.

The panels and Council also serve as insulators protecting the Arts Endowment from political interference. As noted above, the professional panels in each program area make decisions on the merits of the applications and forward their recommendations to the Council. This acts as a buffer and prevents the White House or Congress from influencing specific applications. The Chairman, in opposing such interference, can point to decisions made by panels or the Council as based on quality.[26] Seemingly, this prevents "politics" from influencing grant decisions. However, this neglects the decisions made in the larger context among art forms. If Congress and the President approve the allocation of monies among line-items in the budget, they are directing the Endowment's distribution of its funds among art forms. Inevitably, this will favor one art form over another and result in Program A receiving more support than Program B. This ultimately affects the growth and survival quotient of various art forms.

The programs which are looked upon more favorably are those which are able to make their influence felt in the "corridors of power." It is in this way that politics enters the development of art. An assumption which makes this acceptable is that equal participation serves the public (and the arts, presumably) by enabling all interests to compete equally in defining the public interest, i.e., the development of art. Reality negates this. The more powerful art lobbies are able to insure a certain amount of support for "their" program areas and the process is biased from the beginning. It is not that congress or the president can reject or approve specific grants, it is that they are able to structure the process in favor of broad program areas and to influence the direction of cultural development in the United States.

This assessment of the advisory bodies and, by extension the policy which emerges, depends on what one thinks of the character of the policy.

> . . . whether one thinks a certain organizational arrangement is "good" or "bad" depends on what one thinks of the policy it facilitates. But if some organizational arrangements facilitate certain kinds of policy and other organizational arrangements facilitate other kinds, then organization is also politics in another guise, which accounts for the passion that men so often bring to procedural and organizational matters.[27]

The procedural and organizational matters offer means to facilitate certain kinds of policy by providing multiple points of access for the arts constituencies which the Endowment serves. Representatives of institutions and individual artists serving on the panels and on the Council are an installation of the agency's clientele in the agency. Thus, the determination of arts policy is within the purview of the groups and individuals which the agency serves and represents an institutionalization of "interest group policy process"[28] in the Arts Endowments.

THE CHAIRMAN

The use of advisory bodies and the general administrative character of the agency is very much the prerogative of the chairman. The Chairman of the Arts Endowment, appointed by the President for a four-year term with the advice and consent of the Senate, is simultaneously the Chairman of the National Council for the Arts. The chairman must by statute approve or disapprove each grant recommendation made by the Council. Ostensibly, this gives the chairman ultimate authority. However, the chairmen who have headed the agency viewed their role as nearly automatic regarding the Council's decisions. Chairman Biddle commented, ". . . I would never think of myself as reversing panel-Council decisions, merely I look on my role as a person who provides the experts to deal with these problems rather than as a person who makes the ultimate decisions on quality."[29] Generally, the definition an individual gives to formal organizational roles is a more realistic reading of the position than formal definition; this has been true of the Arts Endowment.

The chairmanship of the Arts Endowment has been held from 1965 to 1980 by three individuals: Roger Stevens, Nancy Hanks, and Livingston Biddle. Mr. Stevens, appointed by President Johnson, was the person responsible for the establishment of the agency. Mrs. Hanks, appointed by President Nixon, was responsible for the meteoric rise in the budget along with basic policy changes which moved the agency to the center of the arts constituency. The third chairman, Livingston Biddle, appointed by President Carter, took the post amidst much speculation over the politicization of the arts and a leveling of appropriations as the agency matured. Each chairman has individualized the agency and one may conclude that each was "right" for the agency at that particular point in time. Roger Stevens was able to devote his energies and political adroitness to see the NFAH into law. In turn, Nancy Hanks had the deftness to acquire increased funding for the agency during Richard Nixon's administration. Livingston Biddle arrived as the agency felt pressures of politicization in terms of appointments and responsiveness to various constitutent groups.[30]

The era of Roger Stevens is generally characterized as one of innovativeness and much flexibility owing largely to lack of precedent and any sort of organizational inertia.[31] A reading of early grants and Council minutes bear this out. Chairman Hanks's tenure was marked by dramatic increases in the agency's budget and a policy shift as she moved the NEA from the periphery of the arts constituency to the center with support for (and from) museums, symphonies, and orchestras. Mr. Biddle's acrimonious beginnings were marked by blatant charges of politicization as the new Carter administration and Congress seemingly gave more weight to political qualifications than quality, non-partisan appointments for both the NEA and NEH.[32] Biddle assumed the position in time to be met with a number of pending criticisms regarding grant distribution, management

disputes, and problems surfacing as funding plateaued
after a rapid growth period. Perhaps, the real story of
the agency is told by Chairman Hanks' tenure.[33]
     The chairmanship of Nancy Hanks was marked by dra-
matic increases in the agency's budget and a somewhat
more institutionalized internal sturcture. The budget
rose from $8.4 million in 1970 to $94 million in 1977,
the period of the Hanks charimanship. This represents a
tenfold increase (see Table 8.2). The panel operations
became more regularized as guidelines were established
for program and subprogram areas. The explanation of
Mrs. Hanks's tenure and its fiscal success is a story of
political entrepreneurship and the story of the
Endowment.[34] In addition to the increased budget, she
also established a more regular grant procedure through
panels and guidelines. Although a good deal of flexibility remains, bureaucratic procedures replaced the
"poetic atmosphere" of earlier years. This process is
now in adolescence as the agency deals with data
processing, investigative reports, and five-year plans.
     Each chairman came with goals or objectives which
they then incorporated into presentations to Congress
and the Office of Management and Budget. The first
chairman, Roger Stevens, used seven goals which outlined
the NEA's policy.

> To increase opportunities for an appreciation
> and enjoyment of the arts through wider
> distribution
>
> To sustain and develop existing independent
> institutions of the arts
>
> To sustain and encourage individual performers
> and creative artists
>
> To increase the importance and awareness of
> the arts
>
> To increase the participation of the people in
> local artistic programs
>
> To provide the people with new opportunities
> in all aspects of the arts, and
>
> To support programs and projects of an inter-
> national nature in the United States and
> abroad[35]

Mrs. Hanks, in addition to promises of more money, came
with three goals in mind.

To increase the availability of the arts

To strengthen the cultural resources

To advance the nation's cultural legacy[36]

She announced these to Congress in January, 1970, while asking for congressional support for the new administration's funding levels. They were last used in the appropriations requests for fiscal 1979. Livingston Biddle decided on five categories to make his case to the Congress and the White House.

Individual creativity and excellence

Institutional creativity and excellence

Living heritage

Making the arts available

Leadership in the arts[37]

In acuality, it appears that these various statements of policy goals (nearly identical in substance) had nothing to do with the success or failure of the Arts Endowment. While official pronouncements, testimony, and occasional interviews make it appear that the agency budgets by these goals, one official confided, "the goals are meaningless--Nancy uses them for obfuscation."[38] While they may be meaningless, they are not meaningless in a symbolic way to Congress, OMB, and cultural interest groups. Regardless, they do not represent goals toward which the agency plans; rather, they are an imposition of a seemingly rational character upon the political arithmetic and economic logic of the budgetary process. This is consistent with the distinction between operative and official goals.[39] Official goals, purposely vague and general, contrast with operative goals which are indicative of what the agency is doing. Operative goals provide the specific content of official goals and reflect choices among competing values within the organization and in the external environment. While Mrs. Hanks promulgated the goals of the agency (to make the arts available, advance our cultural legacy, and strengthen the cultural institutions), the actual distribution of grants among art forms represented what the agency was doing. One need only look at the budgetary profile for the Stevens and Biddle years for a similar contrast. The budget profile has not changed since the Hanks years and the NEA's official goals have also not changed, at least in substance.

The observation that each chairman was appropriate
for the agency suggests a somewhat evolutionary process
for the agency. Biddle has been characterized as an
administrative conserver and "politico" seeking to
". . . retain existing levels of organizational power,
resources, and prestige."[40] Biddle has had to deal with
rising criticism, increasing congressional oversight and
demand for information, and the politicization barbs.
Overall, he has had to reconcile charges of elitism
which, while leveled at the Humanities Endowment in
particular, have a general application to the Arts
Endowment as well. Biddle has handled both issues by
tempering the elitist argument with the promise of
access.

> I think it reaches the whole philosophy of the
> program I am interested in promoting and that
> is that we are dealing with the arts across
> the whole length of the country, and that
> outreach, availability to quality in the arts
> is what is most basic with our program, access
> to quality in the arts.[41]

Regarding the politicization of the arts, he commented:

> I have seen in the dictionary "politiciza-
> tion," but in any event that is a difficult
> word for me to pronounce and comprehend
> because I feel the arts have been in the main-
> stream of our political process ever since we
> began this program back in 1965 when it was
> enacted and before that when it was being
> considered by the Congress in the early
> 1960's. I feel very strongly that this is
> exactly where the arts belong, in the
> mainstream of our political process "with
> democratic process," and that is the way this
> country is governed, and I think it would be
> bad to have the arts in some other area.[42]

BUDGETARY PROCEDURE AND POLICY

The Endowment's place in the cultural patronage
structure was not guaranteed with its establishment.
The initial appropriations were meager and the early
years were hardly overwhelming as budgetary or policy
success. The election of Richard Nixon led to a dramatic change in the agency's budget and policies. Mrs.
Hanks, appointed by Richard Nixon in October, 1969,
managed to have the NEA's budget ceiling lifted and

subsequent budget requests were constrained by the
authorization levels only.   Mrs. Hanks had received
assurances prior to her appointment that financial
backing was forthcoming from the new White House.   The
President was supportive in principle but not exact in
details.   He would approve general requests, but the
details were left to his assistants.

The continued goodwill of the Nixon administration
was made possible through Leonard Garment, Special
Assistant to the President.   He became the Arts Endowment's friend at court and pressed the agency's points
with the decisionmakers at the White House and with the
Office of Management and Budget.   OMB abdicated its
usual paring role and permitted blanket approval of the
NEA's budget requests.   This involvement and commitment
had more than budgetary implications, it had an effect
on policy as well.   As Michael Straight would later
observe, "[t]he development of a coherent policy for the
arts requires principally a commitment on the part of
the White House."[43]

One reason for White House support was the agency's
forthcoming policy shift.   The Endowment would begin
funding the nation's museums and symphonies which, prior
to Mrs. Hanks, had received little or no support.[44]   In
turn, these groups had not advocated the agency's
programs in Congress or with the Executive branch.   It
is not clear if this was because of the lack of funds
available, or a general hostility to this source of
funding.   The effort to swing these constituencies
behind the Endowment's programs was made possible by the
promises of increased support for these groups.   This
represents the classic interest group, legislative,
agency nexus.   The following excerpts tell the story.[45]

In a memorandum to President Nixon, Chairman Hanks
asked him to   ". . . indicate to the OMB your desire to
ask for a $40,000,000 appropriation which would be the
same appropriation as requested in the authorizing
legislation . . ."   Mrs. Hanks noted that:

> This is a substantial increase over sums
> available to the Endowment for expenditure
> this year . . . However, the increase would
> not basically affect the federal budget.   And
> the increase would be essential to the
> Administration's ability to have any impact.

The Chairman noted the support for the program in other
quarters,

> . . . I have been able to ascertain (quietly)
> that the arts groups and civic leaders would
> enthusiastically endorse a program at this
> level . . .   Senators Pell and Javits have

agreed to back a program at this level to the
hilt--and not come in with a request for higher funds. I understand from Michael Straight
that Congressman Brademas and Thompson's
reaction would be the same. . . . I believe
we have a good base on which to build and a
strong constituent waiting in the wings.

This communication to President Nixon from Mrs. Hanks
was followed by one from Leonard Garment. He made the
case for increased appropriations by noting the small
amounts, the assured success, and the political benefit
that would follow.

It is important that the administration be
identified forceful with increased support for
the arts and humanities. In a message to the
OMB indicate your strong desire to ask for the
same appropriation as you are requesting in
the authorizing legislation. . . .

At least two extremely, powerful, and
emotionally persuasive groups are standing by
to put great pressure on the committees and
the Congress for considerable increases (the
symphony orchestras and the museums). In each
of these two cases, we are assured by private
conference if your message holds a hope for
some assistance, no great effort to criticize
the effort will be made.

For an amount of money which is miniscule in
terms of the total federal budget, you can
demonstrate your commitment to "reordering
national priorities to emphasize the quality
of life in our society."

The amount proposed . . . would have high
impact among opinion formers. It is, on the
merits, justified, i.e., the budget for the
arts and humanities is now completely
inadequate. Support for the arts is,
increasingly, good politics. By providing
substantially increased support for cultural
activities, you will gain support from groups
which have hitherto not been favorable to this
administration.

We are not referring to the hard-core radicals
who offer little in the way of constructive
dialogue when they plead for more support for
cultural projects. We are talking about the
vast majority of theatre board members,

symphony trustees, museum benefactors, and the
like who, nevertheless, feel very strongly
that federal support for the arts and
humanities is of primary importance. It is
well for us to remember that these boards are
made up, very largely, of business, corporate
and community interests.

In sum, the president would be able to reap
political benefits from a relatively small investment of
political capital.[46]   Increased support for the arts
represented a low-risk, high-yield addition to the
president's political portfolio. The small investment
is obvious. The Arts Endowment budget is minute
compared to other agencies and, in addition, the
investment was safe. The relevant members of Congress--
Frank Thompson and John Brademas in the House; Claiborne
Pell and Jacob Javits in the Senate--had assured
Chairman Hanks in advance of their support for the
president's proposal. The high-yield calculation is
possible because of the healthy and well-publicized
impact of the agency. As a result, the arts budget
"took off." Support existed in every quarter. The
agency had a guaranteed political coalition enjoying
support from Congress, the President, and a small but
powerful constituency. The remaining question is what
effect did all of this have on the Arts Endowment and
cultural policy?
The budgetary growth made possible a shift in
agency policy which, in turn, made possible the agency's
budgetary growth. The effect of these changes is
demonstrated by examining the agency's budget process
and the resulting budgetary profile. By disaggregating
the agency's budget into program shares, one notices an
irregular profile prior to 1970.[47]   The post-1970 period
is marked by two distinctive features. First, the
patterns of funding became more regular as programs
progressed with steady shares of the agency's budget.
Second, two programs--museums and music--consume a
greater portion of the agency's budget than other programs. (See Table 8.3) These changes in the character
of the NEA's budget reflect the basic policy change.
That change was not one of continuation and elaboration
but, rather, one of a shift in policy focus. As noted
in the agency's five year plan, ". . . a shift in policy
often means redistributing funds." And, more naively,
"[b]udgeting is a means through which policy is transformed into reality."[48]   The reality was that the NEA
would move to the center of the cultural coalition and,
in the process, insure that progress in arts patronage
meant more money for the arts organizations and groups
which had already had the most of everything--political
clout and operating deficits.

TABLE 8.3
1981 Program Budget Shares--National Endowment for the Arts

Program	% Share of Program Budget
Artists-in-Education	3.6
Challenge	9.1
Dance	6.1
Design Arts	3.5
Expansion Arts	6.2
Fellows (Management)	.1
Folk Arts	2.0
Inter-Arts	3.5
International	.2
Literature	3.2
Media Arts	8.4
Museums	8.8
Music	11.1
Opera-Musical Theatre	4.2
Partnership-Coordination	.4
Research	1.0
Special Constituencies	.2
State Programs	16.1
Theatre	7.3
Visual Arts	4.9

Source: Figures were calculated from amounts listed in The Cultural Post, 6 (March/April 1981). They represent the fiscal 1981 allocation by program. Total program funds equal $146,660,000, administrative funds equal $11,900,000, and the total budget for Fiscal 1981 was $158,560,000. The percentages above represent shares of the program monies.

        In this case, the budget lies at the heart of the policy process. An examination of the budgetary history and process presents a coherent picture of the NEA's policy stance and changes. However, what does this mean for patronage and the arts? The policy change demonstrated that funding priorities, hence policy, flow from the political process.[49] Policy choices are made by a combination of actors pursuing objectives; for example, legislators, administrators, lobbyists, presidential assistants. This means that the arts are now politicized. While arts patronage may be a legitimate and necessary function of government, entry into the political process becomes equally as necessary for the arts. Sara Garretson and Carol Grossman observe:

> Perhaps the major lesson to be learned by arts organizations is that public subsidy requires entry into the political process. They must learn the techniques of lobbying by other special interest groups that are competing for funds.[50]

Arts policy now became a creature of the political process with cultural organizations guarding their prerogatives and deciding future directions of cultural development.

CONCLUDING OBSERVATIONS

The Arts Endowment underwent a policy change and shift in institutional focus during the Hanks chairmanship. Major programmatic changes can or will occur in the future. The patterns of funding are established. If policy changes occur, they will be but a continuation and elaboration of existing policy and not a fundamental redirection of the agency. For the Arts Endowment this might mean the provision of general operating support for major art institutions. This would not be a major departure from present policy but would, however, require increased appropriations. Therefore, while there may be an increase in appropriations levels which would suggest policy changes; the direction of the agency's support for the promotion of the arts would not change.

The lack of substantial programmatic changes in the Endowment's support of the arts is predicated on the politicization of the arts. The political pressures which generated and supported a shift in agency policy in 1970 will prevent a major shift in focus. The alliance which shifted the agency's funding priorities now exists as a guardian of the funding patterns. Contributing to this is the internal program competition as program people fight for "their" money. As noted during recent appropriation hearings, while the agency's leadership and the National Council on the Arts set parameters of what they will emphasize, the program directors compete for shares of the pie. "In effect, the programs will be competing with one another for a larger part of the Endowment's budget."[51] The symbolic verification of this will come with substantial line-itemization in the NEA's budget as a way of solidifying patterns even more. Of course, this will have the effect of passing programmatic control to Congress and insure a greater continued politicization of arts policy.

The haves of the arts constituencies saw the priorities of the agency adjusted in line with their needs. With their interests now at stake and priorities flowing from the political process, these constituencies-- generally representing institutional art activity--will work to maintain their share of the budgetary pie. Thus, the result of direct government support for the arts has established the future direction of cultural policy. Government relates to that which relates to it best. The decisions to spend, and where to spend the cultural dollar, stem from the political marketplace and this may not provide the most responsible use of public money for the arts.

NOTES

[1] PL 89-209. For a general discussion of the history of arts support see Lawrence Mankin, "Government and the Arts: From the Great Depression to 1973," (Ph.D. dissertation, University of Illinois, 1976). See also, Joan S. Burns, The Awkward Embrace (New York: Alfred Knopf, 1975).

[2] Michael Straight, Twigs for An Eagle's Nest (Berkeley: Devon Press, 1980). For a discussion of the relation between patronage and style in art, see Edward Henning, "Patronage and Style in the Arts: A Suggestion Concerning Their Relations," Journal of Aesthetics and Art Criticism 18 (June 1960): 464-471. For a discussion of European patronage systems and their implications for the United States, see Frederick Dorian, Commitment to Culture (Pittsburgh: University of Pittsburgh Press, 1964).

[3] The 1965 data are from National Endowment for the Arts, Annual Report (Washington, DC: Government Printing Office, 1965). The 1980 data are from U. S. Congress, House, Hearings, Department of Interior and Related Agencies, before a subcommittee of the Committee on Appropriations for 1979, House of Representatives, 96th Cong., 1st Sess., 1980. The catalytic effect of the agency's monies are part of the claim to be efficacious. The Arts Endowment claims, at least in part, that the increase in personal, corporate, state and local, and foundation giving is due to activity by the Arts Endowment. For a disputed version see, Dick Netzer, The Subsidized Muse (New York: Cambridge University Press, 1978).

[4] Enumeration and a cursory description of the agency's programs are available from the Arts Endowment. See Guide To Programs (Washington, DC: Government Printing Office).

[5] Section 504 of the 1973 Rehabilitation Act guarantees access to all persons regardless of handicap. For a brief discussion of the Endowment's response, see my "New Challenges for the Arts: The Disabled Consumer," paper presented at the Spring, 1979 meeting of the National Capitol Area Political Science Association, Washington, D.C. This also appears in Short Essays, Fall, 1979, published by the National Capitol Area Political Science Association. A glance at any of the National Council on the Arts "Council Books" will illustrate the breadth of agency comment on pending legislation.

[6] Roger Hilsman, To Move a Nation (Garden City, NJ: Doubleday, 1967), p. 17.

[7] Intern discussion with Nancy Hanks, Chairman of the National Endowment for the Arts, April 23, 1976. The other information regarding panels is from Rodney

Campbell, "Ten Years for Tomorrow" (unpublished manuscript, National Endowment for the Arts); informal conversation with Anne Hartzell, National Endowment for the Arts, Spring, 1976; interview with Ann Clark, National Endowment for the Arts, Spring, 1976.

[8]Interview with Anna Steele, National Endowment for the Arts May, 1976.

[9]U. S. Congress, House, Michael Straight in testimony before a subcommittee of the Committee on Appropriations, Hearings, Department of Interior and Related Agencies, 1975, House of Representatives, 93rd Cong., 2nd sess., March 23, 1974, pg. 563.

[10]National Endowment for the Arts, Division of Planning, General Plan (1979). The agency prepared its first five year plan after much prodding by Congress. The plan purports to be an agenda for action of Endowment activities for the next five years, however, it is dataless and appears to be another document extolling agency virtues.

[11]U.S. Congress, House, 96th, 1st sess., pp. 540, 695. See Straight, Twigs for an Eagle's Nest, p. 80, as he indicates that "[i]t was in the panels that Endowment policies were developed."

[12]A total of 155 days was spent in 1978 by Endowment panels in the review of applications. U. S. Congress, Hearings, before a subcommittee of the Committee on Appropriations, Department of Interior and Related Agencies, House of Representatives, 96th Congress., 1st sess., p. 526.

[13]The description of the panel meetings stem from personal observation, discussion with staff, intern fellows, and "A Report to the Committee on Appropriations, House of Representatives on the National Endowment for the Arts and Humanities," U. S. Congress, House, 96th Cong., 1st sess., Vol. 1, pp. 865-1041.

[14]Intern discussion seminar, National Endowment for the Arts, Spring, 1976.

[15]Ibid.

[16]"Report to the Committee on Appropriations, on the National Endowments." This report was requested by Congressman Sidney Yates (D-Ill.) as a means of determining what the Endowments were doing as well as to broadcast the virtues of the agencies. Apparently, it fell short of expectations and had the effect of generating re-rebuttal, surrebuttal, and so forth. They do say some interesting things and some of their conclusions parallel those I made two years earlier in "The Fine Politics of Art: Organizational Behavior, Budgetary Behavior, and Some Implications for Arts Policy," (Ph.D. dissertation, University of Colorado, 1977).

[17]U. S. Congress, House, 96th Cong., 1st sess., pp. 529-530.

[18]U. S. Congress, Nancy Hanks in testimony before a subcommittee of the Committee on Appropriations, Department of Interior and Related Agencies, Hearings, House of Representatives, 92nd Cong., 1st sess., 1971.

[19]Seminar, Intern Fellowship Program, Richard Contee, National Endowment for the Arts, April 12, 1976.

[20]Informal discussion with Anne Hartzell, National Endowment for the Arts, Spring 1976.

[21]Interview with Larry Reger, National Endowment for the Arts, March 11, 1976.

[22]U. S. Congress, House, 96th Cong., 1st Sess., p. 1075.

[23]Interview with Anna Steele, May 5, 1976; interview with Ann Clark, May 3, 1976; and informal conversation, Anne Hartzell, Spring, 1976, all of the National Endowment for the Arts.

[24]U. S. Congress, House, 96th Cong., 1st sess., p. 724.

[25]National Council on the Arts, Minutes of 31st Meeting, July 29, 1973, p. 5-8. (Typewritten.)

[26]On this point, Rourke reasons, "[t]he importance of preserving the independence and integrity of certain kinds of expertise in government is thus very great. . . . But as more and more agencies play a policy making role that requires reliance upon expert or at least nonpolitical standards, the need for professional autonomy begins to assert itself in all phases of bureaucratic policy making." Francis E. Rourke, Bureaucracy, Politics, and Public Policy (Boston: Little Brown, & Co., 1976), p. 134.

[27]Hilsman, To Move A Nation, p. 18.

[28]J. Leiper Freeman, "The Bureaucracy in Pressure Politics," Annals, 319 (September 1958): 10-19; Theodore Lowi, The End of Liberalism (W. W. Norton & Co: New York, 1978); and David B. Truman, The Governmental Process (Boston: Little, Brown & Co., 1952).

[29]U. S. Congress, House, 96th Cong., 1st sess., p. 541.

[30]There have been a spate of articles regarding the controversey over elitism, politicization, and appointments and procedures at both the Arts and Humanities Endowments; this is but a partial list. C. Gerald, "Economist Criticizes Some Governmental Aid to and Effect on Arts," New York Times, April 25, 1978; "U. S. To Review Arts Policy," New York Times, November 25, 1977; David Dempsey, "Funding Culture High and Low and Calling it All Art," New York Times, October 16, 1977; Hilton Kramer, "The Threat of Politicization of the Federal Arts Program," New York Times, October 16, 1977; Haynes Johnson, "A Civilizing Government," New York Times, November 2, 1977; Lon Tuck, "Can They Bring Order to Culture," Washington Post, March 5, 1978; Philip Kadis, "Livingston Biddle," Washington Star,

November 30, 1977; Robert Brustein, "Can the Show Go On?" <u>New York Times Magazine</u>, November 23, 1977; Robert Brustein, "Whither the National Arts and Humanities Endowments?" <u>New York Times</u>, December 18, 1977; John Friedman, "A Populist Shift in Federal Cultural Support," <u>New York Times</u>, May 13, 1979; Grace Gulek, "Filling Humanities Post is an Art," <u>New York Times</u>, June 28, 1977; John Friedman, "Mr. Duffy Goes to the Humanities Endowment," <u>New York Times</u>, August 21, 1977.

[31]See Barry Schwartz, "Politics and the Arts: A Case of Cultural Confusion," <u>Arts and Society</u> 10 (Fall-Winter 1973): 19-26; and my comments in Malcolm Carter, "The National Endowment for the Arts: Will Success Spoil Our Biggest Patron," <u>Art News</u>, 76 (May 1977): 32-48.

[32]See note 30 above.

[33]The preoccupation with Nancy Hanks throughout the chapter and in any discussion concerning the Arts Endowment is warranted. Her tenure at the agency has been the longest and she had, I think, the greatest impact of any of the chairmen.

[34]The phrase is Eugene Bardach's; see his <u>The Skill Factor in Politics</u> (Berkeley, CA: University of California Press, 1972).

[35]Roger Stevens, testimony before a subcommittee of the Committee on Appropriations, House of Representatives, U. S. Congress, House, Department of Interior and Related Agencies, <u>Hearings</u>, 90th Cong., 2nd sess., March 1980.

[36]See the Arts Endowment budget presentation to the Congress any year during Chairman Hanks's tenure.

[37]Livingston Biddle, testimony before a subcommittee of the Committee on Appropriations, House of Representatives, U. S. Congress, House, Department of Interior and Related Agencies, <u>Hearings</u>, 95th Cong., 1st sess., May, 1979.

[38]Interview with Arts Endowment official requesting anonymity.

[39]Charles Perrow, "The Analysis of Goals in Complex Organizations," <u>American Sociological Review</u>, 26 (1961): 854-866.

[40]Kevin V. Mulcahy, "The Current Status of Arts Administration," paper presented at the Annual Meeting of the Western Social Science Association, Denver, Colorado, April 27-28, 1978.

[41]U. S. Congress, House, 96th Cong., 1st sess., pp. 683-684.

[42]<u>Ibid.</u>, p. 617.

[43]Straight, <u>Twigs for an Eagle's Nest</u>, p. 96.

[44]Otto A. Davis, M. H. Dempster, and Aaron Wildavsky, "A Theory of the Budgetary Process," <u>American Political Science Review</u> 60 (1966): 529-547. For a more extended discussion of the definition of incrementalism, see their paper "Yes, Virginia, There Is No Magic Size

To An Increment," Center for the Advanced Study in the Behavioral Sciences, University of California, Berkeley, May, 1975 (Mimeograph). The relatively small share of the federal budget consumed by the Arts Endowment does not undermine my analysis, rather, it helps to explain the political cost benefit analysis for the President. In addition, Davis, et. al., suggest that participants in the budgetary process think in terms of percentages (p. 531).

[45] Leonard Garment became the NEA "aye-sayer" in the White House. Henry Caufield, Professor at Colorado State University defined this characterization for me. The "aye-sayer" role is in contrast to the usual "nay-sayer" role performed by OMB. See Ben W. Heineman, "The Organization and Management of Great Society's Programs," (Washington, DC: The President's Task Force on Government Organization, Executive Office of the President, June 1967, unpublished). The existing Heineman report was the basis for the establishment of the Domestic Policy Council. For an article on the OMB which uses the Heineman report as its basis, see Larry Berman, "The Office of Management and Budget That Almost Wasn't," Political Science Quarterly 92 (1977): 281-303. The memorandum in the following pages are excerpted from Rodney Campbell, "Ten Years for Tomorrow," (National Endowment for the Arts, unpublished manuscript.)

[46] For elaboration of this concept, see Oliver E. Williamson, "A Rational Theory of the Federal Budgetary Process," in Gordon Tullock, ed., Papers on Non-Market Decision Making, Volume II (Charlottesville: Thomas Jefferson Center for Political Economy, University of Virginia, 1967).

[47] The notion of examining the budget process through a disaggregation of data to programmatic shares is from P. R. Natchez and I. C. Bupp, "Policy and Priority in the Budgetary Process," American Political Science Review 67 (1973): 951-63.

[48] National Endowment for the Arts, General Plan, p. 148. See also, Netzer, The Subsidized Muse.

[49] For example, see the following for geopolitical considerations and funding priorities. Goegraphic distribution is of concern to the agency and an arena in which the state arts agencies have eased some of the criticism. Thomas Murphy, Science, Geopolitics, and Federal Spending (Lexington, MA: D. C. Heath, 1971).

[50] Sara P. Garretson and Carol B. Grossman, "The Arts in the United States: Inflation, Recession, and Public Policy," paper prepared for the West Berlin Conference on Culture, Economics and Politics, Germany, 1975.

[51] U. S. Congress, House, 96th Cong., 1st sess., p. 148.

9
State and Local Arts Agencies

Arthur Svenson

Many presidents throughout our history have stressed the necessity of nourishing artistic endeavors, believing that vital benefits would accrue to the social order. In 1788, Washington spoke of the arts as "essential to the prosperity of the state. . . . They have primary claim to the encouragement of every lover of his country and of mankind."[1] John Adams talked of his obligation "to study politics and war" in order to secure for future generations "the right to study painting, poetry, music, architecture . . ."[2] More recently, Dwight Eisenhower, taking note of "the activities which would make our civilization endure and flourish," beckoned the federal government "to give official recognition to the importance of the arts."[3] John Kennedy also recognized the social value of a vital artistic climate; moreover, he stressed the country's responsibility as the "leader of the world" not to be neglectful of, or indifferent to, artistic creativity.[4]

Despite executive exhortations, a significant effort by the federal government to remedy generations of neglect and indifference toward the arts finally occurred in 1965 when Lyndon B. Johnson signed into law a bill which established the National Foundation on the Arts and Humanities.[5] The federal government, for the first time in its history, became a patron of the arts and humanities.[6] At the signing ceremony, President Johnson extolled the legislators of the 89th Congress:

> [This Congress] will consider many programs which will leave an enduring mark on American life. But it may well be that the passage of this legislation, modest as it is, will help secure for this Congress a sure and honored place in the story of the advance of our civilization.[7]

Lest all honor be bestowed on the 89th Congress for this participation "in the advance of our civilization," one should note that similar efforts had already been generated--successfully, too--by other participants: state governments. Although political scientists have often been critical of the states, a number of state innovations in public policy have helped to inspire and guide programs subsequently adopted by the federal government. In this context, state arts agencies and their policy formulations are especially important.

The Utah State Legislature established the first state arts agency (SAA) in 1899. A more programmatic, sustained approach to state patronage of the arts, however, did not materialize until 1960 when, with the encouragement and support of then Governor Nelson Rockefeller, New York state legislators authorized the creation of the New York State Council for the Arts (NYSCA). The fifteen-member Council, operating with an initial appropriation of $50,000, designed and implemented a series of programs intending to assess the state's cultural resources, promote touring programs, support individual artists, and supply technical assistance to certain arts organizations.[8]

One particularly innovative dimension to NYSCA's support of the arts involved its matching-fund mode of operation which required that local arts organizations gather funds from private sources equal to the amount received from a NYSCA grant. The impact of New York's matching requirements was dramatic: not only did other state arts agencies (SAA) follow its lead, but, as Dick Netzer explains, the National Endowment for the Arts (NEA) incorporated the plan "as its standard grant procedure."[9]

By 1965, NYSCA's budget had grown to $562,000 and five additional states--California, Georgia, Minnesota, Missouri, and North Carolina--had established their own SAA. Despite such innovation and growth, however, the catalyst responsible for the emergence of arts agencies in other states was eventually to come from the NEA with its "Federal-State Partnership Program." The program (which began in 1967) made block grants of up to $50,000 available to each state for (1) the stablishment of a state arts agency; and, (2) its continued financial support in order "to furnish adequate programs, facilities, and services in the arts to all people and communities in each of the several States."[10] By 1974, as a result, every state in the Union--plus the District of Columbia, and the territories of American Samoa, Guam, Puerto Rico, and Virgin Islands--had created some form of an arts agency or, as some have been described, "mini-endowments".

In the following section of this chapter, the efforts of SAAs "to advance our civilization" are examined from several perspectives. First, the various justifications and goals of SAAs are reviewed. Second, their structural characteristics and programmatic designs are documented. Third, factors accounting for the relatively recent trend toward decentralized state arts patronage are discussed; in this regard, criticisms of local arts agencies qua arts retailers are also assessed. In a concluding section, the politicization of state arts patronage is examined, as well as its long-range impact upon the vitality of artistic creativity.

STATE ARTS AGENCIES--PRIMARILY IN THE SERVICE OF
AUDIENCE AND ARTIST

Throughout the 1960's and early 1970's, discussions about the state of the arts in this country focused primarily upon two interrelated conditions: the "cultural boom"--a reference to growing, society-wide appreciation of the arts, and the "golden vice"[11] christened by art organizations to describe gross red-ink imbalances between expenditures on art productions and earned income from their subsequent consumption. For a number of state legislatures, particularly those which acted prior to the implementation of the NEA's Federal-State Partnership Program, the emerging needs of audience and artist provided sufficient cause to establish SAAs. Most legislatures, however, required further justification for state arts patronage. Two reasons ultimately proved persuasive: free federal money and urban economic relief.

The cultural boom was a well-documented phenomenon; numerous opinion polls and other survey-research information conveyed the message that public interest in artistic activities--in terms of both appreciation and participation--was on the rise. Comparative attendance records between symphony concerts and professional football events, for instance, revealed that for at least ten urban areas the concert hall attracted more spectators than the gridiron; as for grand opera, La Boheme "blanked" the Oilers and Pagliacci "sidelined" the Jets.[12]

In California, a survey conducted by the National Research Center of the Arts demonstrated that nine of ten residents placed "high value" on the arts and culture and, more significantly, three of four actually engaged in some form of artistic activity.[13] Furthermore, the survey showed that fifty-four percent of Californians were willing to increase their taxes by five dollars to encourage expanded artistic opportunities. This was an unexpected finding since "the survey was conducted during a period of economic uncertainty and recession. . . ."[14]

In terms of the production of art, survey research discovered that as interest in the arts increased so too did the number of art organizations aiming to accommodate higher levels of demand. The decade between 1965 and 1975 signified a period of rapid institutional growth: professional dance companies increased from 10 to 51; professional theatres, from 25 to 101; opera companies, from 23 to 45; major symphony orchestras, from 58 to 105; and touring dance companies, from 27 to 86.[15]

However, in this cultural boom era, problems relating to areal concentrations of artistic activity, as well as growing production costs, were considered severe. In large states like California and New York, centers of cultural acitivity were not easily accessible to significant segments of the public; therefore, opportunities to witness first-rate works of art and live performances of professional groups were limited. To compound this problem, attempts to satisfy rising demand threatened many arts organizations with debilitating financial pressures resulting from the labor-intensive nature of arts production and an inflated economy. At hearings before the House Select Subcommittee on Education in 1973, testimony from a number of experts suggested that "unfortunately . . . in the world of arts, more production to meet increased public demand almost invariably results in greater losses. It is truly paradoxical that the very success of the arts. . . results in their financial downfall."[16] In response to these emerging concerns state legislators from around the country worked diligently and enthusiastically to establish some form of state arts patronage. Some legislators, however, worked even more diligently knowing that federal money was available for such purposes and that urban areas would benefit economically from state arts patronage.

The block grants which the NEA offered to the states in 1967--and every year thereafter in higher increments--were difficult to refuse. Indeed, most block grants by nature seem to employ a rather subtle form of coercion. Political scientist Michael Reagan argues, "It is hard to resist a program that enables one dollar to become two or three, when the same dollar has no 'multiplier' effect of this kind when used for some other area."[17] Such an inducement apparently helped to convince many states to establish SAAs. For some, like Dick Netzer, the federal inducement was so strong that a thorough explanation of the rise of SAAs begins and ends with the NEA. "With a few exceptions, these state arts councils resulted not from an autonomous rise of interest in patronizing the arts on the part of state governments but from the availability of NEA funds for the purpose."[18]

The impact of arts patronage in urban areas offered yet another justification supporting efforts to create SAAs. Many legislators argued that state arts patronage would make at least three positive economic contributions to cities.[19] First, employment opportunities would be broadened. Baltimore's eight leading arts organizations generated nearly 1200 full-time positions--positions unlikely to be eliminated by modern labor-saving technology. Professor Sidney F. Parham explains:

> Although the sizes of symphony orchestras vary, the minimum number required to perform Beethoven's Ninth Symphony is the same as it was in 1828, the year he composed it. Because of technical advance in scenery and lights it takes more poeple to mount the production of <u>Hamlet</u> than it did in 1600. These facts mean that the arts must employ many people who will live and spend money in the community.[20]

Second, urban economies would be invigorated from increased organizational and audience expenditures. Urban areas in New York state alone account for direct expenditures exceeding $400 million annually by resident arts institutions, not to mention the additional millions left by tourists attracted to New York for its cultural opportunities.[21] Third, a healthy artistic environment would help to attract business, corporate, and financial institutions to the city. Corporate headquarters such as the American Express Company remain in New York City in part because the area is "the center of art and commerce and because of the importance of the arts, not only in city life . . . but corporate life as well."[22] (The relationship between culture and the cities is discussed at greater length in Chapter 10.)

Thus, a wide variety of justifications motivated the establishment of SAAs: the cultural boom, the golden vice, the block grant, and the urban economy. Consonant with these justifications, state legislatures articulated broad-based goals for their SAAs, stressing the cultivation of arts appreciation and the nourishment of artistic quality and creativity. State legislatures, however, provided little further guidance in terms of specific policy and program design; those responsibilities were delegated to state arts agencies.

ORGANIZATIONAL STRUCTURES AND PROGRAMMATIC OFFERINGS

Although all states are now officially patrons of the arts, no state legislature shoulders the duties and responsibilities associated with the administration of arts patronage. State arts agencies were created for this purpose, and for good reasons many thought. Politicians should be free from such on-going and consuming tasks, and the arts should be equally free from the entanglements and intrigues of politics. As a member of the New York State Council on the Arts once observed, "We should be enclaves of the arts in government, not enclaves of government in the arts."[23]

To insure sufficient separation between politics and the arts, seventy-seven percent of the fifty-five existing SAAs have acquired positions of decisionmaking independence within state governmental structures—either as autonomous agencies (fifty-two percent) or as autonomous agencies within larger state departments (twenty-five percent). The remaining SAAs function in subordinate roles to larger state departments (five percent), as members of departments which serve purposes other than the arts (nine percent), or as administrative agencies within the executive office of the governor (nine percent).[24]

Within each SAA, primary policymaking responsibilities are assigned to a governing board, usually designated as an arts council or commission. The authority of the board extends in several directions including long-range programs design, the establishment of project categories and associated levels of funding, the formulation of criteria utilized in the distribution of grants, even the resolution of budgetary issues—subject only to the legislature's controlling position as guardian of the purse.

The average number of councilors or commissioners per SAA is fifteen although Louisiana's once had 104, and Oregon's seven. Board members usually serve staggered two- or three-year terms, compensated only by a travel allowance to cover an average of six board meetings in most states, confirmation by the state legislature is a common procedure—and one which is often fraught with controversy. The selection of arts administrators in California provides a revealing illustration of such a controversy.

The California legislature established a state arts agency in 1963 with a fifteen-member Arts Commission serving as its policymaking board. The Governor was empowered to select eleven commissioners, and the State Senate and Assembly the remaining four. Governors Edmund G. "Pat" Brown (1959-66) and Ronald Reagan

(1967-74) utilized their appointment power to elevate
political allies and dilettantes to the Arts Commission.
Expertise in the arts or arts administration did not
substantially affect the recruitment process, and
commissioners and their activities were ridiculed daily
as a result. Governor Reagan's appointees seemed
particularly offensive to many taxpayers, especially
artists, who complained bitterly about a Commission
dominated by "cookie-pushers, ex-beauty queens, and
Hollywood leftovers."[25]

When Governor Reagan left office in 1975, his
successor, Edmund G. Brown, Jr. took immediate action to
remedy the ills which had infected the arts agency.
Under Governor "Jerry" Brown's direction the Arts
Commission was replaced by a nine-member Arts Council,
all members now owing their appointments to the governor
subject to the approval of the state senate. With his
power of appointment, the governor proceeded to
implement a radically new perspective on the composition
of the Council, one which required that working artists
serve as arts councilors. As the Governor explained,
only those who live the life of an artist can understand
and direct the enrichment of California's craft and
beauty. "This is an artist's council--let's have
artists."[26]

Governor Brown's decision to appoint working
artists to the Arts Council quelled the controversy
created by his predecessors; unfortunately for the
Governor--and, say some, for art--his appointment
philosophy embroiled the Council once again in public
controversy. On March 6, 1979, the Governor nominated
Academy Award-winning actress Jane Fonda for the Arts
Council. Despite her artistic qualifications, the
Cailifornia Senate overwhelmingly rejected her appointment citing Fonda's 1972 visit to North Vietnam where
she urged United States pilots "to return home."
Senator Robert Nimmo, a retired Army Colonel, explained
his vote against Brown's nominee in the following
fashion: "By the standards under which I was raised and
served for 29 years, giving aid and comfort to the enemy
is an act of treason. [Miss Fonda] in fact gave aid and
comfort to a country at war with the United States."[27]
Senator Ruben S. Ayala echoed a similar protest: "Anyone who gives aid and comfort to the enemy waives her
[sic] right to serve in an appointive position in state
government."[28] The Governor's rejoinder suggested the
worst; this Council had indeed become an enclave of
government in the arts:

> A number of these Senators were afraid of
> their own election. Some of these big men are
> afraid of Jane Fonda and they felt that her
> art, her voice, her influence if you will, was

> too much for them. . . . We're not going to
> set artistic standards if we become subject to
> log-rolling, cheap political strategies, or
> partisan bickering.[29]

While Governor Brown's philosophy toward the
recruitment of councilors was unusual, working artists
in other states have been appointed to similar types of
administrative positions. In New York, for example,
composer William Schuman (Lincoln Center) and dancer
Alwin Nikolai (New York State Council on the Arts)
assumed administrative and artistic duties simultane-
ously--and successfully.[30] Nationally, however, the
number of artists helping to direct SAAs is small: one
recent survey, conducted for the National Endowment for
the Arts, reports that councils and commissions are
composed largely of persons from fields other than the
arts: business and finance (twenty-two percent), civic
personalities not professionally employed (eighteen
percent), education (sixteen percent), and cultural
administration (fourteen percent).[31]
State arts administrators have designed and
implemented, with considerable creativity, a wide array
of programs aimed at satisfying the needs of artist and
audience. Some SAAs, for example, have engaged artists
to perform and instruct rather atypical audiences.
Poets, musicians, sculptors, and painters have accepted
residency positions in hospitals, prisons, mental-health
facilities, farm-labor camps, and half-way houses in
order to stimulate the creative talent of "institutional
clients" and to enhance otherwise artless institutional
environments. Another innovative and popular program
sends artists and arts organizations (for example, chamber orchestras, dance ensembles, and theatre groups) to
local schools hoping to stimulate an early participatory
interest in, and appreciation for, the various art
forms. SAAs have even sponsored research programs
designed to explore the application of art to the
teaching of traditional academic subjects.
The financial plight of major performing and
visual-arts organizations ranks high among the
priorities of state arts administrators as a
particularly serious problem. Unfortunately, early
attempts by SAAs to aid such organizations actually
exacerbated fiscal pressures. SAA grants were awarded
under conditions requiring the "majors" to undertake
touring and out-reach projects which, while benefiting
hard-to-reach audiences, nevertheless increased
organizational expenditures. Recently, however, in
light of the growing budgetary strength of many SAAs,
financial asssitance for established arts organizations
has reduced their deficits even during a period when
their public-service obligations have expanded.[32]

While the lion's share of SAA expenditures have aimed at sustaining and expanding the productions of major arts organizations, small and developing arts producers, as James Backas reports, have also profited handsomely from state patronage.[33] Many arts producers without national reputations or sizeable budgets manage to share their art with audiences in smaller urban and suburban areas on the strength of "affordable" grants awarded by SAAs. Such grants are wisely distributed explain many councilors and commissioners: they provide quality art, satisfying the needs of more remote audiences, at a minimum cost to the arts agency.

The creativity which SAAs can bring to the program-design dimension of their activities, however, is not without statutory constraints. Not all arts organizations, for example, are eligible for SAA aid. In most states, the distribution of patronage is limited only to non-profit and/or tax-exempt organizations. Several SAAs, in addition, are prohibited from funding an arts organization beyond legislatively-imposed ceilings while still others are mandated by their respective legislatures to support certain organizations or artistic activities. Furthermore, legislatures in over half the states have even prohibited SAA support of individual artists, although patronage can be "rerouted" to individual artists through program categories with more public-regarding designations--for example, "art in public places," "artists in schools," and "artist residencies."

Although primary responsibility over program design rests with the governing boards of each SAA, the actual distribution of grants is a task which is commonly shared with SAA-appointed advisory panels. Panelists, each with expertise in a particular art form, are utilized by a vast majority of SAAs to review and evaluate applications and to recommend awards to the various state arts boards. Grants are usually awarded to artists and arts organizations whose productions satisfy standards of excellence devised by advisory panels and whose impact is judged meritorious by SAA councilors or commissions.

Still, one significant problem associated with SAA grantsmanship stems from feelings of frustration and alienation among otherwise eligible artists and arts organizations who have applied but who have failed to receive state support. The problem becomes particularly vexing in multi-cultural and multi-lingual regions where almost any programmatic decision necessarily excludes some artistic interest from the benefits of state patronage. Moreover, the governing boards of many SAAs are situated in a delicate position: invested with significant policymaking autonomy by the state legislature, arts councilors and commissioners are held accountable for public dissatisfaction with state arts policies and programs. For many SAAs the redelegation of grantmaking authority to local arts agencies (LAAs) has provided significant relief.

THE MOVEMENT TOWARD ADMINISTRATIVE DECENTRALIZATION

Local arts agencies in nineteen states are currently entrusted by SAAs with grant-distribution responsibility. Other SAAs are likely to adopt similar decentralized modes of grantsmanship as the number of LAAs continue to grow (over 2000 now exist) and as the word of their administrative competence spreads. Although several LAAs may have initially been utilized as "retailers" of state patronage in order to defuse the controversy surrounding the grantmanship of some SAAs, experience has proven to the satisfaction of many legislators and arts administrators that artist and audience also benefit from decentralization.

One recent survey of SAA executive directors catalogues a wide variety of factors justifying continued reliance upon LAAs in the grant-distribution process.[34] Many state arts administrators argue that LAAs can discover and assess local artistic talent as well as audience demand more thoroughly than centralized arts agencies; hence, the grantmaking authority of LAAs vis-a-vis SAAs is enhanced on the strength of superior information. State arts administrators also suggest that LAAs can inspire an expanded appreciation of the arts within a community, as local control over artistic and cultural development is made more meaningful through decentralization. Furthermore, decentralization is widely acclaimed as a mechanism to insure a more equitable distribution of state arts patronage; targeting LAAs as grant-distribution centers can counterbalance a pattern of support which concentrates expenditure only in metropolitan areas. Finally, decentralization can release state arts administrators from the time-consuming task of application review and grant distribution so that their energies can be redirected to long-range policy and program design.

The SAAs in Maryland, North Carolina, and New York were the first to institutionlize decentralized grant distribution in the early 1970's. These experiences provided models subsequently adopted in other states. In Maryland, LAAs are required to match every dollar of state money which they receive with three dollars of their own, an unusually rigorous ratio which has nonetheless operated with surprising effectiveness. "It's a very successful program," explains Kenneth Kahn,

Executive Director of the Maryland Arts Council. "[LAAs]
watch over that money very, very carefully. After all,
it's mostly theirs. In Maryland our top priorities for
the eighties are to increase support to the major
institutions and to local arts agencies--our two most
stable institutions."[35] In North Carolina and New York,
distribution of state arts money to LAAs is determined
on a per capita basis; of the two, only North Carolina
requires a dollar-for-dollar match. In New York,
however, the "free" state money has generated local
contributions of equal amounts--evidence, some argue,
which suggests that decentralization has stimulated
substantial community appreciation and promotion of the
arts. Says Juliana Acilla, Director of NYSCA's
Decentralization Program, "The local arts agencies
really know what a seed grant is."[36]

Despite the growing enthusiasm associated with
decentralization, two serious issues have arisen which
threaten its continued utilization. The first involves
the norms between decentralized arts support and the
arts consumers. In a recent study focusing upon the
social composition of the American audience,
sociologists Paul DiMaggio and Michael Useem demonstrate
with persuasive force that "there are no signs that the
democratization of arts funding is bringing a
democratization of arts consumption."[37] The authors
explain that the prediction by Alexis de Tocqueville
last century of unprecedented public appreciation of,
and involvement in, the arts has never materialized--a
prediction dashed against the near monopolization of
artistic consumption by America's socioeconomic elite.
Through a secondary analysis of audience surveys,
DiMaggio and Useem show that better education and
higher-income groups constitute the core of American
arts audiences, not the general public. Not with-
standing the best intentions of policymakers, therefore,
the grantmanship of LAAs does not appear to have
broadened the social composition of the arts
consumers.

The second issue calls attention to the utilization
of decentralization primarily as a tool to advance the
political careers of state legislators, and only
secondarily--if even that much--the needs of artist and
audience. The argument is made that decentralized arts-
support plans channel the resources of SAAs to regions
of a state where no vital artistic community exists, or
at best where only "amateur, even hobbyist artistic
activities can be subsidized."[38] Under such conditions
only the interests of the state legislator are enhanced.
The legislator claims credit from his constituents for
fighting to insure equitable distribution of state arts
support--irrespective of the realities of areal concentrations of artistic activities.

From the perspective of state arts administrators,
however, the justifications supporting decentralization
have not been weakened in light of research on the prevailing social patterns of artistic consumption and the
areal concentrations of artistic production. For both
issues arts administrators would argue that critics of
decentralization should be reminded of the classical
liberal perception of equality as equality of opportunity which is integrated into their policy and administrative decisions. In terms of arts policy, decentralization is not considered a failure because the arts
audience is unrepresentative of lower socioeconomic
groups, any more than the 26th Amendment to the
Constitution should be similarly construed because 18-
year olds vote less frequently than other age groups.
The critical measure of success is the extent to which
equality of opportunity is expanded, not the extent to
which equality of result is achieved. From this
vantage, state arts administrators evaluate the
activities of LAAs approvingly: as administrative arms
of the state, the proximity of LAAs to local culture
better equips them to survey and understand the needs of
the artists and to expand the opportunities for artistic
enrichment of communities.

State arts administrators also explain that the
focus on equality of opportunity, answers critics of
decentralization who argue that LAAs subsidize artists
and audiences where few in reality exist. "Quite true,"
respond state arts administrators, "but the paucity of
opportunities to experience the arts outside major
metropolitan areas is precisely the reality which state
and local arts agencies are endeavoring to correct."
Efforts to correct that reality in 1980 entailed the
distribution of approximately $4.5 million to 719 LAAs.
Arts administrators will also hasten to report that such
expenditures have achieved a measure of success even if
the criterion of "result" is factored into policy
evaluation. As Netzer observes:

> In the last decade hundreds of thousands if
> not millions of Americans have discovered
> through publicly supported programs some form
> of the arts and found it so fascinating that
> continuing experience with that art form--at
> some level--will be part of the rest of their
> lives. The emphasis of the public funding
> agencies on wider availability has made
> ordinary Americans more familiar and comfort-
> able with the arts than their counterparts in
> other large countries seem to be. And this
> development may in time result in significant
> audience expansion. [Emphasis supplied][39]

Thus, despite its detractors, the movement toward administrative decentralization continues to gather support--among legislators and arts administrators. Nevertheless, a development of serious proportions does indeed threaten the capacity of state and local arts agencies to accomplish the goals for which they were designed. This involves the increasing politicization of state arts patronage.

ARTS FOR FUTURE GENERATIONS

Jim Nollman is a composer and musician whose work focuses on themes of conservation and wild-life preservation. Some of Nollman's artistic creations do not conform to conventional conceptualizations of musical form and content. One of his recent compositions, for example, is orchestrated for wolves and turkeys; still another envisions a ballet performance of kangaroo rats in Death Valley, California. Nollman's artistry received official recognition in 1977 when he recieved a $1,000 "special projects" grant from the California Art Council (CAC) to construct and perform underwater musical instruments for the benefit of migrating whales. The grant reflected a serious, on-going effort among CAC members to help insure adequate recognition and support of experimental applications of the arts. Wide-spread appreciation of the Council's efforts in this regard, however, never materialized. After California taxpayers overwhelmingly approved the state's tax-relief initiative, legislators responded with budget cuts in order to compensate local governments for revenue losses of $7 billion. For many legislators, the CAC's patronage of experimental art symbolized waste in public spending. Said one state senator about Council members:

> [My district] would smite you down if they knew you were funding [such] trash . . . because it's not what you and I normal people think is art. This is a way of feeding the underbelly of society . . .[40]

Upshot: the California legislature slashed the 1978-79 arts budget by sixty percent. California's experience with state arts patronage in 1978 demonstrates a problem which disturbs arts administrations in other states. Although formal authority over program design and grant distribution usually resides with SAAs, the contours of state arts policy are often shaped by the policy preferences of state legislatures. In California, legislative preferences were made explicit by dramatic reductions in the Council's spending authority. Since 1978, the threat of similar budgetary cuts has made the state legislature an increasingly less silent partner in the Council's policy and program decisions. Urging other members of the CAC to remain ever aware of the legislature's will, CAC chairman Peter Coyote offered these words of caution: "You can't turn a piano on its side and play it like a guitar."[41]

Analyses of arts patronage in other states point up further example of legislative influence on SAA decisionmaking. In Pennsylvania, for instance, major arts organizations have obtained substantial financial aid directly from the state legislature through line-item appropriations--circumventing program demands accompanying certain grants processed by the Pennsylvania Council on the Arts.[42] A study of the Maryland Arts Council indicates that state arts policy can be adventurous only "if the climate is agreeable and the monies forthcoming."[43] Likewise, an examination of the Arizona Council on the Arts and Humanities shows that Council members seek "avoidance of controversy" in grantmaking in order to enhance their financial base.[44]

Politicization of state arts policy can be particularly frustrating for those artists whose work, in an effort to "add reality to life", does not objectify life.[45] They argue, sadly, that neither private-oriented arts organizations nor SAAs can sustain artistic innovation: the short end of a gamble on the unconventional could spell economic ruin for the private arts organizations, and political repercussions from state patronage of "anti-popular" arts could threaten the availability of already limited funds appropriated to support existing arts programs.

In some states, imaginative new funding methods have been devised and implemented--with the blessings and support of arts administrators--to insulate sources of arts support more effectually from legislative control. The so-called "% of Art" law provides such an effect. Currently on the books in eleven states, this type of law requires that a specified percentage of the cost associated with the construction of a new building must be set aside for the purchase of art work to be integrated into the completed structure. A related procedure for establishing new sources of art support has been to urge the heads of state agencies to earmark a percentage of their departmental appropriations for artistic and cultural expenditures. For example, transportation departments could utilize a percentage of their funds on highway beautification projects, and education departments could institute curriculum changes designed to broaden arts programs in public schools. Yet another method of arts support focuses upon "Resale Royalty" laws. Such an enactment entitles an artist to receive a certain share of the resale price of a work, guaranteeing a potential source of income after the initial sale.

Despite these efforts, however, legislative deference to artistic conventions continues to persist. Perhaps understandably; as Ortega Y Gasset once remarked, "Whenever the new Muses present themselves, the Masses bristle."[46] Unfortunately for the new Muses of our day, legislative depreciation of "dehumanized art" encourages legislative supervision and control of state arts patronage. This weakens the capabilities of SAAs not only to serve the needs of future-oriented artists but to nourish the artistic links with future generations of artists and audiences.

NOTES

[1] "Federal Arts and Humanities Foundations Gain Support," _Congressional Quarterly Weekly Report_, April 30, 1965, p. 837.

[2] Constance Holden, "Arts and Humanities: Culture Agency is Emerging from Infancy," _Science_, December 4, 1970, p. 1060.

[3] U.S. Congress, Senate, Report No. 300, 89th Congress, 1st Session, June 6, 1965, p. 12.

[4] Ibid.

[5] Public Law 89-209, 89th Congress, S. 1483, September 29, 1965.

[6] One should be reminded that in the Works Progress Administration of the 1930's, the federal government functioned as an employer of artists, not as a patron of the arts.

[7] Senate Report No. 300, to accompany S. 1483, Senate, 89th Congress, 1st Session, June 6, 1965.

[8] Dick Netzer, _The Subsidized Muse_ (New York: Cambridge University Press, 1978), p. 80.

[9] Ibid.

[10] U.S. Congress, House, Special Subcommittee on Labor, Committee on Education and Labor, Hearings, _Amendments to the National Foundation on the Arts and Humanities Act of 1965_, 90th Congress, 1st Session, on H.R. 11308, July 18, 26, 1967, p. 81.

[11] Stanley Kauffman, "Can Culture Explode?" _Commentary_ 40 (August 1965): 20.

[12] "The Real Losers in Sports are the Taxpayers--and the Arts," _Los Angeles Times_, January 3, 1978, sec. 2, p. 5.

[13] California Arts Commission, _Californians and the Arts: Highlights from a Survey of Public Attitudes Toward and Participation in the Arts and Culture in California_, January, 1975, p. 8.

[14] Ibid., p. 24.

[15] Paul DiMaggio and Michael Useem, "Cultural Democracy In A Period of Cultural Expansion: The Social Composition of Arts Audiences in the United States," _Social Problems_ 26 (December 1978): 180.

[16] U.S. Congress, House, Senate Subcommittee on Education, Committee on Education and Labor, _National Foundation on the Arts and Humanities Amendments of 1973, Part II_, 93rd Congress, 1st Session, March 14, 15, 16, 1973, p. 172.

[17] Michael D. Reagan, _The New Federalism_ (New York: Oxford University Press, 1972), p. 87.

[18] Netzer, _The Subsidized Muse_, p. 90.

[19] Sidney F. Parham, "States and the Arts: More Than Meets the Eye," _State Legislatures_ 5 (February 1979): 22-25.

[20] Ibid., p. 24.

[21] Ibid.

[22] Ibid.

[23] James Backas, "The State Arts Council Movement," a paper presented at the National Partnership Meeting, June 23-25, 1980, Washington, D.C., p. 47.

[24] National Endowment For the Arts, Study of State Arts Agencies: A Summary Report, 1976, p. 35.

[25] "New Flap Over Nominees to the Arts Commission," Los Angeles Times, September 30, 1974, sec. 4, p. 1.

[26] "Arts Council: Resignations and Rhetoric," Los Angeles Times, January 11, 1978, sec. 4, p. 1.

[27] "Senate Rejects Jane Fonda for Arts Council," Los Angeles Times, July 21, 1979, sec. 1, p.1.

[28] Ibid.

[29] "Brown Calls Rejection of Miss Fonda Gutless Act," Los Angeles Times, July 28, 1979, sec. 1, p. 1.

[30] "California Arts Commission and Its Forward Look," Los Angeles Times, January 13, 1974, sec. 4, p. 1.

[31] National Endowment for the Arts, Summary Report, p.42.

[32] Backas, "Movement," p. 21.

[33] Ibid., pp. 23-26.

[34] Ibid., pp. 52-53.

[35] Originally quoted in Backas, "Movement," p. 50.

[36] Ibid., p. 51.

[37] DiMaggio and Useem, "Cultural Democracy," p. 195.

[38] Netzer, The Subsidized Muse, p. 85.

[39] Ibid., p. 162.

[40] "Arts Council Under Fire in State Senate," Los Angeles Times, August 26, 1978, sec. 4, p. 1.

[41] "California Arts Council Holds Public Forum," Los Angeles Times, July 11, 1979, sec. 4, p. 3.

[42] Edward Arian, "The Problems of a State Arts Council in Achieving Equity in the Distribution of State Arts Funds: A Case Study of Pennsylvania," paper presented at the Annual Meeting of the American Political Science Association, September 1, 1978, New York City, p. 4.

[43] C. Richard Swaim, "Balance in Public Policy: The Maryland Arts Council," paper presented at the Annual Meeting of the American Political Science Association, September 1, 1978, New York City, p. 10.

[44] Lawrence D. Mankin, "Rites of Passage: The First Twelve Years of the Arizona Commission on the Arts and Humanities," a paper presented at the Annual Meeting of the American Political Science Association, September 1, 1978, New York City, p. 16.

[45] Jose Ortega Y Gasset, The Dehumanization of Art (Princeton: Princeton University Press, 1972), p. 31.

[46] Ibid., p. 7.

10
Culture and the Cities

Kevin V. Mulcahy

Culture is a decidedly urban phenomenon. The arts seem to require the rarefied atmosphere of cities to grow and flourish. Not all cities are cultural centers. Yet city life seems to be a necessary if not sufficient condition. Of course culture is produced outside of an urban setting. But this is that peculiar variant known as folk arts. The products of high culture--operas, orchestral and chamber music, dance and ballet, theater, painting and sculpture--are all largely urban. So too are the various retainers of the cultural world: critics, managers, fund raisers, patrons, arts lobbyists, editors, intellectuals. Above all else, cities provide an audience aware of the arts and sensitive to cultural innovation.

In making these assertions, I do not wish to provoke another episode in the ancient hostilities between country and city. American populists have long railed against the parasitical nature of the cities exploiting the food-producing hinterland. They have extolled the superior virtue of rural life, the more so as those values came under attack by the processes of industrialization, urbanization, modernization. Nor has this suspicion of the city been limited to the American experience. Literary critic Raymond Williams expresses some of the traditional ambivalence toward London as the predominant center of British social and economic life.

> For just because the city ordinarily concentrates the real social and economic processes of the whole society, so a point can be reached where its order and magnificence but also its fraud and its luxury seem almost, as in Rome, to feed on themselves; to belong in the city, and to breed there, as if on their own. Thus parasites collect around the real services, as in the legal and social underworlds of seventeenth-century London.

> Around the engrossing lawyers collect the
> confidence-men and the professional sharpers.
> Around the profit-making merchants collect the
> hucksters, the puffers, the overtly
> fraudulent. Around the political authority
> collect the informers, the go-between men, the
> fixers and (in the court as often as anywhere)
> the prostitutes; some from, some on their way
> to, what was called an aristocracy.[1]

Of course city and country stand in a reciprocal
socioeconomic relationship. The one produces food and
raw materials in exchange for the other's specialized
services such as law, finance, communications, and
government. So too with culture. The purpose of this
discussion is to examine the relationship between
culture and the city. This will involve looking at four
topics: (1) the contributions that the arts make to the
economic condition of cities; (2) the role that culture
plays in defining the peculiar character of urban life;
(3) the varieties of urban cultures; (4) some
recommendations for support by municipal governments of
local cultural resources. Culture will be discussed
with reference to cities in general, although examples
from particular cities will be used as often as
possible.

CULTURE AND THE URBAN ECONOMY

Because manufacturing has declined significantly as
an economic activity of the city, the importance of the
service sector has risen dramatically. Among services,
culture has a unique importance for cities: it employs
people who have valuable skills and who like urban life.
The manufacturing activities that led to the original
growth of metropolitan complexes have left for surrounding areas having the available space for large-
scale horizontal assemblage. But cities have always
provided a unique array of specialized services not
available outside the urban core: banking, insurance,
advertising, publishing; highly technical medical,
intellectual, legal, and accounting services. Cities
are also centers of fashion and cuisine where people
come to shop in exotic stores and dine in ethnic
restaurants; to buy art, visit galleries and museums; to
attend concerts, go to plays, operas, the dance.
The economic contributions that the arts make to
the urban economy have been much commented on, if not
always systematically analyzed. Some examples may
suffice to indicate the magnitude of their importance.[2]

New York's 1977-78 theater season realized gross revenues estimated at $104 million; service related expenditures (e.g., restaurants, transportation) $217 million; and indirect expenditures of $347 million. Coupled with related direct expenditures for national touring companies of Broadway productions, this had a total economic impact of $945 million.

A Philadelphia study showed that attracting an additional 100 out-of-town visitors a day to the city's cultural organizations generated $1.2 million in increased retail sales jobs and approximately 111 new industry-related jobs.

Chicago's arts and cultural activities had an annual economic impact on the city totalling $70 million. Direct expenditures associated with arts and cultural organizations totalled $156 million in 1976 including $80 million spent by audiences attending events.

Expenditures among Washington, D.C.'s non-profit arts organizations were estimated in excess of $25 million annually. Economic impact of these direct expenditures exceeds $50 million. More than 3.5 million people attended performances and exhibitions by these organizations in 1975.

An evaluation of the impact of the four-week New York City theater strike in 1975 estimated revenue losses to cab drivers of $468,000, to parking lot operators of $50,000, and to restaurants of nearly a quarter million dollars.

A 1975 survey of Philadelphia's seventy-nine major arts, sciences and humanities showed that in one year these organizations:
    --paid over 3,600 full-time employees
    --spent over $64 million, not including capital improvements
    -- stimulated approximately $64 million in direct spending (The performing arts audiences alone spent $3.8 million on ancillary services such as taxis and restaurants).

A 1977 study of the eight major performing and visual arts institutions in Baltimore found that these organizations:
    -- generated about 1,175 full-time jobs
    -- created $29.6 million of direct and indirect business volume

-- accounted for about $5.7 million of business
real property, equipment, and inventories
-- produced about $3 million of additional
local bank credit
-- induced $1.9 million in local spending (in
addition to admission fees) by out-of-town
visitors.

In Chicago, out-of-town visitors to its seven
museums contributed $76.5 million to the economy,
and in New York City nonresidents passing through a
single museum were responsible for approximately
$187 million in expenditures annually. (These
figures represent direct outlays, and a multiplier
of two is usually used to calculate the indirect
economic benefits as the money changes hands
several times before entering savings or tax
accounts.)

The arts in New York City generated more than $3
billion in expenditures in 1974 and more than $102
million in local taxes. The nonprofit arts
organizations, which pay no taxes, spend $193
million yearly. At least one-quarter of tourist
visits to the city have cultural pursuits in mind,
whether for the theater, Lincoln Center, museums,
art galleries and other such attractions. This
segment of tourism accounts for $400 million in
yearly spending and for more than $16 million in
local taxes.

These data should suggest the benefits to at least
some sectors of the urban economy from cultural
spending. Some researchers have questioned whether "the
whole economy, the municipal government, and the local
public also benefit from this sectoral economic
impact."[3] These are, of course, very difficult
questions to answer conclusively. However, there are
strong reasons to believe that these cautionary
observations are not sufficient to question the
contributions that the arts make to the urban economy.
First, performing arts organizations and museums
are "important to a city's image, enchancing its
attractiveness to residents, vistors, and business
firms."[4] Second, city residents overwhelmingly perceive
cultural institutions as a defining characteristic of
urban life and as a major reason for living in a city
center. Third, industries not always considered
related to the cultural world, such as publishing,
advertising, broadcasting, and fashion draw on artistic
talent or supply artistic material. In New York City,
Broadway's profitmaking theatrical productions and the
commercial art galleries have an obviously close

relationship to the nonprofit theater, musical, and dance companies and museums.[5] Martin E. Segal, when chairman of New York City's Commission for Cultural Affairs, predicted that "New York's art and cultural life--unequaled in the world--will be the major glue of the city's economic life."[6]

Despite these arguments for the contributions of culture to the urban economy, we should beware of reductionism and narrowing of scope. The arguments stressing that the "arts are in the business of business" are indeed correct, but more important as part of a strategy to gain political support for government subsidies. What needs greater emphasis is that the arts provide benefits all out of proportion to the subsidies involved and, like programs for parks, libraries and schools, they merit government support "even if they are not such great shakes at promoting business." Joan Davidson, chairman of the New York State Council on the Arts, thus argued that support for the arts had to move beyond a "meat and potatoes" argument to support for culture as a good in itself. Moreover, a "creative public policy for the arts" should encourage new art forms as well as "recondite pursuits such as performances in out-of-the-way places and hand bookbinding" and "the protection of elegant old working theaters from destruction by new hotels" even though such programs "are not likely to be of much use in filling city coffers."[7]

CULTURE AND URBAN LIFE

In his history of the United States during the period 1877-1890, John Garraty argued that the allure of urban life for rural Americans was not just for economic or professional reasons. "Equally compelling were the harshness and intellectual sterility of rural life and the corresponding attractiveness of the cities." These rural immigrants were attracted by the superior educational facilities of urban communities and their theatre, music and art, as well as by the excitement and stimulation offered by city life with its "fleshpots and titillating vices."[8] A study by the Massachusetts Commissioner of Labor Statistics in 1879 documented the "superior social life of the cities" and suggested that the drift of population to the cities could be attributed to the "defective social element of our country life." According to one rural educator: "The lack of pleasant, public entertainments in this town has much to do with our young people feeling discontented with country life."[9] It was not just seeing Paris that

made it difficult to keep the boys down on the farm;
seeing Boston had much the same result.

The urban rose has lost some of its bloom in recent
years and cities have been critized for a lack of
community, the displacement of personal values and the
depersonalization of life. Many of these criticisms are
quite understandable reactions to the sweeping
structural changes brought about by urbanization and
industrialization. But much anti-city rhetoric depends
on a nostalgic romanticization of the small town (Our
Town) and ignore what Marx labeled (if unfairly) "the
idiocy of rural life." Yet, even if we accept much of
what urban critics assert, the importance of culture as
an urban amenity is further enhanced. "People are
compensating for the dehumanizing consequences of a
highly technological civilization and its concomitant
alienation by having increasing recourse to cultural
activities."[10]

Whatever the disadvantages of urban life, cities
are certainly home to artists. Eighty-eight percent of
Americans who consider themselves artists live in urban
areas (compared to seventy-four percent of the total
population). "It seems that the social and economic
characteristics of cities tend to encourage support for
artistic professions."[11] Cities are also home to a
sizeable "arts bureaucracy." This consists, firstly, of
the various employees of cultural institutions: not
only the performing artists but the directors, managers,
personnel officers, accountants, union business agents,
and members of the governing boards of symphonies,
operas, ballets, theaters, and art museums. Then there
are the secondary cultural institutions which are
concerned with artistic education and criticism: the
schools, colleges, conservatories, libraries, teachers
of voice, dance, acting, music, the visual arts and, of
course, the critics. Lastly, there is the cultural
clientele: the consumers of what is written, painted,
sculpted, composed, or otherwise artistically
conceived.[12] "These consumers are made up of various
types of audiences from the symphony-goer to the patron
of the art museum to the viewer of the experimental film
in the city library."[13] What these audience members
have in common is a commitment to culture and while
those so committed can be found everywhere, they are
more likely to be found either in specialized
communities (such as college towns and artist colonies)
or in cities.

Culture has also become recognized as an important
dimension in popular perceptions of the "quality of
life." The National Research Center for the Arts
reported that ninety-three percent of the population
judged arts facilities such as theaters, museums and
concert halls to be personally important for their

lives. People also saw cultural facilities as important community facilities and ones that made their communities more attractive as places in which to live and work. Tables 10.1 and 10.2 detail these findings.

The data in Table 10.2 are particularly suggestive of the importance that cultural amenities have for establishing a city's desirability for business and individuals alike. A 1977 Fortune survey reported that company executives' personal preferences and employees' style of living are the most important considerations for determining the location of corporate headquarters. Cities are particularly attractive to firms that have highly-educated, well-paid, skilled and mobile personnel. A Rand Corporation/Kettering Foundation study, published in 1977, concluded that a primary determinant of economic development was residential attractiveness, especially in the areas of education and the arts.[14] The executive secretary of the Seattle Arts Commission has observed that ". . . a culturally healthy city has a better chance of being an economically healthy city; people want to live in a city with a vital cultural life." Indeed, cities like Seattle, San Francisco, Minneapolis, Louisville, Baltimore, and Atlanta have earned national reputations as eminently "liveable" for having active downtowns and stable neighborhoods while "they have experienced an outpouring of cultural activity."[15]

THE CITY AS A CULTURAL ASSET

Although the economic vitality of urban centers has declined in recent decades, their cultural vitality has remained strong. Consequently, culture plays a proportionately greater part in defining the raison d'etre of a city than has been the case in the past. But, the "urbanity" of a city is related to culture in a broader sense than the activities of the performing and visual arts. The urban scene, at its best, provides accessible office-building plazas, varied commercial streets, inviting public parks that offer opportunities (literally spaces) for social interchange. If these sites are aesthetically distinguished, as well as physically attractive, they serve as both cultural symbols and economic resources.

Rockefeller Center and Madison Avenue in New York City, the Mall and the National Gallery of Art's East Wing in Washington, D.C., Embarcadero Plaza and Golden Gate Park in San Francisco, Westwood Village and Venice Beach in Los Angeles, Bourbon Street and the French Market Place in New Orleans are different examples of

TABLE 10.1:
Personal Importance of Cultural Facilities

How important is it to you that your community or neighborhood should have:	Very	Somewhat	Not very	Not at all	Not Sure
a theater	39%	33%	16%	10%	2%
a concert hall	38	32	18	11	1
an art museum	40	33	16	10	1

Source: National Research Center for the Arts, Arts and the People (New York: American Council for the Arts, 1973), p. 4.

TABLE 10.2:
General Importance of Cultural Facilities

Whether or not you are personally interested, how important do you think such facilities are to:	Very	Somewhat	Not Very	Not At All	Not Sure
the quality of life in the neighborhood or community	50%	35%	9%	5%	1%
the business and economy of the neighborhood or community	38	36	12	8	6
attracting residents who will improve the neighborhood or community	43	28	14	11	4

Source: Arts and the People, p.4.

timulating urban spaces. They are backdrops against
which a wide variety of cultural activities (broadly
defined) take place.[16] "The lacing of art into the
fabric of the daily environment is probably the most
underdeveloped area of the arts."[17] Encountering art in
the daily working environment can be an important form
of education. Art in public places can not only create
a special environment but change the attitudes of the
people who come into contact with it. In evaluating a
controversial Calder stabile installed by the city of
Grand Rapids, Michigan, the local newspaper observed
that it had "painlessly increased people's interest [in
art] without making them self-conscious of having
'culture.'"[18]

Yet another cultural feature of most cities is the
fact that they are old--at least compared to the typical
suburb. And, many older inner-city districts are
strikingly different in architecture and conception when
compared to contemporary suburbs and suburban-style
cities. Downtown Los Angeles, for example, had become a
geographic expression for where the major freeways
intersected. As business and commercial development
moved to newer centers out along the freeway system, the
original "center city" decayed. The construction of a
new music center in this downtown area signaled its
renascence. There are new major office complexes and
hotels (although some of the structures are criticized
for being hermetically-sealed islands, built without
relation to the surrounding area). More important, the
downtown and its major commercial thoroughfare
(Broadway) is being rediscovered, refrequented, and
reappreciated for some of its diverse ethnic
neighborhoods and cultural mixes: Chinatown, Little
Tokyo, Korea Town. Broadway itself has become a focal
point for the Mexican community: not just a place to
shop but a cultural and social experience. This "old
L.A.," that is, the area built before World War II, has
also become appreciated as a cultural phenomenon in
itself. A study by the School of Architecture and Urban
Planning at UCLA made the following observation
concerning the cultural assets represented by the older
inner-city.

> One of the most advantageous features of older
> downtown environments such as Broadway is the
> fact that they are old! Behind the dirt and
> deterioration of many of these buildings (and
> in some instance, whole blocks) is the charm,
> grace and human scale that seem to have been
> forgotten in much of our new developments.
> The character and attention to detail of many
> of these old buildings cannot be duplicated
> elsewhere, especially in newly developing

suburbs. It is an amenity unique to the downtown environment. . . .[19]

Historic preservation associations and other arts groups have often been in the vanguard of reawakening many cities to the value of their older neighborhoods. The sparks of local pride and civic self-awareness that were kindled have also sparked valuable reinvestment. The arts council of Galveston, Texas, formed a coalition of local businesses and neighborhood groups to develop the Strand, a nineteenth-century warehouse district. An initial investment of $200,000 led to $3.5 million invested in housing, shopping and services to transform the Strand into a prosperous shopping, residential, and tourist center.[20] Examples such as this could be multiplied throughout the cities of the United States: the Pioneer Square district of Seattle, the Boston waterfront, the Lincoln Center area of New York City, Capitol Hill in Washington, the Fan District in Richmond, the French Quarter in New Orleans. These are but a few examples of successful local efforts at neighborhood revitalization to which the cultural community has made a significant contribution.

Some of this "cultural development" of urban neighborhoods has been resented by local residents, sometimes including artists themselves. As Greenwich Village, long an American synomonym for bohemianism and the avant-garde, became the victim (or lucky beneficiary) of enbourgoisement in the 1950's, the need for a new art neighborhood became clear. This led to a southward migration of artists: south of Houston Street, north of Canal Street--what became known as SoHo. Artists, illegally at first, came to occupy the large loft spaces in nineteenth-century, cast-iron buildings that had previously been occupied by light-manufacturing facilities. The attraction was a lot of space for a little money--and the location was in close proximity to the traditional Village arts neighborhood. Some galleries opened; bars and restaurants followed. At first, these catered to artists, soon to the more general cultural world, eventually to the public at large. With SoHo's emergence as New York City's premier art zone, the residential lofts became legalized and the neighborhood, with its wonderful architecture of the period 1800 to 1890, became designated a national landmark. By the 1970's, SoHo had also become the object of intense real estate speculation that saw many of the early artist-renovators priced out of their lofts. "SoHo lofts where you might expect to find artists are often occupied by would-be-hip young professionals who want to be near all the perking excitement."[21] SoHo is for many a tourist attraction providing entertainment for a "culturally-aspiring" segment of the population. "Tourists and media-hype have so distressed some SoHo artists that the only bearable solution was to move away."[22] Adjacent, as yet unchic, artist neighborhoods fear being "SoHoized"--that is, being transformed into an aesthetic themepark, a cultural Disneyland.

The commercialization of cultural envirionments is not a phenomenon limited to SoHo: the histories of Greenwich Village, North Beach in San Francisco, Venice Beach in Los Angeles suggest a wider pattern. After artists discover a neighborhood, it becomes discovered by artistic fellow-travellers and, eventually, by tourists. Cultural redevelopment leads to commercial exploitation. The artists move out and the affluent hip move in. Cultural production gives way to leisured consumption. But such a process is not inevitable and need not be taken to extremes; and, cities are often bettered in the process. Old neighborhoods are revitalized and the artists move on to discover new areas--from Venice to downtown L.A.; from North Beach to South of Market; as from SoHo to TriBeCa and NoHo. These artists serve as urban pioneers making over decayed, or obsolete, sections of cities. "By making SoHo the site of a lot of elaborately deployed energy-- aesthetic, eonomic, social--the art world has rescued the area from a slow slide into oblivion."[23]

Such urban revitalization is less celebrated by artists inconvenienced by their very success. It is even less the cause for celebration among the neighborhood residents displaced--and dispersed--to make room for the more successful. Both the Music Center in Los Angeles and Lincoln Center in New York required whole neighborhoods to be razed for their construction and the residents relocated. Such residential shifts are perhaps an inevitable part of a city's ongoing transformation, and the cultural complexes built are part of large-scale area redevelopment--for downtown L.A. and New York's Upper West Side. However, the interests served by these cultural institutions are widely perceived as being white and middle class while the residents displaced were decidedly minority and poor. Not surprisingly, the association of cultural institutions with redevelopment projects could be seen as "cultural imperialism" by those who do not immediately share in their benefits.

When Courtney Callender was deputy commissioner of the New York City Department of Cultural Affairs, he observed that prior to the late 1960's, the boards of trustees of that city's cultural institutions were almost exclusively white and affluent. "Of blacks, Hispanics, and . . . Euro-ethnics, there were virtually none, and certainly none who were looked on as spokesmen for their own non-establishment constituencies."

Moreover, virtually all of the major cultural institutions are located in mid-Manhattan to the exclusion of the so-called "outer boroughs." From a cultural standpoint, "the city" meant Manhattan (as far north as Ninety-Sixth Street and an enclave in Morningside Heights around Columbia University), while the outer boroughs of Brooklyn, Queens, Staten Island, and the Bronx, which contain the vast majority of New York City's population, were the cultural hinterlands. "The fact that your neighborhood, whether it was Bensonhurst or Morrisania or Kew Gardens or Tottenville did not boast even miniature versions of 'the city's' resources also went unquestioned."[24]

In a tone similiar to Mr. Callender's, Junius Eddy, then of the Ford Foundation, attacked what he called the "cultural enrichment" programs that have been offered by city governments as part of well-intentioned efforts at improving opportunities for ghetto youth. He describes such efforts as:

> . . . a kind of loosely organized exposure of poor youngsters (mainly nonwhite) to enriching experiences from the Western middle-class cultural tradition intended to compensate for presumed deprivation in their own lives and backgrounds. One does not have to deny the true richness of the Western cultural tradition to point out the presumptiousness, arrogance, and racism inherent in this simplistic approach to the culturally different person in our pluralistic society.[25]

What Mr. Eddy suggests is that, instead of exporting culture to the ghetto, municipal arts agencies should support arts groups indigenous to the ghetto neighborhood. Arts programs run by local artists and sensitive to community values can celebrate the "richness of cultural life and tradition in the ethnic subcultures of American society."[26]

Indeed, an emphasis on cultural pluralism has been part of neighborhood arts programs in such cities as San Francisco, New York, Cleveland, St. Louis, and Milwaukee. For neighborhood residents cultural programs are an added contribution to the quality of their personal lives and can assist in creating a sense of group identity. Culture can thus enhance the pride of minority urbanites and help to solidify ethnic neighborhoods within cities that are largely of a different cultural tradition.

> As the blacks, the Puerto Ricans, and the Mexican-Americans, particularly, began to seek

out the roots of an ethnic or racial heritage
which the dominant society had systematically
ignored or denigrated, the nature of the
community based arts movement began to change.
The arts became an obvious and powerful
vehicle in this cultural renaissance, a
vehicle through which minority-group artist-
leaders could begin to voice the social and
economic concerns of their communities, to
assert a new-found historical identity, and to
reflect the new sense of ethnic pride and
awareness they believe is essential to their
survival in white America.[27]

The important contribution that community arts
organizations can make in fostering neighborhood
cohesion and social development among minority residents
needs greater recognition by city governments. Los
Angeles, for example, does not have an established
neighborhood arts program. "There is no official body
to assist with funding and proposal development,
coordinate programs, provide technical and research
support, and help clear away the typical bureaucratic
obstacles to local programming."[28] San Francisco, on
the other hand, created a successful and innovative
Neighborhood Arts Program in 1967 as a service agency of
the city's Art Commission. This program provides
technical and production assistance to community arts
organizations for use in neighborhood cultural
projects.
Community arts agencies should be an integral part
of a Department of Cultural Affairs in every city. In
addition to the services described above, such an agency
should act as a clearinghouse for all proposed community
arts programs (like neighborhood arts festivals) and
help find local public facilities for such programs--for
example, parks, daycare facilities, post offices,
housing projects.[29] Moreover, a community arts agency
can work with business groups to provide funding and
sites for cultural programs. The Urban Innovations
Group of UCLA suggests the following benefits of
programming in such nontraditional locations.

By including opportunities for artistic events
in the planning and construction of business
and commercial centers and of major public
buildings and parks throughout the country,
music, drama, dance and art can be brought
directly into the work and recreational
settings where many Americans spend the
greater part of their lives.[30]

Through public programs like these cities can help to make the arts an integral part of the lives all of their citizens. The use of neighborhood sites can also increase the accessibility of the arts--especially to the poor and minorities who are unfamiliar with "elite" cultural institutions. Yet, support for neighborhood arts programs does not have to be at the expense of established arts organizations. Community facilities and programs should supplement and complement the offerings of the traditional arts. "A balanced and planned program for the decentralization of arts facilities could meet the needs of both urban and suburban populations by making a diversity of cultural modes readily and freely accessible."[31] Lastly, neighborhood arts programs represent a commitment to cultural democracy: a society in which a diversity of cultural expressions are encouraged and supported. "A cultural democracy provides for the acceptance of one's historical, ethnic and racial identity just as a political democracy respects the individual's legal and economic rights."[32]

THE VARIETIES OF URBAN CULTURE

While culture is inextricably intertwined with urban life, not every city is culturally equal or equivalent. Certain cities have established national reputations for unique cultural offerings. A few examples should suffice: Pheonix's Hurd Museum with its collection of Southwestern Indian art, Santa Fe's summer opera and chamber music festival, Cleveland's symphony orchestra, Providence's Trinity Square Repertory Theatre. Certain other cities have established reputations as regional arts centers with a wide variety of first-class cultural organizations. A few that could be mentioned are: Houston with its symphony and opera; Salt Lake City with the Utah Symphony, Ballet West, and Mormon Tabernacle Choir; Minneapolis with its art museum, symphony, and Guthrie Theatre; Seattle with an opera season that is ninety-eight percent subscribed, the highest per capita concert attendance in the country, and its internationally recognized Wagner Festival. A few other cities can claim to be cultural capitals: Chicago with its Institute of Fine Arts, Lyric Opera, and symphony (arguably the nation's best); Boston with its symphony, art museums, and university arts programs; Philadelphia with its orchestra, art museum and the Curtis Institute (arguably the nation's premier conservatory); San Francisco with its symphony, art museums (especially the Asian collection at the De Young), and opera.

These listings are not meant to be inclusive-- either of the cultural amenities in the cities mentioned or of all the American cities that are serious about culture. It is only meant to suggest the degree of cultural diversity and diversification in the country and that it is possible to classify American cities according to the extent of their cultural development and influence. Three types of cities would be those of local, regional, and national importance.

New Orleans is a good example of a city of local cultural importance. It is an original among American cities with its Latin character, unique architecture, distinctive cuisine. The French Quarter is a celebrated entertainment district known especially for jazz clubs; Mardi Gras is a festival of revelries the likes of which are simply unknown elsewhere in the country. All of these attractions have made New Orleans a popular center for tourists and conventions. On the other hand, the cultural scene in New Orleans has only a local significance. Of the city's dozen or so full-time arts organizations; only the Opera and Symphony have real significance.[33] The others, even the well-known Le Petit and innovative Gallery Circle theaters, are either small in scale or cater to a highly specialized audience. Where the city was once an important operatic capital, the New Orleans opera now presents five productions, performed twice each month from October through May--excluding the Mardi Gras months of January and February. The opera orchestra comes from the New Orleans Symphony; all of the lead singers are imported, the chorus is semi-professional, most costumes and sets are rented. The Opera sells about ninety-five percent of its seats; seventy percent through season subscriptions. While the audience has a reputation for being knowledgeable and enthusiastic, the Opera is a purely local organization offering a few works from the standard repertory. If financially stable, it has only a limited artistic scope and a narrow base of support.

The New Orleans Symphony, by contrast, is the largest cultural organization in Louisiana with an active auxiliary. But this auxiliary membership is largely confined to the local social elite, and the orchestra runs a large and persistent deficit. Plans have been made for the Symphony to increase the scope of its activities: touring in a wider area, performing more, cultivating a larger audience. The idea is that the New Orleans Symphony should become a regional organization drawing on the audience, talent, and funds of a larger area than it now encompasses. The catch is that any expansion would require substantial additional funding and the money is simply not forthcoming. But

even aside from the money, the cultural scene in New
Orleans is not characterized by a strong commitment to
artistic excellence. One local resident (and supporter
of the arts) put it this way:

> Safety first seems to be the rule of thumb,
> and innovate programming is in short supply.
> The fault, if there is one, lies with both the
> audience and the arts organizations. New
> Orleans audiences are most easily pleased by
> the familiar, the recognizable, the upbeat
> form of entertainment, and shun intellectual
> complexities and unharmonious modulations.
> The arts groups recognize this and pander to
> it, understandably if they want an audience,
> but regretably for Bartok and Pinter.
> Conservatism in the arts is to be expected,
> even anticipated, in a city where more people
> attend a single football game than go to every
> single cultural event over a year.

Los Angeles, unlike New Orleans, has a distinctly
regional rather than merely local influence. It
dominates the Southern California region whose
population of over twelve million people makes it second
in size to the New York metropolitan area. The new
Music Center not only spurred a dramatic urban
revitalization drive but also became a visible symbol of
the city's commitment to the arts. The stereotype of
Los Angeles as a "cultural wasteland," as popular among
some Northern Californians as among some Easterners, is
simply not borne out by the facts.

The Los Angeles area has been home to a number of
serious artists such as Arnold Schoenberg and Igor
Stravinsky, Christopher Isherwood and Aldous Huxley, as
well as a better-known legion who came to work in
Hollywood. The Los Angeles Philharmonic under its past
two music directors, Zubin Mehta and Carlo Maria
Guilini, and through the patronage of Mrs. Dorothy
Chandler, is ranked among the top six orchestras in the
United States. The "California School," associated with
the names of David Hockney, Richard Dieberkorn, Edward
Ruscha has become a major influence on the visual arts;
of equal importance is the architecture of Rudolph
Schindler, Greene and Greene, Charles Eames, Richard
Neustra. Commercial galleries have grown up on
LaCienega, Santa Monica, and Melrose Boulevards while
Venice Beach has emerged as a full-fledged artist
colony. Local art museums are important cultural
institutions: the Norton Simon in Pasadena for its
permanent collection, the L.A. County for its special
exhibitions, and the newly established Getty Museum for
its as yet untapped riches available for acquisitions.

Repertory theater is strongly represented at the Mark
Taper Forum, the Ahmanson, and John Anson Ford. Local
educational institutions, especially U.C.L.A.,
Ambassador College, Cal State Northridge, and El Camino
College, sponsor ambitious artists series. Smaller
communities within the Los Angeles Basin, such as
Pasadena, Glendale, Long Beach, have symphonic
orchestras and other cultural institutions.
    The Urban Innovations Group at U.C.L.A.'s School of
Architecture and Urban Planning summarized the following
strengths and weaknesses of the Los Angeles Cultural
scene.[34]

Strong Points

- a symphony of national and international
  importance
- a strong repertory theater
- many small, experimental theaters
- three major arts museums
- many painters and sculptors of national
  reputation
- a strong crafts tradition
- an ethnic murals movement

Weak Points

- lack of coordination among arts groups
- weakly supported neighborhood arts groups
- no full-scale, resident opera company
- no full-scale, resident dance company
- no tradition of cultural activities in
  public places
- no tradition of art in and around buildings
- no tradition of preservation and
  restoration

    In many ways, the Los Angeles cultural situation is
comparable to that of other regional centers--some arts
organizations of the first rank and some glaring
deficiencies. However, there is one aspect of Los
Angeles that distinguishes it from all other cities and
strongly influences its cultural development--that is
Hollywood. More a functional than a geographic
description, Hollywood is a denotation not only for the
movie industry but also the entertainment business
generally including television and records. Hollywood
has been a mixed benefit for culture in Los Angeles. On
the one hand, it has given the city a visibility to
creative artists of all kinds, and the entertainment
business has created some large fortunes that have
patronized the arts. On the other hand, Hollywood is a
commercial enterprise and the economics of the market

and the uninspiring values peculiar to mass entertainment have overshadowed efforts at serious culture. The two best film schools in the country (USC and UCLA) are in Los Angeles, as well as the only professional conservatory of film (American Film Institute). But there is little creative outlet for young film makers (except perhaps in commercials). Hollywood itself lacks a tradition of the film as an experimental and avant-garde art form. Los Angeles must outgrow Hollywood if it is to become a national cultural center.

New York City is not only a place of national cultural importance but one of international stature as well. For better or worse, New York serves as a standard-setter and showcase for the nation's cultural life. There is some resentment against New York being accorded such a premier position, not a little of it due to the parochialism of some New York City residents who are seemingly unaware of the richness of cultural activities beyond the Hudson River. There is certainly a great deal of distinguished cultural activity in cities other than New York. There are several orchestras across the country that are superior to the New York Philharmonic (those in Boston, Chicago, and Philadelphia); important conservatories exist besides the Julliard (the Curtis Institute in Philadelphia is one); full-scale opera exists besides the Metropolitan (at least in Chicago and San Francisco); the Museum of Modern Art and the Metropolitan Museum are not the country's only major picture collections (those at the Chicago Art Institute, the National Gallery in Washington and the Philadelphia Museum are also first-rate).

But as music critic Samuel Lipman has noted: "the brightest and the best of musical talents are drawn to New York for major periods in their lives as students and performers, and nothing has happened in recent years to affect New York's central role in the dissemenation of information and publicity about cultural matters."[35] Indeed, it is as the headquarters of the arts management business and as the grantor of an imprimatur of cultural approval that signifies much of New York's symbolic importance. But most important is the sheer magnitude of cultural organizations that are located in New York. Of the 1,500 such professional organizations, it should suffice to list twenty to give some indication of their diversity and importance.

> American Ballet Theater, American Museum of Natural History, Carnegie Hall, Chamber Music Society of Lincoln Center, Dance Theater of Harlem, Eliot Feld Ballet, Frick Museum, Joffrey Ballet, Martha Graham Center for Contemporary Dance, Metropolitan Museum of

Art, Metropolitan Opera, Museum of Modern Art,
New York City Ballet, New York City Opera, New
York Philharmonic, New York Public Library,
Paul Taylor Dance Foundation, Morgan Library,
Twyla Tharp Dance Foundation, Whitney Museum
of American Art.

Such a concentration of arts organizations in one
city can lead to a cultural imbalance draining off
talent and energies from other regions. New York is not
alone in creating such a situation; London and Paris
dominate the cultural lives of Britain and France far
more than New York City does in the United States. It
should also be noted that the arts organizations located
in New York are really national in scope. For example,
in the period 1974-76, 322 cities in 46 states received
loans from 18 New York City museums; 501 cities in 46
states were visited by 28 New York City performing arts
organizations; the American Museum of Natural History
estimated that sixty percent of its visitors came from
outside New York City; two-thirds of the Metropolitan
Opera's requests for tickets also came from outside New
York City.[36] In a sense, New York City's cultural
resources (like the governmental and cultural institutions in Washington, D.C.), belong to the nation as a
whole. While not a political capital like London,
Paris, or Rome, New York is our cultural capital. As a
cultural capital, New York qualifies as an equal to its
European counterparts and, in certain fields (dance and
art, for example), their superior. Any chauvinism among
New York's indigeneous population should not lessen the
pride that all Americans can take in that city's
cultural achievements. It is a national landmark on a
par with the Grand Canyon and Mount Rushmore. Its
cultural institutions are assets which merit broad
public support so that they might be more widely
experienced and enjoyed.
Culture is clearly alive and well in American
cities. Besides New York, Boston, Philadelphia,
Chicago, and San Francisco can claim national importance
as artistic centers. Los Angeles, Seattle, Salt Lake
City, Houston, Minneapolis, Cleveland are thriving
regional centers for the arts. Too often, however,
cities rely solely upon importing artistic events or
offering traditional cultural programming with little
innovation or community support. Not every city can, or
should, aspire to a regional or national cultural
importance. But this does not mean that the local arts
need be either second-rate or a diversion for the local
cognoscenti. Cities should seek a level of cultural
development that builds on existing arts organizations
and seeks a broad base of support.

The small city of Temple, Texas (population 33,431) developed an integrated, diverse cultural program with relatively wide participation. "Using the published guidelines of the Association of Councils of Arts, they (Temple civic leaders) organized a local council and using their influence to make the council a recognized local body. Called the Cultural Activities Center (CAC), one of the group's goals was to concentrate on the 'family unit.' CAC would try to influence, cajole, or otherwise develop arts activities that would involve people of all socioeconomic classes." The Temple CAC engages in a large number of programs: publishing a monthly newsletter of scheduled events; sponsoring a local art fair where local artists display and sell their work; supporting an independent theater group which also sponsors visits by touring companies; funding numerous other groups including a railroad museum, a boys' choir, a piano ensamble, an art appreciation group. Temple also participated in the state Arts Council's on the "Artists-in-the-Schools" program. "While not without its problems, the Temple program does indicate what can be accomplished . . . when business, local government, and private citizens combine resources. A community need not be large or located near major institutions (such as a university) to develop an ambitious arts program."[37] Unfortunately, programs such as this have been rare in cities (and not just in Texas) and too few arts councils exist that can provide the leadership necessary for local cultural development.

TOWARDS MORE LIVEABLE CITIES: SOME RECOMMENDATIONS

Despite the demonstrated importance of culture for the urban economy and quality of life, most cities (New York, San Francisco, and Seattle are among the exceptions) have not been overly generous in their support of local arts organizations. Dick Netzer makes the following observation about the condition of public support for the arts at the local level.

In most of the United States, the alleged intensity of local pride in the orchestra, opera company, art museum, or resident theater company does not manifest itself in initiatives on the part of state or local politicians to commit state or local funds to the institutions' support. For the most part, local pride is compatible with letting NEA bear the burden of providing public funds for the support of the primary institutions."[38]

Netzer's judgment is perhaps too severe. Cities, of course, grant exemptions from property and sales taxes to nonprofit arts organizations. Many cities maintain museums at public expense or heavily subsidize those that are private. In the early 1960's, San Francisco was the first city to use proceeds from a hotel occupancy tax to support a variety of cultural activities in the city. Some cities--New York, Chicago, and San Francisco--have also used federal CETA (Comprehensive Employment and Training Act) funds to assist unemployed and underemployed artists and arts technicians. But the urban cultural programs just cited are distinct exceptions. As the National League of Cities pointed out in its report on national municipal policy, cities are faced with "major problems in establishing the arts as an essential municipal service." Among these problems are the following:

> Traditionally, the arts have been looked on as a private sector activity, and therefore neglected as a resource in urban policy and as an appropriate area for further public investments.

> There exists a lack of public understanding of the economic needs of arts organizations and artists.

> In many cities, there is no coordinated planning or program development to ensure that the arts are accessible to all citizens.[39]

The League's report also addressed itself to the question of urban aesthetics--making cities attractive and inspiring places to live, work, and play. Among its policy recommendations were the following which specifically related to the role of municipal culture in urban aesthetics:

> States and cities should review tax policies and zoning and building codes to encourage attractive use of land, good standards in architectural design and site planning, and cultural opportunities. Zoning codes and municipal procedures should not only remove obstacles, but also maximize opportunities for cultural experience.

> Public buildings, transportation facilities, and other improvements should provide leadership in good design.

> Cities should consider, in cooperation with
> appropriate professional organizations and
> citizen interests, the use of design panels to
> review existing community development and
> proposed public and private improvements and
> recommend ways to enhance community
> aesthetics. Such design panels should be
> coordinated with overall cultural planning in
> the community.[40]

What has emerged with absolute urgency from a
variety of studies is the need for a municipal cultural
agency that "can coordinate the city's arts activities,
foster its overall cultural development, and create a
comprehensive policy for the city." The Urban
Innovations Group of U.C.L.A. argued that a department
of cultural affairs would stimulate the development of
the arts by:

> (1) supervising city aid to cultural
> institutions, (2) helping to determine funding
> allocations, (3) administering free programs
> to the public, (4) providing technical
> services to cultural organizations, groups,
> and individual artists, and (5) coordinating
> the efforts of other city agencies that affect
> cultural activities . . . Also, the
> department should work closely with such
> agencies as the city planning department and
> community redevelopment agency in overall
> planning efforts to encourage the arts
> component in development strategies.[41]

The U.C.L.A. group also stressed the importance of
neighborhood arts programs modeled on those in San
Francisco that through educational programs and
community cultural centers "could help to generate the
kind of cultural climate in which the neighborhoods arts
can flourish."[42] A study of arts policy in Texas
concluded that even small cities (population under fifty
thousand) can develop an active community arts program
if there is vigorous local leadership--particularly by
members of the local elite. Unfortunately, such private
leadership was found to be rare and strong arts councils
are not usually found in smaller communities.
These University of Texas researchers recommended
that each local government should create an independent
public arts agency with both authority and operating
funds. Such an agency should be responsible for
coordinating the efforts of local arts organizations in
securing private funding and support from the state arts
council and the National Endowment for the Arts.[43] The
Texas study noted what had been noted so often

elsewhere. "An artistically rich community can be a factor in attracting and keeping employees;" and, "as part of a larger civic concern for the nonmeasurable quality of life, the arts can be a selling point for a community."[44]

Those "liveable cities" that have been mentioned (Seattle, San Francisco, Minneapolis, Louisville, Baltimore and Atlanta, among others) have attracted national attention for their vibrant downtowns and flourishing cultural organizations.[45] Mayor Maynard Jackson of Atlanta explained the connection between culture and the cities as follows:

> The arts are the very highest expression of urban life; and the cultural enrichment that is only possible in an urban setting is the highest and most eloquent justification of the city itself; for the arts and the city are inseparable. . . . The arts reveal us to ourselves. They show us who we are and where we are going, whether as a neighborhood, a city, or a nation. The arts are an expression of community identity in its highest form.[46]

Culture then is not a "frill" or "luxury." It is at the very essence of city life and constitutes a basic civic entitlement. Cities are places where people live, and people want to live in cities with a vital cultural life.*

*I wish to acknowledge my debt to Richard Wheeler of Claremont Men's College and to my colleagues Ramon Arango, James Bolner and Adam Hayward for their comments on earlier drafts of this paper. Responsibility for the final disposition is, of course, solely mine.

NOTES

[1] William MacDougall, "Where Culture Puts a City Back on the Map", U.S. News and World Reports, February 9, 1981, p. 62.

[2] These data are derived from the following sources: The Taxpayers' Revolt and the Arts (Washington, DC: U.S. Conference of Mayors, 1978), pp. 2-5; Toward More Liveable Cities: A Report for the President's Task Force on Urban Policy (Washington, DC: National Endowment for the Arts, 1977), pp. 7-8; George C. Koch, "The Culture Industry" (mimeograph, Department of Commerce, Employment and Training Administration, 1979). See also David Cwi and Katherine Lyall, Economic Impact of Arts and Cultural Institutions A Model for Assessment and Case Study of Baltimore (Washington, DC: National Endowment for the Arts, Research Division Report # 6, 1977).

[3] Paul DiMaggio, Michael Useem and Paula Brown, Audience Studies of the Performing Arts and Museums: A Critical Review (Washington, DC: National Endowment for the Arts, Research Division Report #9, 1977), p. 40.

[4] Dick Netzer, The Subsidized Muse: Public Support for the Arts in the United States (New York: Cambridge University Press, 1978), p. 95.

[5] New York Times, October 16, 1978, p. 95.

[6] New York Times, January 11, 1976, sec. 4, p. 5.

[7] New York Times, March 15, 1980, p. 18.

[8] John A. Garraty, The New Commonwealth (New York: Harper Torchbooks, 1968), p. 183.

[9] Quoted in ibid., p. 184.

[10] John Meisel, "Political Culture and the Politics of Culture," Canadian Journal of Political Science 7 (December 1974): 601.

[11] Where Artists Live, 1970 (Washington, DC: National Endowment for the Arts, Research Division Report #5, 1977), p. 3.

[12] William O. Winter, "The University, The City, and The Arts," Public Administration Review 30 (July/August 1970): 409-10.

[13] Ibid., p. 410.

[14] Studies cited in The Taxpayers' Revolt and the Arts, pp. 5-6.

[15] Toward More Liveable Cities, p. 1.

[16] Harvey S. Perloff, and others in the UCLA School of Architecture and Urban Planning, The Arts in the Economic Life of the City (New York: American Council for the Arts, 1979), p. 99.

[17] Ibid., p. 104.

[18] Ibid.

[19] Ibid., p. 109.

[20] Toward More Liveable Cities, p. 3.

[21] Carter Ratcliff, "SoHo: Disneyland of the Aesthete?" New York Affairs, Vol. 4, No. 4 (1978): 68-69.

[22] Ibid., p. 70.

[23] Ibid., p. 68. For discussion of zoning for artists' housing and studios, see Cathleen McGuigan, ed., Cities, Counties and the Arts (New York: Associated Councils of the Arts, 1976), pp. 38-40.

[24] Courtney Callender, "Bringing It All Back Home: Community Access to the Arts," New York Affairs, Vol. 4. No. 4 (1978): 88.

[25] Junius Eddy, "Government, the Arts, and Ghetto Youth," Public Administration Review 30 (July/August 1970): 400.

[26] Ibid., 401; see also Cities, Counties and the Arts, pp. 17-21.

[27] Ibid., p. 403.

[28] Perloff, Arts in the Economic Life of the City, p. 34.

[29] Ibid., p. 127.

[30] Ibid., p. 122. See also Cities, Counties, and the Arts, pp. 23-24.

[31] Ibid., p. 119.

[32] Ibid., p. 32.

[33] Much of the information about the New Orleans cultural scene is drawn from an independent study by Virginia Besthoff, a resident of that city.

[34] Perloff, Arts in the Economic Life of the City, pp. 13-15.

[35] Commentary (May, 1980), p. 68.

[36] These data are drawn from New York as a National Cultural Resource (New York: Commission for Cultural Affairs of the City of New York, 1977), pp. 27, 10.

[37] This discussion comes from Albert Blum, and others in the Lyndon B. Johnson School of Public Affairs, Public Policy Toward the Arts in Texas (Austin: University of Texas, 1978), pp. 33-36.

[38] Netzer, The Subsidized Muse, p. 91.

[39] National Municipal Policy (Washington, DC: National League of Cities, 1978), p. 124.

[40] Ibid., pp. 46-47.

[41] Perloff, Arts in the Economic Life of the City, p. 72.

[42] Ibid., p. 123.

[43] Blum, Public Policy Toward the Arts in Texas, pp. 36, 38.

[44] Ibid., p. 37.

[45] For a fuller discussion of this subject, see Kevin V. Mulcahy, "The Administration of Cultural Affairs: The Case of New York City," paper presented at the Annual Meetings of the American Political Science Association, San Francisco, September 1-3, 1975.

[46] Quoted in Toward More Liveable Cities, p. 1.

11
Public Broadcasting and the Arts in Britain and the United States

Richard S. Katz

PUBLIC SUPPORT OF THE ARTS

Government can support the arts in a variety of ways. The previous chapters have been concerned primarily with programs involving direct subsidies. In some cases, as with state and especially local programs, these subsidies are motivated by the same desire as support of convention centers or tourist attractions-- that people will be attracted to, and business stimulated in, a particular area. In other cases, the desire is simply to encourage artistic endeavors at levels and to audiences beyond those that would be supported by the free market. These programs may take the form of direct grants to artists or artistic companies. Alternatively, the cost of attending an artistic performance may be reduced for some or all patrons, as through the Arts Council of Great Britain's program of "reverse touring," bringing people from the periphery to the center rather than sending artists on tour. Finally, private capital may be lured into artistic investment and artists encouraged to try risky ventures through the potential subsidy of a guarantee against loss.

These are relatively new forms of patronage, dating in Europe for the most part since World War II and in the United States since the mid-1960's. Other forms of indirect subsidy have a longer history. Among these are reduced postage rates for printed matter which allowed mass circulation magazines to flourish and greatly bolstered the market for short stories; tax exempt status to shield the income of many museums, orchestras, and theaters; and tax shelters for their contributors to encourage private donations. In all these cases, however, while the government has modified some market conditions, it has allowed the free play of economic forces and popular taste to determine the ultimate fate of each project. By and large, these programs have been

structured to minimize, or even to preclude, governmental exercise of artistic judgment.

Beyond direct and indirect subsidies, governments
can also support the arts by creating a climate favorable to their advancement. Music and art appreciation
classes introduced into the public school curriculum can
increase the size of the future adult audience.
Presidential or Royal command performances, honors given
to artists, or simply attendance by a prominent official
can give an artistic enterprise an aura of establishment
respectability and valuable media exposure. Here, there
is more room for artistic judgment as a president
chooses what plays or concerts to attend and which
artists to honor, or as a school board or individual
teacher decides what kind of art or music children
should be encouraged to appreciate.

The greatest government involvement in making
artistic judgments comes when the government moves from
patronage in the sense of "giver of aid" to a more
traditional sense of "purchaser of work." Governments
have always engaged in this form of patronage.
Architects, painters, and sculptors would be hired to
decorate public buildings. Of somewhat more recent
origin, works of art would be purchased for display in
publicly owned museums. Musicians would be hired to
perform at public ceremonies. While the government
would then exercise the same discretion based on taste
that is exercised by any purchaser of art, the impact of
the "government's taste" was limited by the relatively
small scale of its purchases.

In recent times, however, the magnitude of this
direct involvement by government in the purchase of art
has grown tremendously both in magnitude and in scope.
Instead of buying a specific piece of art, commissioning
a particular work, or engaging performers for a limited
series of performances, artists may become regular state
employees. This has become particularly common with the
performing arts in Western Europe as well as being the
natural model in the socialist bloc. The degree to
which artistic decisions are made on explicitly political grounds of course varies; but when the government
acts as impresario, public officials must exercise all
the discretion ordinarily exercised by a private producer or employer of artists.[1]

Although any public agency may engage in any of
these forms of artistic patronage from time to time,
arts councils have tended to concentrate their efforts
on subsidies and to a lesser extent on creating a favorable climate for the arts. In many cases, they have
seen themselves, and have been seen by others, as
providing a service to the artistic community. Other
agencies have been more actively employing artists and
mounting productions in the course of providing some

service to others. Most notable among agencies of this
sort, particularly with reference to the performing
arts, have been public broadcasters.

The potential of public broadcasters to influence
the arts is tremendous and stems from two fundamental
characteristics of the broadcast media. The first is
their insatiable appetite for material to fill air time.
A single station operated only from 7:00 AM to 11:00 PM
with a reduced schedule on Sundays (and most broadcasters have far more extensive schedules) would require
over 100 hours of material each and every week.
At that rate, the complete plays of Shakespeare would
fill only a few days; the complete works of Beethoven
would take only a bit more than a week. Broadcasters
constantly need new dramatic scripts and new music, thus
furnishing a steady market for their creators. They are
also massive employers of performing talents.

Beyond this, broadcasters can play a major role in
shaping the artistic climate of their communities. More
people may see an opera broadcast one evening on
television than could see sold-out performances at the
Metropolitan Opera House in a decade. Broadcasting can
give greater access to art and culture to those who
appreciate them than can any other medium. It also has
the potential to introduce vast audiences to levels of
cultural experience they would not ordinarily seek out
on their own. Broadcasting can both create a demand for
the arts and make a major contribution to satisfying it.

The ability of public broadcasters to do these
things varies from one art form to another. Radio can
do little to satisfy a demand for painting or sculpture,
although lecture series might stimulate demand or
heighten the public's appreciation of these forms. It
is well adapted, however, for the dissemination of
music. Television, while capable of carrying music,
seems more suited for arts with heavy visual components
--ballet, opera, and theater. Moreover, public broadcasters also vary in their interest in particular art
forms. North German Radio, for example, has been particularly active in promoting radio drama,[2] while the
British Broadcasting Corporation's radio programs have
been more promoters of music. Finally, the ability of
public broadcasters to foster art at all varies with
their economic and political circumstances and with
their relative positions within the broadcasting
industry as a whole.

The rest of this chapter will be devoted to
comparison of two public broadcasting systems that
differ quite markedly on these dimensions. One is the
British Broadcasting Corporation (BBC) which operates
two of the three television networks available in
Britain as well as four national radio networks. The
other is the American system of the Corporation for

Public Broadcasting (CPB) in conjunction with the Public Broadcasting Service (PBS--an organization and network of public television stations) and National Public Radio (NPR).

PROBLEMS IN PUBLIC BROADCASTING

The general problems raised by government support of the arts reappear with relation to public broadcasting--often in exaggerated form. This exaggeration results from the coincidence of three factors. First, there are the restrictions placed by government on entry into the broadcasting industry. Problems of potential interference impose limits on the number of channels available. While advances in the technology of sound radio have allowed this number to expand greatly, the precedent for government licensing has been firmly set and in any case the number of television channels available in any particular area is usually far below the number of individuals who would like to operate stations. Since the government is forbidding some individuals from broadcasting, it assumes a responsibility for the quality of the service provided by those it does license. This is especially true when the government operates broadcasting facilities itself or through public corporations.

Second, because broadcast programs are transmitted into their homes, people tend to be more sensitive to material they consider improper or offensive than they would be in a theater. Moreover, the audience is less self-selected than is the theater audience. Since people often come across programs quite by chance while turning the dial of their radio or television rather than deliberately seeking them out, it is more likely that someone will be offended by questionable material. Then too because the broadcast audience is so large, particularly when one is dealing with national networks, each incidence is magnified in importance.

Third, the directness of government involvement in public broadcasting makes it unusually sensitive. Although public money is involved in subsidy programs as well as in cases of socialized cultural production, in the case of subsidies the government does not exercise direct creative control and so can deny responsibility for "occasional lapses of judgment" by recipients of grants. Public broadcasters ordinarily do not have this luxury.[3]

These three factors exacerbate difficulties that are common to all government arts programs. The first is the danger of censorship and political control.

Although with broadcasting this problem is usually discussed with reference to news and public affairs programming (the Nixon White House attempt to stifle national public affairs programming on PBS and the conflict between the BBC and the British government over programs like A Question of Ulster are examples), it can readily extend to drama as well. This problem is particularly acute for public broadcasters because they act as producers and not just as funders of programs. Since they are supposed to exercise artistic control, it is far easier for them to mask political judgments under the label of artistic discretion. At the same time as censorship is to be avoided, public broadcasters (like all spenders of public funds) must expect to be held accountable by the political authorities.

A second difficulty is that the concentration of economic power in the hands of government as patron-in-chief will lead to a standardization and to a corresponding stifling of creativity. All patrons of the arts indulge their own taste in deciding to support one project rather than another. But when one patron dispenses a predominant share of the support, will not artists be forced to pander to that patron's taste regardless of their own desires? Moreover, if that patron is institutionally prone to be conservative (as is nearly always the case with government bureaucracies) will this not dull the cutting edge of artistic production? Again the problem is especially acute for public broadcasters since the economics of networking forces a concentration rather than a dispersion of funds. In this case, the desire to trust proven talent may all but shut out new individuals (and new ideas) until they have worked their way through the ranks. The danger is that by the time they have "made it," they will have been socialized to conformity.

The third difficulty concerns the level of taste, or mix of levels of taste, to which programming should be aimed, and in particular concerns the legitimacy of trying to raise the level of the public's taste. In fact, the way this problem has just been posed implies that there are superior and inferior, not just different, tastes and this assumption is subject to dispute. Are some genres more worthy of support than others? Should classical music be favored over rock and roll, opera over musical comedy, Shakespeare over Norman Lear? People are apparently far more willing to have their money spent to support orchestras in concert halls for the benefit of those who already enjoy them than they are to have orchestras imposed on "their" mass media of radio and television. If radio and television are a mass media, perhaps they should be aimed at current mass taste, rather than trying to educate a mass audience to appreciate those art forms currently enjoyed by the elite. On the other hand is the danger, as seen by the BBC's first director general that, "he who prides himself on giving what he thinks the people want is often creating a fictitious demand for lower standards which he will then satisfy."[4]

The fourth difficulty concerns the legitimacy of using public monies to subsidize a public enterprise in competition with private entrepreneurs. For most government arts programs this is of little relevance since the private sector is either nonexistent or the recipient of government aid. In the case of broadcasting, however, public and private sectors compete in an arena in which private entrepreneurs can survive very well unaided. Indeed, even with steep taxes and strict regulation of advertising time, one British commercial broadcaster described his franchise as "a license to print money." Commercial broadcasting in the United States is even more lucrative. If the private sector can provide television and radio programs, why should commercial broadcasters be shut out of the market in favor of public agencies which then depend on government support for their funds?

A fifth difficulty relates to the intended beneficiary of the program, the artist or the general public. For most subsidy programs, this is a marginal concern since both the public and the art constituencies benefit from each grant--albeit in differing relative degrees. Broadcasters, however, have to face this dilemma more directly when, for example, deciding between purchasing rights to a foreign program or to rebroadcasting old material or paying for a new production. The former alternative may well provide the public with a superior product, and is certain to allow a fixed program budget to stretch farther, but it is of little direct benefit to the current domestic arts community. The latter alternative, while providing greater employment for artists, sacrifices at least the short-run interests of the public.

A sixth difficulty--one which only confronts public broadcasters is how the money for their support is to be raised. For most arts programs, the only possible source of money is general tax revenues. For broadcasters, however, there are a variety of other possibilities. These include a license fee charged to all owners of radio and/or television receivers--a large enough group to make non-commercial broadcasting economically feasible while providing some insulation from government control through appropriations bribery or blackmail--and taxes on the manufacturers of radio equipment or the operation of commercial stations--justified by their use of the public airwaves to make private profit.

BRITISH BROADCASTING: HISTORY AND STRUCTURE

The British Broadcasting Company was chartered in
1923 as a corporation wholly owned by British manufacturers of radio equipment and given a monopoly over
radio broadcasting. As in the United States where
regular radio broadcasting had begun in 1920, the
primary motivation was to create a market for radio
receivers and the original BBC was to be financed
primarily from royalties on them. In large measure, its
structure was a reaction to the reigning chaos of
American broadcasting where unregulated stations were
springing up and interfering with one another.

The British Broadcasting Company was replaced in
1927 by the British Broadcasting Corporation (the
current BBC) with John Reith, the company's managing
director, retained as the corporation's director-
general.[5] The form of a public corporation was adopted
for the BBC to provide insulation both from politics and
from business. At the head of the BBC stands its Board
of Governors who are appointed by the Crown by Order-in-
Council on the advice of the responsible minister.
Originally this minister was the Postmaster General, but
it is now the Home Secretary; the Prime Minister has
regularly been involved as well.[6] Once appointed,
however, the Governors are no longer responsible to a
ministry. While the government retains the power to
compel or forbid any broadcast or class of broadcasts,
the stature of the BBC is such that this power is almost
never used.[7] Rather, the Governors and the senior staff
whom they appoint from outside the regular civil service
system exercise independent discretion in making policy.

While not a government department, the BBC is
nonetheless part of the state structure. Its External
Services are paid for by direct government grant. For
the rest of its income, it depends primarily on a
license fee set and imposed by the government with the
legal sanctions. While well separated from the day-to-
day pressure of normal politics,[8] the BBC is subject to
some scrutiny by the House of Commons Select Committee
on Nationalized Industries. Moreover, its charter is
granted for limited periods with committees of enquiry
and government decisions about its future. Consequently, the BBC is sensitive to more broad-gauged
political trends.

The BBC has always seen its mission as providing
national broadcasting services. Until 1930, it operated
one radio program. In that year, a second program,
called "Regional" but also aiming at national coverage,
was instituted. A third radio program was instituted
after World War II and a fourth in 1967. Also in 1967,
rested in London and all local broadcasts, wherever

made, were produced by members of the regular BBC staff. Television broadcasting began in 1936 only to be suspended during the war. When it was resumed, the model of a national service was again applied. The BBC's broadcasting monopoly was broken in 1954, with the passage of the Independent Television Act, and a commercial television system began operating in 1955.[9] The BBC started operating a second national television channel in 1964.

By 1974 the aim of national coverage had been well met--excepting Radio 1 which operated only in the Medium frequency band where signal propagation deteriorates badly after dark. Radios 2, 3, and 4 in the VHF band could be received by 99.3 percent of the population of the United Kingdom (ranging from a low of 94.4 percent in Wales to 99.7 percent in England), while the UHF television services of BBC-1 and BBC-2 were available to 97.3 percent of the population (ranging from 86.7 percent in Northern Ireland to 98.3 percent in England).[10] The VHF service of BBC-1 reached 99.5 percent of the population with at least 97 percent served in each of the four national regions.

The BBC license fee has risen steadily as service has expanded, but until recently the increases (and total fee) were relatively small. BBC expansion was financed through the growth of the number of licensees and the proportion buying the higher priced TV and then color TV licenses.[11] In the 1970's, however, the market has approached saturation while rapid inflation reduced BBC finances. For example, despite a forty percent increase in the license fee to L34 granted in 1979, the BBC's debt grew from under L30 million in early 1979 to L100 million in early 1980. At that time, the BBC announced that it would have to save L130 million from its budget of L1,000 million over the next two years-- including cuts to wipe out a L40 million operating deficit, the postponement of expansion plans, and the permanent loss of 1500 jobs.

The other major source of problems confronting the BBC is commercial competition. The period following the loss of its television monopoly in 1955 was difficult and occasioned a substantial revision in BBC program policy on television. More recently, its monopoly over sound radio has also been breached and in 1980 a Conservative, free enterprise-oriented government planned to allow a second commercial television network. This has aggravated the BBC's difficulty in retaining qualified staff, who after being trained at BBC expense (the commercial broadcasters have no similar training program), leave for higher salaries. This situation forced the BBC to concentrate more of its resources on meeting the competitive challenge in television at the expense of educational and all sound radio broadcasting.

BBC program policy for each network is set centrally. In radio, the Managing Director (Radio) and the Director of Programmes set overall policy while the three network controllers (one for Radio 1 and Radio 2 and one each for Radios 3 and 4) select and schedule the particular programs to be carried. A similar structure is used for television with two network controllers, assisted by the Programmes Planning Group, deciding which new programs of those proposed by the production departments to make, which old material to repeat, which outside programming to purchase, and which to schedule. To assist in policy-making, the BBC has created a number of functional and regional advisory committees, and a General Advisory Council.

While overall decision-making is highly centralized, the production of individual programs is highly decentralized. Producers propose program ideas and budgets to the head of their department or group (for example, drama group, light-entertainment group, music and arts department) who select proposals to be forwarded to the network controllers. Once a program is selected for productions, its producer is given a budget and freedom to make the program--select talent, contract for use of the BBC's central and/or eleven regional production facilities, and so forth--subject only to the BBC system of "reference-up." That is, a producer is obliged to refer to his department head (and the department head to his superior) any problem he believes will cause serious controversy or any questionable interpretation of BBC policy. This has allowed experienced producers to guide the inexperienced and a kind of case-law evolution of BBC policy. At the same time, it is up to the individual producer to decide whether he needs this kind of guidance.

AMERICAN BROADCASTING: HISTORY AND STRUCTURE

Public broadcasting evolved quite differently in the United States. As in Britain, the original broadcasters were radio manufacturers interested in stimulating a market for their product. Unlike Britain, however, no consortium was given a national monopoly. Instead, stations were licensed locally. Although there was widespread antipathy towards advertising--(Secretary of Commerce Herbert Hoover declared, for example, that it was "inconceivable that a medium with such a potential for service should be drowned in a sea of advertising chatter."), the first sale of time occurred in 1922. Advertising soon became the main source of broadcasting revenue in a system operated primarily for private profit. Licenses were issued and the industry regulated from 1927 to 1934 by a Federal Radio Commission, and since then by the Federal Communications Commission (FCC). Legislative oversight is exercised by the commerce committees in both houses of Congress.

While some radio stations were operated by non-commercial entities (usually universities), most of the desirable frequencies were assigned to private business. There was an unsuccessful attempt made in the 1930s to void all existing licenses and reserve one fourth of all new licenses for educational and noncommercial broadcasters (the Wagner-Hatfield Bill), but only years later did the FCC go so far as to reserve some FM channels for educational purposes. In 1950, of the 108 television stations on the air, none were noncommercial or educational. Finally in 1952, FCC Commissioner Frieda Hennock succeeded in getting the commission to reserve eighty VHF and 162 UHF channels for educational or noncommercial use. Of the nine largest cities, with twenty-five percent of the population, only Boston, Chicago, and San Francisco were assigned VHF educational channels.[12]

The first noncommercial television station, KUHT licensed to the University of Houston, was on the air in 1953. By 1961, there were sixty-two stations, over two-thirds of which were licensed to universities, school boards, and state boards of education. At the end of 1976, there were 270 stations, 110 of which were operated by some form of educational entity.[13] In contrast to the BBC's 99 percent level of penetration, an American public television signal was received by an estimated 90.3 percent of the television households, ranging from 100 percent coverage in several smaller eastern states such as Connecticut, Delaware, and Mississippi to under ten percent in Montana and Wyoming. The comparable figure for public radio was only about sixty percent. (Both are computed on the basis of lower standards than those used in Britain).

In its early days, American public broadcasting was very closely identified with instruction even when stations were owned by community service corporations rather than educators. The drive for reserved channels was spearheaded by educators and argued for in the name of education. The first "network" of public television stations was the Educational Television and Radio Center, which began operations in 1954 "bicycling" programs among its nine (of the ten existing non-commercial stations) members.[14] In 1959, this organization, with Ford Foundation support, moved to New York and became the National Educational Television and Radio Center (later NET). The first direct federal financial support for public television came in 1962 with the Educational Television Facilities Act. Thus, in contrast to the BBC where instructional programming was one part of an overall service, the origins of American public broadcasting were explicitly educational and to this day professional educators are in at least nominal control of over one-third of the public television stations.

The Ford Foundation provided a big push away from purely instructional programming before 1967. Then came the 1967 Carnegie Commission Report on Educational Television[15] and the passage of the Public Broadcasting Act. This act established the Corporation for Public Broadcasting (CPB) as a public corporation with a board appointed by the President on the advice and consent of the Senate. CPB was funded through the regular appropriation process--unlike the British license fee or the dedicated tax on the sale of televisions suggested by the Carnegie Commission. CPB was charged with the responsibility to assist in the production and procurement of programming, to develop an interconnection among the public television and radio stations to allow simultaneous broadcasting, to assist in station development, and to insulate the public broadcasting system from political pressure. On the other hand, CPB was forbidden to own or operate broadcasting facilities, or the interconnection that it was to develop. Much more than with commercial networks, program production and decisionmaking was to be decentralized.

CPB created the Public Broadcasting System (PBS) as an independent corporation in 1969 to run the television interconnection. In 1971, National Public Radio (NPR) was similarly created (with the additional authority denied to PBS to produce programs itself.) Relations between CPB and the individual stations were never terribly good and deteriorated rapidly in 1972 amid charges that the CPB board had yielded to pressure from the Nixon White House concerning programming decisions. One result was the reconstitution of PBS in 1973 as a membership organization of public television stations. An analogous Association of Public Radio Stations (APRS) was founded subsequently. More recently, a National Association of Public Television Stations has been formed to take over the long-range planning, representational, and lobbying functions of PBS. The objective was to relieve PBS of the need to go to Capitol Hill, so that day-to-day programming decisions would be an insulated from political pressure as possible. APRS and NPR, in a reverse move, have merged into a single organization.

A major problem confronting the public broadcasting system has been the conflict between local autonomy and the need for central planning. Many of the stations, and PBS as an organization, have tried to limit CPB's role to one of passing money through to them. They argue that the Federal Communications Act, as well as the spirit of the Public Broadcasting Act and the Carnegie Commission report, give sole responsibility for program decisions to the stations. CPB, on the other hand, has argued both a right and responsibility to exercise some discretion in the allocation of the federal funds it is given and a need to insure that programming is produced to meet the needs of some minorities who might be overlooked by the stations. CPB argues that this is necessary because of the way PBS makes its program procurement decisions through the Station Program Cooperative (SPC). A recent example of the dispute has been over programming targeted for native Americans. Such programming has been rejected by the SPC (no doubt because native Americans do not constitute a sizeable audience in the service areas of most PBS stations) but has been supported by CPB. Another example was the conflict over The Righteous Apples, a program targeted for urban teenagers. Although this program was very unpopular with station managers, it appeared to be reaching its targeted audience and CPB decided to fund a second year over the objections of the stations.

Money has been the other problem and it has two aspects. The first relates to the system's desire to be insulated from the political pressure inherent in the annual appropriations process as when President Nixon vetoed the 1972 CPB authorization. In 1975, a system of longer-term authorizations based on a matching formula (in 1981, one federal dollar for every two nonfederal dollars) was instituted. This allows longer-term planning by the system, but does not remove the threat of political control as Reagan administration attempts to rescind advance authorizations illustrate. The other aspect relates to the income of the stations and PBS for operations and program procurement. CPB is obliged to pass as least fifty percent of its funds through to the stations in the form of unrestricted Community Service Grants (CSGs). These are allocated in proportion to nonfederal fundraising and for television and ranged in fiscal 1979 from $4.7 million for WNET in New York to $108,000 to KEET in Eureka, California.[16] Overall, the CPB-NPR-PBS systems had an income of nearly $600 million in fiscal 1979--about fifteen percent under the BBC's income of L315 million for the year ending March 31, 1979.

In principle, all programming decisions in the American system are made by the local stations. In fact, production of quality programs requires resources that exceed the capacity of individual stations.[17] Some programs are underwritten by corporate or foundation grants. The station is nominally in control of program content; but, if only because of the law of anticipated reactions, a station must be sensitive to the under-writers' interests. This is especially so with programs like Masterpiece Theater which involves the purchase of programs made elsewhere. In this case, the underwriter is likely to be directly involved in program selection. Choice of particular musical programs have been particularly influenced by underwriting. Because Gulf Oil (headquartered in Pittsburgh) provided funding, PBS carried Previn and the Pittsburgh. Withdrawal of underwriting support by Raytheon coupled with a grant from Atlantic Richfield, was instrumental in the decision to drop Evening at Symphony with the Boston Symphony Orchestra in favor of a series featuring the Philadelphia Orchestra. Similarly, the sale of Texas's Lonestar Brewery to Miller Brewery resulted in loss of underwriting for Austin City Limits. Often these decisions are made by a single corporate officer indulging his personal taste. While the program staff of PBS exercises nominal discretion over such programm-ing (and will often initiate attempts to procure underwriting for a particular program), the ultimate decision rests with those controlling the purse strings.

The SPC has been the primary vehicle for financing production of programs without full underwriting. Would-be producers submit descriptions of their material, often with pilot films. In early SPCs, only PBS stations or affiliated organizations like The Children's Television Workshop could submit proposals. More recently, Congress has mandated access for indepen-dent producers. The SPC itself is a simulated market taking place in a number of "rounds". Before each round, every station is told the price it would have to pay for each program if it joined the group already "voting" for it. Before the first round, prices are set on the assumption of eighty percent acceptance. The prices are computed by apportioning the purchase price of each program among the stations opting for it in proportion to their CSGs. If, between rounds, a station joins the list of would-be buyers of a program, its price goes down for all the bidding stations; if a station drops a program from its shopping list, the price goes up for the remaining stations. Bandwagon effects are quite likely--especially if rich stations like WNET (representing over six percent of the total buying power of the system) or WGBH (representing over three percent) move in concert. In the first few rounds, a program is purchased only if the combination of stations opting for it reaches a minimum level. Programs with very little support are dropped. After that, a series of purchase rounds begin in which, if the price of a program stays the same or goes down, all the stations that bid on it are committed to buy it. Although a station may join the group purchasing a program after the SPC market is over, only stations sharing in the cost of a program's production may show it over the air.

The SPC system gives great weight to the desires of the rich stations whose decisions can have a perceptible influence on the price other stations must pay for a program. Smaller, rural stations with limited budgets, while paying very little for the programs they choose, often have little effective choice but to buy the programs their richer more urban counterparts select. Needs of minority audiences not found in the big cities are frequently ignored. In order to encourage the purchase of minority programming, CPB in 1979 and 1980 offered up to one million dollars in four to one matching funds to reduce the SPC price of qualified proposals.

Just as corporate underwriting has led to selection of safe and noncontroversial programs, so the SPC exerts a strong pressure for "the cheap, the safe, and the known."[18] An entirely disproportionate share of the innovative programming on PBS has been financed by direct grants from CPB. The Corporation's policy of cutting such funding after a few years, leaving the program to sink or swim in the SPC, has been an additional source of conflict between CPB and PBS.

THE SYSTEMS COMPARED: LEVELS OF SUPPORT

Support of the arts, or of particular arts or artists, by public broadcasters may take many forms. In 1930, the BBC saved the Covent Garden Opera from extinction by becoming the principal shareholder in a reorganized syndicate. They also underwrote the Sadler's Wells and Carl Rossa Opera companies and an attempt in the early 1930's to organize a Welsh National Orchestra. The BBC continues to sponsor the Henry Wood Promenade Concerts and the Sir Robert Mayer Children's Concert. More often, the BBC and CPB-PBS-NPR systems provide payments for services. They hire artists either on salary or for individual performances. They pay royalties on the works performed. The attention gained from a broadcast appearance can be an appreciable aid in soliciting contributions, selling tickets, negotiating recording or film contracts. (Indeed, indirect benefits of this sort can be so great that the Boston Symphony Orchestra offered to partially underwrite its own appearances on Evening at Symphony.) It is difficult to estimate the total economic value of these kinds of support.[19] However, some indication of the differences between the two systems can be formed by looking at their support for serious music. The differences are extremely large and unrelated to overall financial resources--the two systems have nearly equal incomes and operate equivalent numbers of transmitters. On the other hand, the differences are closely related to their organizational systems.

The BBC has been the principal sponsor of serious music in the United Kingdom. In 1975, about one-third of the country's orchestral resources "consisted on the BBC's various 'house' orchestras . . . altogether the BBC Symphony Orchestra gives more public concerts in London than any of the other four London Orchestras."[20] With over 500 full-time musicians, the BBC spent more than twice as much on orchestral music as the Arts Council of Great Britain. In the year ending March 31, 1976, this amounted to roughly three million pounds. The BBC regularly provides over 4,000 engagements for solo artists each year as well as broadcasting, and paying for, roughly thirty operas and at least one performance by every British orchestra. Original works of music are also commissioned such as Benjamin Britten's opera "Owen Wingate" and music by Malcolm Arnold, David Bedford, and Gordon Crosse.

The contrast between Britain and the United States could hardly be greater. American public broadcasters have no regularly employed orchestras. Total spending on serious music programs produced for PBS in fiscal 1976 was only about half what the BBC spent on its orchestras alone and only approaches the BBC orchestra level when all music programs are added, including such things as Drum Corps International Championships, Keep America Singing, and Dance in America. And even here the American figures, which totalled roughly $6.2 million are not comparable to the British since they include all production costs, not just compensation to the musicians.

A number of factors contribute to this difference. One is structural. Because of the American practice of licensing local stations (rather than national networks) and the obligation to foster local autonomy, the American system of public broadcasting is obliged to spend a much larger proportion of its funds on facilities and administration than does the BBC. Each of the licensees must have cameras and studio facil-ities--even though they may produce only a few hours of local material each week. Similarly, each must have a manager, program director, and other administrative staff. While salaries and costs are roughly comparable (For example, the Director-General of the BBC and the presidents of PBS and CPB all have nearly equivalent salaries), the CPB-NPR-PBS systems are top-heavy with upper-middle management. The BBC senior staff--whether defined as those earning more than L12,500 or by position (For example, "Head of Make-up Department, Television," "Head of Gramaphone Programmes," or "Chief Assistant Pay Policy") as well as the network controllers and production department heads--is composed of about 220 individuals. In 1980 PBS stations employed 196 individuals (average salary $36,404) and NPR stations employed 184 individuals (average salary $21,932) in the positions of chief executive or station manager alone.

Another factor is contractual. Early in its history the musician's unions reached an agreement with the BBC to limit the amount of recorded music ("needle time") that could be played. The amount of program material purchased from abroad is similarly limited. This naturally means that live performances or performances specifically recorded for broadcast by the BBC are in constant demand. No similar limitation exists for NPR or PBS, so that a staple element of their programming, and particularly of the programming of local public radio stations, can be commercial recordings. PBS has also imported a large proportion of its dramatic programming from Britain. This has naturally upset American actors and producers, but so long as it is underwritten by private corporations there is little they can do. When CPB proposed to use federal funds to participate in the BBC production of the plays of Shakespeare, however, the propriety of spending government funds to support foreign actors was questioned. CPB countered that this was a rare opportunity to provide the public with superb programs at a bargain price. Only the appearance of outside support ultimately defused this issue.

In indirect support, the BBC and PBS have been more comparable. The BBC is widely credited with building a sizeable audience for serious music in Britain.[21] It continues to introduce new audiences to opera, dance, drama and symphonic music. PBS performs a similar function, although for a smaller audience. Nonetheless, a Joffrey Ballet audience survey commissioned to evaluate the impact of its appearance on the PBS Dance in America series found that fifty-nine percent of first-time attenders attributed their attendance to the television program.

THE SYSTEMS COMPARED: PROGRAM PHILOSOPHY

BBC program policy has evolved through four basic phases, each reflecting a different conception of the corporation's functions in British society, each responding to a changed environment, and each manifesting a distinctive pattern of programming. Because of BBC reporting practices, this evolution can be most clearly illustrated in the realm of the arts with regard to serious music--but the basic trend applies to all programming.

The first stage was the pre-war era, dominated by the missionary zeal of John Reith. His aim was to provide a balanced, national service that would "carry into the greatest possible number of homes everything that is best in every department of human endeavour."[22] When the BBC had only one radio channel, it carried a mix of programming--broadcasts for the schools, serious music, light entertainment, drama. When a second channel began operation, it too carried the full range of programs. Each channel was scheduled to provide a contrast to the other, but each carried roughly the same proportion of serious music. Reith was opposed to alternative services, each catering to a distinctive audience. Program policy was "elitist", and admittedly so, aiming to "give the public something slightly better than it now thinks it likes."[23] Culture and entertainment were deliberately intermixed with the intention of gradually introducing individuals with little or no experience with serious music to ever more demanding works.

This policy was apparently successful in greatly expanding the audience for good music in Britain. But it depended on a number of conditions that proved to be transitory. The first was the confidence of Reith, his associates, and the class they represented that they really knew what was "good" art. The second was the BBC's monopoly position; the popularity of programs could be a secondary concern when there was no alternative service that might be more popular. The third was the apparent willingness of the public to defer to their "betters" on questions of taste.

These circumstances began to change dramatically during the period immediately after the Second World War. The availability of American Armed Forces Radio during the war led to renewed pressure for a program of light entertainment that would appeal to mass tastes. A third radio channel was added and the idea that each channel ought to carry the full range of broadcast matter was dropped.

> Before the war . . . the listener was deliberately plunged from one extreme to the other. The devotees of Berlin (Irving) were suddenly confronted with Bach. Many listeners were won for higher things in this way, but many were irretrievably lost. For the weakness of the process was that so many intolerances were set up.

> Since the war we have been feeling our way
> along a more indirect approach. It rests on
> the conception of the community as a broadly
> based cultural pyramid slowly aspiring
> upwards. This pyramid is served by three main
> Programmes, differentiated but broadly over-
> lapping in levels and interest each Programme
> leading on to the other, the listener being
> introduced through the years increasingly to
> discriminate in favour of the things that are
> more worthwhile.[24]

While the goal of raising the level of public taste
remained, the strategy changed and the BBC gradually
lost confidence in its ability to ignore mass taste.

From the point of view of serious music, the major
innovation in this system was the Third Programme.
While the "middle brow" channel, the Home Service,
continued to have the same balanced program as the pre-
war National and Regional programs, the Third was an
explicitly elite program. This policy of "classifying
program content by height of brow"[25] was a major
departure in BBC policy and enraged Reith, who called it
"an absolute abandonment of what I stood for."[26] Its
audience was extremely small; instead of the ten
percent the BBC originally hoped for, the Third
Programme audience in the mid-1950's was closer to one
percent. It was, however, tremendously popular with
that one percent who were the intellectual and political
rulers of Britain. The Economist lauded the Third
Programme as an outstanding example of "events which
reflect a happier aspect of society," while similar
praise was echoed by The Times.[27]

In the early 1950's, BBC television programming was
much like early radio programming had been. The novelty
of the medium coupled with the BBC's monopoly position
guaranteed an audience. Under these circumstances a
balanced program, with heavy infusions of culture, was
possible. In 1955, however, a commercial competitor
began operating and the BBC soon found it could no
longer deride the notion that raw popularity should play
a major role in program policy. In response, a third
phase of program policy began in 1958 that involved a
number of changes. The television budget exceeded that
of sound radio for the first time in 1958-59 and the
amount of "high brow" culture on television declined.
The Third Programme on radio was cut back with music
content dropping roughly fifteen percent. Serious music
virtually disappeared from the Light Programme--falling
from about eight percent of total air time to about two
percent.

More important than these programming changes,
however, was the change in attitude that underlay them.

Where early post-war program content had been classified
by "height of brow," now the BBC began to think of its
audience in classes as well.   Indeed, the 1964 BBC
Annual Report described each program in terms of the
section of the community to which it was expected to
appeal.   Gone was the missionary drive to lure the
public to better things.   Instead, serious matter would
be provided on a separate channel for "the significant
minority whose tastes, education and mental habits
enable them to take pleasure in close and responsive
listening to broadcasts of artistic and intellectual
distinction."[28]   Gone too was the confidence that some
things truly were better than others.   People who "are
gardeners, or enjoy cricket, or breed whippets, or like
listening to Seventh Century music, or are amateur arch-
aeologists, or collect old detective stories. . . ."[29]
all were seen to have equally worthy interests.

In 1964, BBC-2 began broadcasting, and the system
of dividing programming and audience continued.   With
BBC-1 locked in competition with Independent Television,
most of the cultural programming shifted to BBC-2.   This
channel, for example, now carries Open University programming and roughly four times as much music as BBC-1--
while that channel has over twice as much "light entertainment."   Even within each category, BBC-1 fare is
generally lighter than that on BBC-2.   The segregation
of programming reached its logical conclusion, however,
on radio.   A fourth national program was begun in 1967-
68 and reached full development in 1970-71.   Radio-1 is
the pop music channel while Radio-2 specializes in other
varieties of entertainment music.   Radio-4 is the
network of the spoken word.   While most of its
programming involves game shows, panel discussions,
situation comedies and serials, it also carries drama
and readings from great books.   Finally, Radio-3 is the
successor of the Third Programme.   Roughly seventy
percent of its programming is serious music with Open
University programs accounting for about ten percent
more.   Altogether, about ninety percent of the serious
music broadcast by the BBC, either by television or
radio, is on Radio-3.

Education, in a broad sense, has always been a goal
of the BBC and the BBC has carried explicitly
instructional programming, both for in-school use and
for the continuing education of adults, since its
beginning.   Instruction, however, has never been more
than a minor part of a full broadcasting service.   The
BBC grew as a monopoly with its only competition before
1954 coming from foreign commercial stations aimed at
Britain such as Radio Normandy or Radio Luxembourg.
Since then the BBC has faced commercial competition;
but, it has been secure with a large (if minority) share
of the audience, an established place as one of the

major institutions of British society, and a reliable
source of income in the license fee. None of this has
been true of American public broadcasting.

In the United States, commercial broadcasting
developed first. There were three strong national networks operating when the first noncommercial television
station went on the air and they had preempted most of
the best frequencies. Indeed, until 1964 most televisions sold in the United States could not receive the
UHF signals of most noncommercial television stations
without a special adapter. Similarly, noncommercial
radio was assigned to the FM band which, if technically
superior for music broadcasting, was also receivable by
only a minority. The origins of American public broadcasting were explicitly instructional and instructional
broadcasting remains a major part of many public
television and radio stations' output. The stations of
the Maryland Center for Public Broadcasting, for
example, have more instructional hours than BBC-1 and
BBC-2 combined and it is not even a school or board of
education-owned licensee. Moreover, as public
broadcasting has moved beyond instruction, it has seen
itself--and been seen by others--as an alternative and
supplement to commercial broadcasting, never as a complete service in itself.

It is almost impossible to talk about PBS or NPR
programming policy because one of the guiding principles
of that policy has been local control. In 1977, for
example, there was no single program carried by all PBS
stations. Moreover, because its history is so much
shorter than that of the BBC, it is hard to identify
distinctive periods in American public broadcasting.
However, some general trends may be identified and with
them some areas of controversy.

Prior to the establishment of the PBS interconnection, there was no public television system in the
United States, only a number of independent stations
bicycling programs among themselves. While Ford Foundation support allowed National Educational Television
(NET) to expand dramatically, both in number of members
and variety of programming, its materials were still
heavily instructional. Some programs, like The French
Chef from WGBH in Boston, were to become classics, but
most locally-produced programs were amateurish "talking
heads" shows with miniscule audiences.

The interconnection made national programming
possible; that in turn made corporate underwriting of
more expensive and more professional programs possible.
Corporate underwriters were especially attracted to
prestige programs that would enhance their images
without arousing controversy. Cultural programming
expanded dramatically as a result. Masterpiece Theater,
In Performance at Wolf Trap, and Evening at Symphony are

three series paid for wholly or largely by corporate donations. By fiscal 1975, corporate underwriting paid for nearly half of all cultural programs distributed by PBS.

Establishment culture, particularly if British, fitted the self-image of the educators running PBS stations. So did public affairs programming which had the additional advantage of being cheap to produce. While no national nightly news on the commercial network model was produced, regular discussion programs by William F. Buckley, Sander Vanocur, and Robert MacNeil were distributed. When the commercial networks stopped live coverage of the Senate Watergate hearings, PBS carried on alone.

Children's programming was the third major element of the PBS package. In 1964, over half of all instructional programming was produced locally. Spearheaded by the phenomenally successful Sesame Street (first broadcast in 1968) and The Electric Company (debuting in 1971), the balance shifted dramatically toward national distribution, reaching eighty percent in 1976.

With the exception of children's programs, the balance of the PBS schedule was clearly aimed at the upper-middle class. This created two problems, both of which represented indirect attacks on the broadcast of high culture. The first problem came from Congress in the form of pressure to do more for minorities and women. This pressure extended to hiring practices and training programs, but was also directed at program policy. In response, a number of targeted programs began to enter the schedule, funded primarily by CPB direct grants, secondarily through the SPC, and only in very minor degree by corporate underwriting. The major argument used by PBS was that Sesame Street and The Electric Company were minority service programs representing many hours, much money, and large audiences. Except for these programs, the audiences for minority targeted programs were tiny, even by PBS standards. The national Nielsen audience rating for October, 1976, for example, showed only .9 percent of the television households watched as much as six minutes of Black Perspective on the News, .1 percent watched Villa Allegre, .4 percent watched Woman while other minority programs were below measurable strength. By June, 1980, Villa Allegre's audience had increased nine-fold, but was still under one percent.

This should not be surprising considering that the targeted audiences, except for females, are minorities. It reflects another problem facing public broadcasting: that is its reputation as an elitist "cultural ghetto" with resulting small audiences for its programs. That PBS will have smaller audiences than commercial broad-

casters is a necessary consequence of its alternative
role. If a PBS program or type of program is especially
popular, it tends to shift to the commercial sector as
with televised tennis or mini-series. Small audiences,
however "special", make it difficult for the system to
argue that it deserves public funds or to raise outside
matching funds from either corporations or individuals.
This realization has led to modifications in program
policy to increase popularity and to increased concern
with audience size and demographics. Thus folk,
country, and gospel music, along with the Drum Corps
International Championship, joined opera and symphony in
the music category. Sports like tennis and soccer
appeared with increasing frequency. Even comedy such as
Monty Python's Flying Circus, Fawlty Towers, and The
Ernie Kovacs Show entered the program schedule.

Unlike the minority programs which tend to be
either explicitly educational or public affairs in
orientation, and therefore in conformity with the self-
image of public broadcasters, entertainment programs
revealed a deep split in the PBS community. Some
stations refused to air them--much to the annoyance of
many of their viewers--on the grounds that they were
"solely for entertainment." Others argued that the
question was one of quality rather than intent; that the
plays of Shakespeare were not written "to provide
literature courses for future generations;" and that
viewers, starved for quality programming of any sort,
deserved to "be 'entertained' by something a little more
stimulating than Laverne and Shirley."[30] While some
stations insist more strenuously than others that their
educational mission be paramount, there has been a
definite trend to broaden the conceptions of what is
educational and what is cultural.

The controversy over entertainment programming
highlights a related problem concerning scheduling.
Before the telephone interconnection was established,
PBS stations could not simultaneously broadcast a
program. While the interconnection made common scheduling possible, local autonomy provides a great impedi-
ment. Proponents of a common carriage and common
scheduling policy could point to a number of advantages.
Common carriage would make national promotion of
programs and audience development easier. It would also
facilitate corporate underwriting since donors could be
assured a national audience. Nonetheless, no program on
the PBS interconnection was carried by all stations in
April, 1977. Even the leading programs, Masterpiece
Theater and Sesame Street were carried by only 93.4 percent and 94 percent of the stations; if one looks at the
percentages carrying the same episodes at the same time,
they drop to 75.2 percent and 62 percent respectively.
The average program was carried by only a minority of

stations at any particular time. In 1979, PBS began experimenting with a common carriage policy under which all stations were asked to carry a two-hour block of PBS programs in the same order (not necessarily with the same starting time) on Sunday through Wednesday; stations were left free to schedule Thursday through Saturday as they saw fit. Intensive negotiations were required to find programs satisfactory to all stations, and the common-carriage line up represents the most popular general audience programs. The vast majority of stations accepted the common-carriage plan with the result, for example, that live carriage of Masterpiece Theater had jumped to 90.1 percent in October, 1980. The average audiences for common-carriage programs increased more than twice as rapidly as those for other programs. But even this success poses problems for PBS. The limit of common carriage has probably been reached with proponents of local independence unwilling to give up any more scheduling autonomy and the stock of mutually agreeable programming exhausted. Moveover, common carriage goes counter to one of the main arguments for the multi-channel satellite interconnection recently inaugurated by PBS--that it would allow the local stations more options in scheduling. This conflict between local autonomy and central scheduling will certainly continue in the 1980's.

For NPR, program policy is even more difficult to discuss, notwithstanding that NPR is empowered to produce its own programs while PBS is not. There is far more variety among NPR stations. Although the majority specialize in music of some kind, some concentrate on classical music (for example, WGBH Boston), while others emphasize jazz (for example, WBUR Boston). There are also stations that concentrate on news and information (WNED-FM and WGBR-AM Buffalo). Still others specialize in service to a particular community (KTDB Ramah, New Mexico, with more than half its programming in Navajo). A far smaller proportion of local programming comes from NPR and, given the accessibilities of local gramaphone music programs, the majority of it is in the field of information All Things Considered and Options were the most widely carried NPR programs at the end of 1977.

THE SYSTEMS COMPARED: AUDIENCE

The direct financial support given to the arts by public broadcasters comes at the production stage and is, for any single program, independent of audience. Continued financial support--corporate, individual and governmental--depend on audience. Moreover, the in-

direct support given to the arts in cultivating a market
for further artistic work, creating a climate of opinion
favorable to the arts, educating the public, and providing a means for them to satisfy their demand for music
and drama depends directly on audience.

The BBC is in a quite different position regarding
audience size than are its commercial counterparts.
Commercial broadcasters, in order to increase profits,
must try to maximize their share of the audience (and
the absolute number of people tuned in) at every particular moment since the fee that can be charged for
advertising varies with the size of the audience. Moreover, the demographic characteristics of the audience
are important. Listeners and viewers with large disposable incomes are "worth" more to advertisers. This is
especially true in the United States, where there is
competition among commercial stations. The BBC, in
order to justify the license fee, needs only to satisfy
as many people as possible (or at least an adequate
number of people) some of the time. For the BBC, the
audience is the consumer; for a commercial broadcaster,
the audience is the product.

Consequently, public broadcasters have much greater
freedom in deciding program policy. They can deliberately appeal to a series of minorities, one at a time,
rather than to the vast majority all at once. Both the
British and American systems have taken advantage of
this freedom to provide programming for such minorities
as farmers, and Indians (native Americans in the United
States; speakers of Hindi in Britain), lovers of avant-
garde jazz, devotees of public affairs, and those
interested in non-mainstream sports. The nature of the
systems is that minorities which are very small in
numbers, but concentrated, are better served by the
decentralized American system; while large, but
dispersed, minorities are better served by the British
system of national programs.

The position of American public broadcasters is
intermediate between those of the BBC and commercial
broadcasters. They are not selling an audience and so
need not maximize its size at all times. On the other
hand they depend on a government appropriation and must
try to provide a service to a sufficiently large and
heterogeneous group in order to justify the use of
public funds. In particular, given congressional policy
directives, public broadcasters must serve various
minorities. At the same time, however, the CPB
appropriation is a matching formula based on nonfederal
fund-raising. To maximize this requires appeal to the
upper-middle class--those who control corporate largess
and who have disposable income to donate to public
broadcasting. Nonetheless, it remains true that neither
American nor British public broadcasters must con-

tinually maximize their audiences. It is not
necessarily counter to their interests that a person
tune in one program and then change channels or turn off
the set. This does run counter to the interests of
commercial broadcasters.

With particular regard to cultural programs, however, the primary audience decision is whether to
program for those who already appreciate the arts and
need only be given a quality product and told where to
find it, or alternatively to attempt actively to convert
new audiences to appreciate good music, drama, and so
forth. Related, is the question of how system structure
and more general program policy have an effect on the
audience for the arts.

The BBC's original policy quite clearly was to lure
people into appreciating artistic achievement of higher
quality than they would ordinarily seek out. This
policy was more or less abandoned by the mid-1960's
when, for example, the Assistant Chief (Orchestra and
Choral) of the BBC Music Division required quotation
marks to refer to "good music", and was quick to add "we
do not and should not tell the license-holders what is
good for them."[31] Its effective demise paradoxically
dates from the development of the Third Programme. The
Third was, and Radio-3 continues to be, a haven for the
cultural elite--but it also became a kind of cultural
ghetto. Excellent broadcasts are available for those
who seek them out--but most people never do. Indeed,
before the complete separation of the third and fourth
networks, it was observed that the same concert broadcast on Radio-4 would achieve a much larger audience
than it had when carried originally on Radio-3. The
same phenomenon applies to television, with BBC-1
audiences regularly larger than those to BBC-2, although
the presence of a significant amount of entertainment
programming on the latter network has prevented complete
segregation of its audience.

The American public television system suffers from
exactly the same problem of "ghettoization" with regard
to its adult programming. While an occasional program
will be very popular in a few metropolitan areas--espe-
cially those with VHF stations--PBS programs generally
play to audiences of under five percent of the
television households. Only about forty percent of the
television households tuned in to any PBS station for as
long as six minutes during an average week in June,
1980. Even the top rated stations had only fifty-seven
percent tune-in even once. In part, this is the fault
of PBS's disadvantageous frequency assignments; of the
top twenty-five stations, only five were VHF. The
greatest problem, however, is the public perception
(which is borne out by the facts) that PBS caters to an
elite audience. Even when PBS programs that have been

extremely popular with mass audiences elsewhere (for example, <u>Upstairs, Downstairs</u>), they are ignored by most Americans. Instead, the PBS audience comes from two distinctive types of households. One provides the audience for children's programs and fairly closely approximates the overall population--except in age. The audience for cultural programs, however, is quite atypical of the general public with homes where the head of the house has done some graduate work more than four times as likely to watch as homes where the head of house has less than a high school education.

The audience for NPR is much smaller than that for PBS. In the week of Roper's 1978 audience survey only 7.5 percent had listened to a public radio station; 20 percent had listened to a public radio station at least once; and, only 28 percent reported that they had ever heard of NPR. The same educational and class biases exist in the NPR audience. While taste for the arts is not restricted to the upper classes, it is highly correlated with class. This leads one to believe that the audience for culture on PBS and NPR is restricted to those who already enjoy it. So long as pop music is reserved to commercial radio and situation comedies and action adventure programs are reserved to commercial television, this audience is unlikely to expand.

NOTES

[1] Whether this phenomenon is truly new depends in part on one's point of view. Much of the great art of the Renaissance--for example, the major works of Michelangelo--was produced on commission from the kings and popes of the time. While these people were the government, the distinction between the pope or king in his private capacity and in his capacity as temporal ruler was far less sharply drawn than it is today. Moreover, there was not the expectation that rulers should reflect in their public actions, especially with regard to art, anyone's judgment except their own.

[2] Martyn A. Bond, "Radio Drama on North German Radio and the BBC," Journal of Broadcasting 17 (Fall 1973): 475-92.

[3] American public broadcasting, however, was structured so as to afford some insulation from direct accountability for the expenditure of public funds. In the case of a PBS program, for example, federal funds may have gone to CPB, been passed to the stations, then to PBS, and then to a single producing station. At each stage, the public money will have been so mixed with private funds as to make it very difficult to specify whose dollars paid for what.

[4] John Reith, Broadcast Over Britain (London: Hoelder and Stoughton, 1924), p. 34.

[5] Indeed Reith, without the advice or approval of the company's shareholders, was one of the prime movers of the change.

[6] House of Lords Deb., 5th series, 176 (1952), 1310.

[7] Report of the Committee on the Future of Broadcasting, Cmnd. 6753 (London: H.M.S.O., 1977), pp. 42-46.

[8] For example, parliamentary questions concerning program content have been ruled to be out of order.

[9] See H.H. Wilson, Pressure Group (London: Secker and Warburg, 1961).

[10] Report of the Committee on the Future of Broadcasting, pp. 370-73.

[11] The license fee was 20 shillings from 1922 through May, 1946 when it was increased to L1 for radio only or L2 for radio and TV. By 1976 it had risen to L8 for black and white and L18 for color. At that time, the BBC fees were the lowest in Europe--often under half, and in one case for color and seven cases for black and white under one-third, those charged elsewhere. The requirement of a license for radio only was abolished in 1971.

[12] A commercial VHF channel assigned to New Jersey was subsequently purchased to become WNET in New York.

[13] On December 31, 1976, the distribution of public television licensees and stations was as follows:

Type of licensees	No. of licensees	No. of stations
Community	60	75
University	53	76
State Authority	18	83
State Board of Ed.	6	18
Local School District	7	18

[14] "Bicycling" is the distribution of programs by physical transporting film or videotape from one station to the next.

[15] Public Television: A Program for Action, the Report and Recommendations of the Carnegie Commission on Educational Television (New York: Harper & Row, 1967).

[16] The PBS station in Guam received a CSG of $85,783. CPB has passed roughly fifty percent of its appropriation to PBS stations in the form of CSGs. NPR stations have gotten roughly eight percent.

[17] Most of the following discussion refers directly to television. The same conclusions apply to radio except that radio broadcasters are better able to make use of recordings.

[18] Michael C. Reeves and Tom W. Hoffer, "The Cheap, Safe, and Known," Journal of Broadcasting 20 (Fall 1976): 549-65.

[19] One estimate, however is available. In 1973-74, the BBC is estimated to have spent L25 million on "drama, serious music and arts features." Lord Radcliffe-Maud, Support for the Arts in England and Wales (London: Calouste Gulbenkian Foundation, 1976), pp. 107-08.

[20] Eric White, The Arts Council of Great Britain (London: Davis-Paynter, 1975), p. 170.

[21] B. Maine, The BBC and Its Audience (London: T. Nelson and Sons, 1939), p. 47; Benjamin Itor Evans and Mary Glasgow, The Arts in England (London: Falcon Press, 1949), p. 16; Edward E. Bridges, "The State and the Arts," The Romanes Lecture, Oxford University, June 3, 1958, pp. 20-21.

[22] Reith, Broadcast, p. 34.

[23] British Broadcasting Corporation, BBC Handbook, 1928 (London: BBC, 1928), p. 711.

[24] Sir William Haley, The Lewis Fry Memorial Lectures, University of Bristol, May 11, 1948.

[25] Report of the Committee on Broadcasting, 1960, Cmnd. 1753 (London: H.M.S.O., 1962), p. 24.

[26] John Reith, The Reith Diaries, ed. C. Stuart, (London: Collins, 1975), p. 455.

[27] The Economist quoted in Kenneth Adam, "The Programme and Its Critics," in The Third Programme, (London: BBC, 1947), p. 30; Times (London), February 11, 1958, p. 3.

[28]British Broadcasting Corporation, BBC Handbook, 1964 (London: BBC, 1964), p. 41.

[29]Hugh Greene, Third Floor Front (London: Bodley House, 1969), p. 61.

[30]Bill Carter, "Double Standard and Pretentiousness Keep Ernie Kovacs Off the Air," The Sun (Baltimore), May 2, 1977, sec. B, p. 4.

[31]Hans Keller, "Music Planning: Its Responsibilities," in British Broadcasting Corporation, BBC Handbook, 1965 (London: BBC, 1965), p. 15.

12
Cultural Diplomacy: Foreign Policy and the Exchange Programs

Kevin V. Mulcahy

American educational and cultural policy abroad has been described as the "neglected aspect" of this country's relations with the rest of the world. When Charles Frankel (soon to be Assistant Secretary of State for Educational and Cultural Affairs) made this observation in 1965, he was concerned with clarifying the objectives of government-supported cultural exchanges. He believed that American efforts in this field had been among the most successful of our diplomatic activities and that these cultural programs were "presumably planned with central objectives of national policy in mind."[1] But the question that Professor Frankel asked fifteen years ago still remains to be answered: "What are the objectives of government-sponsored educational and cultural programs abroad?"

Cultural programs are usually listed along with political and economic relations as part of the politics among nations. But specific goals and the means by which these are to be achieved are too often lost in either vague talk of promoting international good-will or in tactical considerations of how to use cultural programs for immediate political profit. Cultural programs have also been caught up in a wider debate about what properly characterizes cultural diplomacy. Basically, educational and cultural exchanges are part of the normal interactions and discussions between nations as are trade, travel, and immigration. As such, cultural exchanges stand on their own and should foster better relations within the family of nations (although not necessarily support for a nation's foreign policy). What the exchange programs seek to facilitate is a better understanding of American society by exposing other nationals to the diversity of cultural activities found here. In this sense, cultural programs (faculty and student exchanges, performing arts productions, museum shows, book exhibits, lectures) should be distinguished from those activities designed to explain

269

and defend American political objectives abroad or to
counteract Communist propaganda. The exchange programs
represent "cultural diplomacy" while the latter
activities are part of "informational diplomacy".

The distinction between these two diplomatic
activities has not always been clearly understood, and
has been even less often observed in practice. This
accounts for much of the confusion about the nature of
cultural diplomacy--its objectives and practices. Most
basically, exchanges must be distinguished from
"propaganda". Both are legitimate activities of
governments as they seek to project their interest
abroad. Propaganda has an admittedly negative
connotation, but as used here simply refers to the range
of information and psychological activities (such as
films, news stories and broadcasts) that seek to explain
to other people what American foreign policy is about.
Such informational diplomacy has an explicit, immediate
political content; cultural diplomacy does not: its
methods are indirect and its goals are long-range.
Informational diplomacy uses the techniques of public
relations (and sometimes psychological warfare) while
cultural diplomacy is rooted in education and example.
In effect, the premise of cultural diplomacy is that
allowing American cultural activities and leaders to
speak for themselves abroad is the best advertising for
the virtues of a free society. That the goal is
political--projecting a favorable image of American
society abroad--has been appreciated but that the
methods of cultural diplomacy--the free exchange of
ideas, events, and peoples--are nonpolitical has been
less well-understood and perhaps even less appreciated.

This chapter will examine the nature of cultural
diplomacy in general and the origins of American
cultural exchanges specifically. This will be followed
by an analysis of the various administrative agencies
that have been involved in this cultural sphere: the
Bureau of Educational and the Cultural Affairs, the
United States Information Agency, the International
Communication Agency. Some assessment will be offered
about the efficacy of the cultural exchanges in
diplomacy. The concluding section will offer some
recommendations about the administration of cultural
exchanges.

CULTURE AND FOREIGN POLICY

Cultural diplomacy is as old as relations among
different political systems. In ancient times both
Greece and Persia used culture as an aspect of their

warfare. The benefits of Roman civilization--its language, learning, order, prosperity, and amenities-- were a powerful tool in the conquest of Italy and of the greater part of the known world. To be a Roman was to participate in its cultural traditions, especially Latin language and literature. Roman citizenship was a prize that was eagerly sought by the empire's subjugated peoples and many of its ostensible enemies. As the empire expanded and matured, Rome came to indicate not just a geographic location but a universal cultural concept. A Roman was not one who resided on the banks of the Tiber but who participated in Latin culture. The preservation of a common cultural linkage became a powerful bond that held together the Roman empire's ethnically diverse members.

Since the nineteenth century, European nation-states have used culture as part of more general foreign relations. France was the first Western nation to create an extensive program of officially organized cultural relations involving extensive religious, educational, and philanthropic works especially in the Near and Far East. French cultural influence is still strong today in the Levant, in Indochina and in the former French colonies in Africa. Official cultural missions were supplemented by private organizations such as the <u>Alliance Francaise</u> which since 1883 has exported French language and culture through schools, books, and lectures.[2] That these efforts at disseminating French civilization were not entirely cultural in scope should be obvious. Supporters of "civilizing efforts" in the French colonies saw inculcating a love for the French language as a means of insuring political dominance.

Great Britain formally entered the field of cultural diplomacy in 1934 when the British Council was formed. The Council's official purpose was to "make British life and thought more widely known abroad, to encourage the study of the English language, and to render available abroad current British contributions to literature, science, [and] the fine arts." Such official activities followed the lead of private organizations such as the English Speaking Union and Rhodes Scholarship Society, groups which still seek to maintain close bonds between Britian, the Commonwealth countries, and former British colonies (one of which, of course, is the United States). Any supposed affinity among the "English speaking peoples," as Winston Churchill was disposed to claim, can be a bit farfetched. Yet, if Sir Winston is credited with having "mobilized the English language" to defend Britain during the bleakest period of World War II, it is perhaps more accurate to credit him with having secured the necessary support of the Dominions and the United States for the war effort. Appeals to a common cultural heritage and democratic political tradition, as well as emotional ties to what had been for some Americans, Canadians, Australians and New Zealanders an ancestral "home," also played a strong part in ensuring the alliance.

Culture has its uses as an instrument of foreign policy in ways other than the cultivation of ties among "close relatives" in the family of nations and the dissemination of national artistic products. As already indicated, cultural diplomacy has furthered colonialist ends as nations have used their civilizing mission, or some other form of the "white man's burden," to justify the occupation of foreign territories. Cultural colonialism has usually been associated with the French and British, as well as the Spanish and Portuguese, in Africa and Asia; but it has also been a European phenomenon as represented by the English in Ireland and the Hapsburg Empire among the Magyars and Slavs. The Nazi regime used cultural politics in a particularly aggressive manner to claim an identity among all German-speaking peoples regardless of nationality and to assert the cultural superiority of the so-called Aryan race over others, particularly the Slavs and Jews. Both peoples were branded as racially inferior (untermenschen); the Jews were to be exterminated culturally and physically; Slavs were to become slaves of their culturally-superior masters.

The Nazi regime has not been alone in the systematic appropriation of cultural symbols and ideas to further foreign-policy objectives. The Soviet Union seeks to create a favorable image abroad of "Soviet culture" and life in the U.S.S.R. and to assert its superiority to "bourgeois culture" and the values of Western democracies.[3] Frederick Barghoorn stresses this two-fold nature of Soviet cultural diplomacy.

> Its mission is not merely the positive one of projecting the aspects of Soviet reality selected by the Soviet authorities for domestic and foreign disclosure and glorification. It has, in addition, a negative mission of considerable significance, which consists in vituperative criticism of aspects of foreign cultures deemed to be incompatible with Soviet values, as well as censorship, distortion, or denial of positive aspects of bourgeois cultures which according to officially determined Soviet definitions of capitalism, are not supposed to exist.[4]

Much of this smacks of the Cold War rhetoric fashionable in academic circles two decades ago. However, there has been a growing skepticism about

Soviet foreign policy objectives. This skepticism has extended to Soviet cultural programs especially in view of the fate of dissident intellectuals such as Alexander Solzhenitsyn and Andrei Sakharov. While we need not become unduly suspicious of Bolshoi dancers, we might well inquire about the character of government-sponsored cultural exchanges in general.

AMERICAN CULTURAL EXCHANGES

The United States was late in establishing an official program of international cultural relations. The first American initiative in this field came as a response to Nazi Germany's "cultural offensive" in Latin America during the 1930's. The American government countered these propaganda activities at the Pan American Conference for the Maintenance of Peace in Buenos Aires in 1936 with a proposal for a Convention for the Promotion of Inter-American Cultural Relations. This convention (unanimously approved by the Conference on December 23, 1936) provided for the exchange of university professors, graduate students, and teachers under joint governmental sponsorship. The preamble to the Convention stated the following goals.

> Considering that the purpose for which the Conference was called would be advanced by greater mutual knowledge and understanding of the people and institutions of the countries represented and a more consistent educational solidarity on the American continent; and that such results would be appreciably promoted by an exchange of professors, teachers, and students among the American countries, as well as by encouragement of a closer relationship between unofficial organizations which exert an influence on the formation of public opinion . . . the Governments represented . . . have resolved to conclude a convention for that purpose. . . .[5]

Much of what characterized later American efforts in cultural diplomacy are presaged in this preamble. These characteristics are the following: exchanges were to strengthen cultural relations and intellectual cooperation between the United States and other nations; that the exchanges should be truly reciprocal in nature and should involve unofficial groups (for example, labor unions, youth groups, social services organizations); and, that the exchanges would promote better relations with other nations and the improvement of the American image abroad. On May 23, 1938, the State Department sponsored a meeting on Inter-American Cultural Cooperation to announce its intention to establish a Division of Cultural Relations. In their opening remarks, Department representatives described the purposes of the Division:

> . . . to provide Government leadership in initiating and conducting an organized, coordinated, long-term national effort to strengthen U.S. cultural relations with other countries, beginning with the countries of Latin America where a cultural treaty obligation was pending. The Department wanted to assure the group that it expected to rely on the private sector as the major partner in shaping policies for the new Department-sponsored program, and to be able to publicly announce from the outset that the decision to establish a Division of Cultural Relations in the Department was based on discussion with and approval by the major national philanthropic, educational, and cultural entities of the country. . . . The Department impressed on the group that because of the increasing tempo of Nazi inroads in Latin America, "time is of the essence."[6]

As in the Convention signed at Buenos Aires, the Meeting on Inter-American Cultural Cooperation stressed the long-term value of educational exchanges, the importance of participation by private groups, and the urgency necessitated by the international political situation. The cultural exchange program had decided political overtones. It sought to improve American foreign relations and originated as part of a larger effort to consolidate inter-American unity through a "Good Neighbor" policy. Moreover, these cultural exchanges were prompted by the perception of external threats from the German "cultural offensive" in the Americas described by cultural affairs officer, J. Manuel Espinosa, as "well organized and well-subsidized, and designed to counteract and weaken U.S. cultural relationships with the Latin American countries and discredit U.S. motives and purposes in the area."[7] Thus, cultural propaganda was to be fought with cultural exchanges. From the beginning then American cultural diplomacy was judged according to two, not necessarily complementary, standards. On the one hand, cultural programs were conceived as essentially nonpolitical and concerned with the promotion of mutual understanding among nations. On the other hand, the programs were

seen as instrumental in consolidating a country's
international political objectives. The use of cultural
assets was thus comparable to, if not equal to, the use
of economic and military advantages.

Cultural diplomacy is certainly not the only public
policy that has been judged by more than one standard.
Nor is it unusual in politics for narrow goals to be
justified in terms of lofty abstract principles. The
exchange programs, however, have been marked by sharp
conflicts between practices and principles--largely the
result of rhetorical justifications for international
exchanges as purely altruistic in motivation. At the
first meeting of the newly formed Advisory Commission on
Educational Exchange in September, 1948, its chairman,
B. Harvie Branscomb (Chancellor of Vanderbilt
University), asserted that the argument for international exchanges did not rest on considerations of
political gain or national interest. He declared:

> It will be by cooperation among those nations
> and peoples who believe the spiritual
> heritages of the races are worth preserving
> that the present difficulties will be overcome
> and the problems of our times
> resolved. . . . The program of educational and
> cultural exchange--not cultural penetration--
> rests then on a simple and familiar
> principle. Neighbors who are to cooperate
> need to become acquainted. In the modern
> world all nations are neighbors, and all need
> to cooperate. . . .[8]

A 1963 U. S. Advisory Commission report entitled A
Beacon of Hope also warned against associating
educational and cultural exchanges with political
activities. "If we were to make the mistake of suppos-
ing that the primary purpose of the exchange program is
to serve narrow political ends, the effectiveness of the
whole program would be seriously undermined. It is not
that kind of program, and in imagining it to be so we
would defeat our own ends. . . ."[9] Despite these
disclaimers the exchange program was, of course,
involved with politics if only because it was sponsored
and funded by the government. In 1942 Undersecretary of
State Sumner Welles posed the following question:
"Should a true cultural relations program be used to
implement the foreign policy of any one country; or
should it provide a vehicle for the interchange of ideas
and the deepening of understanding in order to aid
people in the determination of their destiny?"[10] The
answer to this largely rhetorical query is both.
Cultural exchanges are an aspect of foreign relations
although the benefits sought would be better

thought of as being realized in the long-run rather than immediately.

The exchanges are not useful for realizing pressing political objectives but they may help to educate other people about the freedom of expression found in an open, pluralist society. Such an educational process usually has a longer perspective than most programs and yields more indirect returns in positive attitudes toward American values. Henry Kellerman makes this point very forcefully. "Fundamentally humanitarian and avowedly 'nonpolitical,' the educational and cultural relations sponsored by the Department of State was established because international communication and understanding through cooperative person-to-person relations was considered to be a necessary aspect of foreign relations."[11] This is not to deny the importance of "mutual understanding" as a goal in itself. The "person-to-person" relationships cultivated through exchange programs can create a reservoir of good will among its participants and those with whom they communicate. (But not always. Nkrumah of Ghana and Gotzpadegh of Iran had distinctly unpleasant impressions of American society as students which colored their foreign policies concerning the United States in later years.) The U.S. Advisory Commission on Educational Exchanges argued this in the following statement issued in 1949.

> The firm friendship between the United States and the other American republics is due in part to the individual friends that we and the Latin American countries have made through the exchange of persons program. By exchanging representative individuals, the United States and the other countries have given each other a chance to know the good and the bad about each other.[12]

The Advisory Commission's claim is admittedly limited and much has happened since the statement was issued to raise questions about the degree of U.S.-Latin American amity. More fundamental questions could be raised about the actual effectiveness of people-to-people programs for creating understanding where none previously existed. It could be that educational and cultural exchanges serve to reinforce opinion among elites which are already favorably disposed. Exchanges, like exposure to other cultures generally, can also serve to diminish certain national stereotypes, give judgments a real-world basis, and provide experiential references for those who influence public opinion. What the exchange programs have never been is politically disinterested; they have almost always arisen as a response to international political crises. The "inter-American beginnings of U.S. cultural diplomacy" were a response to pre-World War II German initiatives. The Cold War that commenced in the late 1940's between the United States and the Soviet Union further politicized the exchanges programs as these were seen increasingly as part of a "Campaign of Truth" to counter Soviet propaganda.

> The purpose of the campaign was to strengthen the unity of the free nations and to emphasize the coincidence of their interests with those of the United States; to build up the image of the United States as an enlightened and strong power; and to develop and maintain psychological resistance to Soviet propaganda against the United States.[13]

These are valid foreign policy objectives. The problem, however, is whether the "instrumentalities of culture" are well-used in such efforts. Commenting on the use of educational and cultural exchanges as part of the war-effort against Germany, Ben Cherrington, the first director of the State Department's Division of Cultural Relations (and long-time Director of the Foundation for the Advancement of the Social Sciences at the University of Denver), noted that such a practice can have undesirable consequences for a program of cultural relations. "As time went on, the distinction between unilateral propaganda on the one hand and reciprocal cultural cooperation on the other hand, so clearly perceived and adhered to in the previous years, became increasingly blurred."[14]

THE ADMINISTRATION OF CULTURAL EXCHANGES

The administrative unit of the State Department responsible for cultural relations went through a variety of reorganizations and name changes in its forty year history (1938-78). The most familiar bureaucratic designation is Bureau of Educational and Cultural Affairs (or CU--an abbreviation for cultural). CU was always something of an anomaly in the State Department as the frequent reorganizations and name changes would suggest. Cultural relations were most often subordinated to whichever foreign policy operation was important at the time. Rhetorical flourishes to the contrary, cultural exchanges as a vehicle for mutual understanding were rarely judged to be useful in themselves.

The nascent Division of Cultural Relations was quickly absorbed into the war-effort after Pearl Harbor. In 1942 the Division's cultural information programs were accelerated and, at the same time, subordinated to vast wartime agencies--particularly the Office of War Information and, its Latin American counterpart, the Office of the Coordinator of Inter-American Affairs. Under Nelson Rockefeller's direction the latter had responsibility for "cultural and commercial relations affecting Hemisphere defense." There was also a more systematic organization of the cultural relations program with the appointment of cultural officers in U.S. embassies to implement the Division's program. By the close of 1943, cultural officers held appointments in twenty-two nations: twenty Latin American countries and in Spain and Turkey (both important neutrals). The first full-time cultural officer was appointed to China in 1945, although a cultural exchange program was initiated with China almost immediately after the American declaration of war.[15] By the end of 1945, eight more appointments had been made: two in the Middle East (Syria and Egypt) and six in Europe (Belgium, France, Greece, Holland, Italy and Portugal).[16] The major program activities of the Division of Cultural Relations were those involving the exchange of professors, students, group leaders and subject-area specialists. The Division of Cultural Relations "played a large and important policy and facilitative role both in the United States and abroad with regard to radio broadcasting and programming, motion pictures, books and translations, art and music activities, cultural institutes, U.S. libraries, American-sponsored schools, technical training projects, and related programs. . . ."[17] The director of the CU History Project summarized the effectiveness of these programs as follows:

> The accomplishments of the Division of Cultural Relations during the period from Pearl Harbor until the end of the war were quite impressive both strengthening the broad and continuing goals of the program as pursued since the late 1930's, and in reducing Axis influence in Latin America countries. The Department of State was at the center of the total war effort, and the Division was the focal point in the Department in coordinating the cultural relations activities of the various permanent war emergency agencies involved in one way or another in such activities.[18]

The most significant cultural relations activity
that came out of the war effort was not, however, in the
areas previously discussed. With Germany's
unconditional surrender in April, 1945, the United
States exercised, jointly with France, the U.K., and the
U.S.S.R., supreme governmental authority. The cultural
programs in Occupied Germany were part of a total
military, political, and economic operation which could
be implemented by force, if necessary, to assure
compliance with official U.S. policy.

> It is worth remembering that although the
> exchange program was eventually absorbed by
> the worldwide cultural exchange program of the
> Department of State, based on the principle of
> reciprocity, the German program started out as
> a unilateral American-initiated, American-
> funded, and American-directed implement of
> United States policy serving primarily United
> States interests, first under the aegis of the
> Office of U.S. Military Governments (OMGUS)
> and subsequently of the Office of the
> U.S. High Commission (HICOG).[19]

The cultural exchange program conducted by the
United States in occupied Germany in the late 1940's and
early 1950's defies comparison with any other exchanges
(except in occupied Austria and Japan). Most
fundamentally, it was not conducted in the true spirit
of an exchange; in place of reciprocity and mutuality,
there was re-education. Its goal was not to share
cultural experiences but to create a new German society
modeled on Western democratic concepts. The entire
apparatus of military and civilian control was harnessed
to reorient the German people toward a democratic
system. In this case, cultural exchanges were
explicitly used as instruments of foreign policy. The
immediate objective was to demilitarize German society
and restore it to the family of nations. This was a
unique case in the use of cultural diplomacy.

> Here was a case without precedent. For the
> first time in modern history a victor used the
> vast range of his cultural resources and the
> potential of his citizens in a common and
> contributing effort to assist the vanquished
> in rebuilding his national institutions and
> his relations with the entire world. . . . To
> many Americans, even when allowing for the
> accommodation of certain political objectives
> in U.S. exchange policy, the use of
> educational and cultural exchanges as an
> instrument of occupation policy serving the

political, economic, social, cultural, and
even military aspects of U.S. policy, and
performing a highly interventionist function
in the internal affairs of another country,
may have meant to flout the established and
pronounced principles of U.S. cultural
exchanges.[20]

After the initial policies of deNazification of
German social, cultural, educational, and political
institutions and the prosecution of war criminals, the
American military government emphasized that Germany's
"physical, political and cultural reconstruction" was a
prerequisite for European recovery. A directive to the
Commander-in-Chief of the U.S. Forces of Occupation (JCS
1779), issued on July 15, 1947, ordered that "the re-
education of the German people is an integral part of
policies intended to help develop a democratic form of
government and to restore a stable and peaceful
economy."[21]

This reeducation of Germany was conceived as an
instrument of U.S. foreign policy. German aggression
would be less likely in the future if a new Germany
could be built on a foundation of democratic values,
attitudes, and institutions. The following excerpt from
a 1949 letter written by Acting Secretary of State James
E. Webb to the Military Government's Cultural and
Educational Adviser, Herman B. Wells (president of
Indiana University) summarizes the goals that were to be
pursued in the reeducation of the German people.

The Department has recognized quite early and
has so stated that the task of educating the
German people away from authoritarianism and
aggression and toward democracy and peace
remains the hardest and longest of all our
responsibilities in Germany and, in the long
run, the most decisive. The United States
Government would have failed the American
people no less than the democratic elements in
Germany in their justified hope for lasting
security, if this task were to be regarded as
consummated with establishment of a government
by democratic processes, and if it desisted
from further efforts to advise and assist the
German people in the proper and effective use
of their new freedom and of the democratic
institutions and tools which it helped provide
for them.[22]

Dr. Wells saw these goals as best realized through
the exchange process; he favored Germans going to the
United States. "The selection of persons who might

qualify extended across all sectors of cultural, professional, and civic life, with preference given to those concerned with educational, religious, scientific, informational, and cultural affairs, such as students, teachers, religious leaders, and young administrators in education and religion."[23] In the period 1945-1954 (when full bilateralism was established in the cultural exchange program) more than twelve thousand Germans and two thousand Americans participated in what was the largest educational and cultural exchange program undertaken by the U.S. government. The emphasis on intellecutals was rooted in the belief that twelve years of Nazi rule had effectively stultified the free expression of ideas in Germany. The exchange program would serve to restimulate the circulation of ideas and reorient the thinking of German intellectual leaders and the generation of young Germans beginning their education. Of course, it was also believed that these intellectual leaders would be in a position to influence German public opinion to accept a pro-American viewpoint.[24]

The immediate post-World War II years saw not only an unprecedented use of cultural exchanges to reeducate occupied countries but a reorganization and reformulation of exchanges as part of the conduct of foreign affairs. In 1945 President Truman transferred the international information functions of the two wartime propaganda agencies, the Office of War Information and the Office of the Coordinator of Inter-American Affairs, to the State Department. These functions were combined with those of the Division of Cultural Relations to form the Office of International Information and Cultural Affairs (OIC) renamed a year later as the Office of International Information and Educational Exchange (OIE). This office reported to the Assistant Secretary of State for Public Affairs.[25]

Shortly after this reorganization, the Fulbright Act (Public Law 79-584) was passed. Introduced by Senator J. William Fulbright of Arkansas, the act sought to promote international understanding through a binationally administered program of academic exchange. The Department of State was authorized to enter into executive agreements with foreign governments and to use foreign currencies acquired through the sale of U.S. war surplus left in various countries to finance academic exchanges. The Fulbright Program, as it became known, was an immediate success and has continued to be immensely popular with students, teachers, and host institutions.[26] It was widely applauded as a fitting humanitarian gesture and it reflected widespread optimism about the international amity that would reign in the post-war world.

After 1947 initial post-war optimism gave way to a greater wariness in international relations. The Cold

War provided the context within which Congress extended authorization for the international educational and cultural program with the passage of the United States Information and Educational Exchange Act of 1948 (Public Law 80-402). Called the Smith-Mundt Act after its sponsors, this legislation committed the United States government for its first peacetime commitment "to conduct international information, education, and cultural exchange activities on a worldwide, long-term scale" in order "to promote a better understanding of the United States in other countries, and to increase mutual understanding between the people of the United States and the people of other countries." What prompted this campaign was fear about threats to U.S. security abroad and Soviet propaganda as part of those threats. The legislative mandate that the exchange programs seek "to promote a better understanding of the United States" was in fact a commitment for their use, especially the information program, as "a hard-hitting propaganda campaign in response to that of the Soviets."[27]

Pursuant of the Smith-Mundt Act, the cultural division was once again reorganized. (The various reorganizations discussed here are summarized chronologically in Table 12.1.) Two offices were created: the Office of Educational Exchange (OEX) and the Office of International Information (OII). OEX was assigned the Division of International Exchange of Persons and the Division of Libraries and Institutes; OII was assigned Press and Publications, Broadcasting, and Motion Pictures. In 1952 these two offices were consolidated into a shortlived semi-autonomous organization within the State Department, the International Information Adminsitration with the International Educational Exchange Service constituting one of its five divisions (The other four were libraries, press and publications, broadcasting, motion pictures.).[28] While all these reorganizations may seem like so much bureau shuffling, it also involved important issues for cultural diplomacy. Should the "educational and cultural exchange" programs be administered along with the "information media" programs? Did not the former aiming at international understanding have a long-range perspective while the latter was essentially public relations (propaganda) seeking short-run political successes? What kind of administrative arrangement was best suited for the conduct of cultural diplomacy?

One answer came at the beginning of the Eisenhower Administration with a major organizational change recommended by Secretary of State John Foster Dulles and the President's Advisory Commission on Governmental

TABLE 12.1
Organizational History of the State Department Bureau
of Educational and Cultural Affairs, 1938-78.

1938-44	Division of Cultural Relations[a]
1944-46	Division of Cultural Cooperation[b]
1946-47	Office of International Information and Cultural Affairs (OIC)
1947-48	Office of International Information and Educational Exchange (OIE)[b]
1948	Passage of Smith-Mundt Act
1948-52	Office of Educational Exchange (OEX)[b]
1952-53	International Information Administration[b]
1953	Creation of United States Information Agency (USIA)
1953-58	International Educational Exchange Service (IES)[b]
1958-61	Bureau of International Cultural Relations (CU)[c]
1961	Passage of Fulbright-Hays Act
1961	Appointment of Assistant Secretary for Educational Cultural Affairs
1961-78	Bureau of Educational and Cultural Affairs (CU)
1978	Creation of the International Communication Agency (ICA)

Source: Adapted from J. Manuel Espinosa, Landmark
Events in the History of CU (Washington, D.C.:
Department of State, Bureau of Educational and Cultural
Affairs, 1973), pp. 15-18.

[a]Supervised by the Under Secretary of State through the Assistant Secretary responsible for administrative and budgetary matters.

[b]Under the supervision of the Assistant Secretary for Public Affairs.

[c]Supervised by the Special Assistant to the Secretary for International Cultural Relations (with the rank of Assistant Secretary)

Organization (the Rockefeller Commission). Reorganization Plan No. 8, submitted to Congress on June 1, 1953, created the United States Information Agency (USIA) as an agency operationally independent of the State Department (although receiving policy guidance from it) and transferred to it all of the activities of the

International Information Service except those of the
International Educational Exchange Service. IES (and
the UNESCO National Commission staff) remained in the
State Department under the Assistant Secretary for
Public Affairs. However, under an agreement signed on
June 24, 1955 between the State Department and USIA, the
administration of exchange programs overseas was
assigned to USIA. The exchange of persons program
remained in the State Department only because of the
recommendation of a committee chaired by Senator Bourke
Hickenlooper (R-Iowa) that this would avoid "giving the
educational exchange of persons a propaganda flavor."

This reorganization provided partial answers to
some of the questions posed above but not ones that were
satisfactory--either politically or administratively.
Indeed, the Rockefeller Commission later reversed itself
and recommended that the functions of CU and USIA be
combined and placed in the State Department under an
Under Secretary for International Cultural and
Information Affairs. While this plan never
materialized, a separate Bureau of International
Cultural Relations was formed in 1958 with
responsibility for exchange programs and other functions
(including the UNESCO staff) which had been in the
Bureau of Public Affairs. That same year Robert
H. Thayer was named Special Assistant to the Secretary
of State for International Cultural Relations. CU was
further strengthened when President Kennedy appointed
Philip H. Coombs (Program Director for Education at the
Ford Foundation) as the first Assistant Secretary of
State for Educational and Cultural Affairs in 1961.

The 1950's had not been a good decade for the
cultural exchange program. After initial successes
during World War II in Latin America and after the war
in Germany, cultural exchanges were downplayed as USIA's
more aggressive programs came to characterize the
period. Educational and cultural affairs were not
deemed as important in foreign policy-making. Indifference to these activities left the program without clear
policy guidance and requests for funds were given low
priorities in departmental budgets allocations and by
appropriations committees.[29] As hard-hitting ideological
warfare with a concern for immediate impact was relaxed,
the value of the more subtle approach of the exchange
program--even with its longer time perspective--was
better appreciated. Two new efforts in cultural
diplomacy testified to this shift in emphasis. One was
the State Department's sponsorship in 1958 of a cultural
presentations program under the International Cultural
Exchange and Trade Fair Participation Act. The other
was the creation of the East-West Center at the
University of Hawaii (formally the Center for Cultural
and Technical Interchange Between East and West) and

funded by CU "to promote better relations between the
United States and the nations of Asia and the Pacific
through cooperative study, training, and research."
    Most significant of all for strengthening the
exchange program was the passage of the Mutual
Educational and Cultural Exchange Act (PL 87-256),
called the Fulbright-Hays Act for its sponsors, Senator
J. William Fulbright and Representative Brooks Hays
(both of Arkansas). The Fulbright-Hays Act states its
objectives as follows:

> The purpose of this Act is to enable the
> Government of the United States to increase
> mutual understanding between . . . countries
> by means of educational and cultural exchange;
> to strengthen the ties which unite with other
> nations by demonstrating the educational and
> cultural interests, developments, and
> achievements of the people of the United
> States and nations . . . to promote
> international cooperation for educational and
> cultural advancement; and thus to assist in
> the development of friendly, sympathetic, and
> peaceful relations between the United States
> and the countries of the world.

This legislation gave the exchange program a new
mandate. "The Act, in effect, restored international
educational and cultural exchange programs as a
recognized area of our official foreign relations."[30]
    While the Fulbright-Hays Act may have symbolized a
new era for the cultural exchange program, it did not
settle the administrative and policy anomalies that
typified the exchange program. Administratively CU was
a specialized functional division within the State
Department; it was similar to the Bureau of Oceans and
International Environmental and Scientific Affairs or
the Bureau of International Organizations Affairs (to
which the UNESCO staff had been transferred in the early
1970's). The Bureau was managed by an assistant
secretary usually of some political or professional
distinction such as Harry McPherson (1964-65) who went
on to become a powerful White House aide and Charles
Frankel who was a distinguished philosophy professor at
Columbia University. Assistant Secretary Philip Coombs
(1961-62) had been an economics professor and Ford
Foundation official, and the earlier post of Assistant
Secretary for Public and Cultural Affairs (1944-45) was
held by poet Archibald MacLeish, the former Librarian of
Congress.
    The Bureau was also administered by three deputy
assistant secretaries, an office of the Executive
Director, and an Office of Policy and Plans. Among

various advisory commissions, the most important has been the U.S. Advisory Commission on International Educational and Cultural Affairs--nine presidential appointees who recommend exchange policies and appraise the program's effectiveness. The operating responsibilities of the Bureau centered around facilitating various types of personal exchange between nations. These included: International Visitors Program (sponsoring foreign leaders coming to the United States); Youth, Student, and Special Programs (exchanges involving secondary school and college students, and young professionals and political leaders); and International Athletic Programs (involving the exchanges of coaches and teams). The Bureau also provided staff support to the Board of Foreign Scholarship in the conduct of the worldwide academic exchange program. The Office of International Arts Affairs encouraged museum exchanges and assisted performing arts groups in touring abroad.

Essentially, CU provided personal contact between individuals in the United States and other nations--particularly leaders (or leaders-to-be) of influential groups. It could thus be argued that the Bureau of Educational and Cultural Affairs was not really a foreign policy agency since it was a step removed from immediate political considerations. USIA, on the other hand, was decidedly political. It was designed to defend U.S. foreign policy and to explain life in the United States to other countries. The Information Agency was "to tell America's story to the world" (for example, through the Voice of America which has accounted for about thirty percent of USIA's budget), but not within the United States where USIA was forbidden to operate. (Congress did not wish the American people to be "propagandized.") USIA was meant to be a public relations agency for the American government in dealing with foreign nations. CU would facilitate the exchange of people and artistic exhibits which would "speak for themselves" without political editorializing. It was meant to be an "International Endowment for the Arts and Humanities" exporting culture abroad. In other words, there was a distinction between information and culture with the political USIA engaged in advocacy and the nonpolitical CU working to create understanding. CU's cultural diplomacy rested on an implicit assumption that, as nations better understand each other, they would be more favorably disposed to the United States and its international objectives.

While too much can be made of CU's "nonpolitical" character, it was a widely articulated self-description. "Our program is to promote international goodwill and understanding." "We don't have a national policy on culture and I don't believe that we should." "I don't

like to use the word 'image' in what we want to
represent overseas. We try to facilitate
understanding." "It's good propaganda because it isn't
propaganda."[31] These are sentiments that were typically
expressed by CU officials and, even allowing for what is
considered an appropriate response, they reflect
sincerely-held beliefs. Cultural exchange officials do
assert a difference between what they do and what is
done by the information programs. But this is off the
mark. Even the strongest defenders of the "purity" of
cultural exchanges as a value in themselves also claimed
their "pragmatic" worth in promoting a more sympathetic
understanding of the United States. On the other hand,
better understanding need not necessarily involve good
will and better understanding does not necessarily
translate into political support if there are conflicts
of interest and goals.

That the exchange program has pragmatic (if not
immediate) foreign policy objectives should not be
surprising--even to the cultural exchange purists. But
what the program lacked was clear policy guidance,
programmatic direction, and organizational mission.
From 1953 the mechanisms of cultural diplomacy suffered
from severe structural weaknesses.[32] First, there was a
major anomaly in the policymaking process. CU,
supposedly removed from international political
considerations, was located in the State Department
while USIA, which was directly involved in international
politics, was outside the Department. Second, the
organizational split between CU and USIA "seemed to
imply that USIA's dissemination of information abroad
about U.S. society was not related to CU's efforts to
build understanding of the United States overseas."
Third, USIA and CU activities became increasingly
similar as the information programs took on a longer-
range perspective--that is, one that was less concerned
with immediate political objectives. Fourth, the
administrative arrangement whereby CU programs were
executed overseas by USIA officials was organizationally
illogical.

Senatorial insistence ensured that the cultural
exchange programs remained in the State Department to
help keep them distinct from USIA "propaganda." USIA
administration of these programs abroad would presumably
not taint them since these would be embassy activities
under State Department supervision. But not only did
this deprive CU of control over its own overseas
programs, it required USIA officials who did administer
these programs to be both engaged defenders of American
foreign policies and detached supporters of
international understanding.

Twenty-five years of administrative confusion was
supposed to be rationalized with the creation of the

International Communication Agency (USICA) on April 1, 1978 by authority of Reorganization Plan No. 2 of 1977. The International Communications Agency, and the seven-member U.S. Advisory Commission on International Communications, Cultural and Educational Affairs, consolidated the functions of USIA and CU; USICA also has the task of reporting to the President and Secretary of State on worldwide public opinion as it is relevant to the conduct of U.S. foreign policy. As with the old USIA, the International Communications Agency is independent of the State Department. The goals of USICA are to tell the world about American society and U.S. policies, in particular the commitment to cultural diversity and individual liberty that exists in the United States. President Carter summarized the major objectives of the agency as follows:

> Give foreign peoples the best possible understanding of our policies and our intentions, and sufficient information about American society and culture to comprehend why we have chosen certain policies over others.
>
> Help insure that our Government adequately understands foreign public opinion and culture for policymaking purposes, and to assist individual Americans and institutions in learning about other nations and cultures.
>
> To prepare for and conduct negotiations on cultural exchanges with other governments, aware always that the most effective sharing of culture ideas and information comes between individual people rather than through formal acts of governments.[33]

About one-third of the International Communications budget of approximately $425 million (FY 81) goes into each of these areas--that is, the exchange programs, information activities, and the Voice of America (VOA). Table 12.2 summarizes the organization of the International Communications Agency with its program area and principal offices.

The educational and cultural exchanges fall into the following categories:

Academic. The Fulbright Program involves the annual exchange of approximately 2,000 U.S. and foreign pre-doctoral students and 1,600 professors, senior scholars and researchers. (There is also an exchange of about 800 elementary and secondary school teachers sponsored by the Department of Education.) The academic exchange program is supervised by a twelve-member, presidentially-appointed Board of Foreign Scholarships.

TABLE 12.2
Organization of the International Communication Agency

Director---Advisory Commission in International
   Communication, Cultural and Educational Affairs

Deputy Director; General Counsel; Director, Office of
   Congressional and Public Liaison; Executive
   Secretariat.

Associate Director for Broadcasting (VOA)
   Deputy Associate Director
   Director, Office of Programs
   Director, Office of Administration
   Director, Office of Engineering and Technical
   Operations

Associate Director for Programs
   Deputy Associate Director
   Director, Office of Program Coordination
    and Development
   Director of Television and Film Service
   Director of Press and Publication Service
   Director of Exhibits Service
   Coordinator, Foreign Press Centers

Associate Director for Educational and Cultural Affairs
    ---Board of Foreign Scholarships; East-West Center
   Deputy Associate Director
   Director, Office of Cultural Centers and Resources
   Director, Office of Institutional Relations
   Director, Office of Academic Programs

Associate Director for Management
   Deputy Associate Director
   Director, Office of Administrative Services
   Director, Office of Comptroller Services
   Chief, Office of Inspections
   Director, Office of Equal Employment Opportunity
   Chief, Office of Audits

5 Regional Directors: Africa; American Republics; East
Asia and Pacific; North Africa, Near East, South Asia

Source: U.S. Government Manual (Washington, D.C.:
Government Printing Office, 1980)

Foreign Leaders. U.S. Chiefs of Missions extend invitations to foreign leaders in government, labor, mass media, science, education, among other fields, to visit their counterparts in the United States. Almost 500 foreign leaders visit annually; local hospitality is arranged by volunteers associated with the National Council for International Visitors.

American Specialists. In response to specific requests from abroad, American experts (about 200 annually) participate in conferences with their counterparts abroad.

Performing Arts. Major companies in the fields of music, drama, and dance are assisted in touring abroad (for example, as part of the U.S.-U.S.S.R. Exchange Agreement) and museums are assisted with loans and travelling exhibits.

Grants-In-Aid. Financial awards are made to private organizations whose work abroad serves to facilitate U.S. government objectives of mutual understanding. In recent years, there have been about 225 such awards annually totalling about $10 million.

East-West Center. An autonomous agency at the University of Hawaii, the Center for Cultural and Technical Interchange between East and West received about $15 million from the ICA in 1981. All of these exchange programs have as their purpose "to give citizens of other countries a better sense of what the United States stands for and why, and to give the American people a more accurate idea of their neighbors across national boundaries."[34]

CULTURAL EXCHANGES AND CULTURAL DIPLOMACY

When proposals were made in 1939 for appointing cultural attaches to administer the activities abroad of the newly created Division of Cultural Relations, Assistant Secretary of State George S. Messersmith reacted negatively. He said:

There are certain totalitarian states which, as you know, are very anxious to appoint cultural attaches . . . They are no more than poorly concealed political agents, most of them acting along subversive lines . . . Tentative efforts have been made by the totalitarian states to send cultural attaches to the American republics . . . If we were to send cultural attaches there and they were received, the American Republics would similarly have to receive cultural attaches

from Italy, Germany, etc. . . . From the
political standpoint, therefore, the
consideration of the appointment of cultural
attaches is out of the question.[34]

While Messersmith's arguments were persuasive at
the time, the policy was reversed in 1941 when cultural
relations officers, later called cultural affairs
officers but never officially "cultural attaches," were
appointed to serve in foreign missions. These officers
were to be the princpal liaison with all aspects of
cultural, intellectual, and educational life in the
country to which they were assigned. Many of the early
cultural officers were distinguished scholars on
temporary assignment with the State Department, as well
as career diplomats. The tradition of appointing
cultural officers from the academic world has persisted
throughout the program's history. For example,
Dr. George Vaillant, archaeologist and director of the
University of Pennsylvania Museum, served in Peru from
1943-44; Dr. Margaret Clapp, president of Wellesley
College for seventeen years, served in India from 1968
to 1971; Dr. Joseph Palombara, chairman of the
Political Science Department at Yale University, was the
cultural affairs officer in Italy from 1978 to 1980.

While the style "cultural affairs officer" rather
than "cultural attache" may have been merely a matter of
official usage, the distinction between cultural affairs
officer (CAO) and public affairs officer (PAO) was more
than nominal. The distinction was rooted in the 1953
administrative reorganization whereby the cultural and
educational exchange programs remained in the State
Department but their overseas administration was a task
for the United States Information Agency. (Part of what
was termed a "Rube Goldberg" administrative system
whereby USIA reported directly to the President but
received policy guidance from the Secretary of State.)
In a medium-size mission, for example, the Public
Affairs Officer would be a senior official (sometimes
with the diplomatic designation of Counselor)
responsible for a section of the embassy known as the
United States Information Service. Under the PAO's
supervision, cultural and informational activities were
directed by a CAO and IO (or Information Officer) of
equal administrative rank. The IO would be responsible
for all media-related activities (such as press
releases, film and tape distribution) while the CAO
would be responsible for the State Department's exchange
of persons program, a library, and a binational cultural
center. One former CAO adds the following
responsibilities:

> The role of the cultural attache may be
> regarded as that of a catalyst in the cross-
> fertilization of ideas between the academic,
> artistic, and intellectual comunities of the
> United States and his country of assignment.
> This may involve hearing and giving lectures,
> attending concerts and art exhibits; making
> American cultural values better known wherever
> he is while tracking down the sources of the
> most significant intellecutal activity that is
> taking place in the country during his
> presence therein.[35]

Many cultural officers were said to have rankled
under the statutory arrangements that made them
responsible to the State Department for policy-guidance
and sense of purpose while administratively subordinate
to USIA. There may also have been a certain measure of
distaste at the intermingling of the cultural exchange
programs with the Information Service's "propaganda."[36]
The creation of the International Communication Agency
ended the administrative cross-purposes resulting from
the division of functions between CU and USIA. ("Former
USIA Director George Allen once said that only the U.S.
government could invent a system under which one agency
sends the fiddler abroad and another the fiddle."[37])
But what about propaganda? Essentially, all public
information personnel--whether CU, USIA, or USICA--are
engaged in activities which, however different in
emphases, methods, and time perspectives, are intended
to inform and influence foreign public opinion. If one
defines propaganda as "any organized or concerted group
effort or movement to spread a particular doctrine or
system of doctrine or principles" (Webster's New
International Dictionary, 2nd ed.), then all the
cultural relations programs can be judged propaganda
since they are desinged to promote the U.S. government's
foreign policy goals. But, using this standard,
could not all political argument be placed under the
rubric of propaganda? And would that be accurate?

American exchange programs are sensitive to
political currents and reflect broad goals of
international politics. This has been so despite the
misguided (if well-meaning and deeply-felt) claims of
the advocates of cultural exchanges that these programs
are nonpolitical and should be kept administratively
separate from the information programs lest they be
"contaminated by propaganda." Whatever may be the wisdom
of the U.S. government's military, economic, or diplomatic actions, it has a right to explain itself and to
make its motives clear to people abroad. Members of the
international community can make what judgments they
will about the information received. The exchange pro-

gram represents another aspect of American foreign policy that exists quite independent of its short-range political undertakings: the belief that the values of a democratic political system, with free institutions and a pluralistic culture, will speak for themselves to visitors from abroad. This is not to suggest that the American domestic situation is without flaw, nor does it necessarily mean that all will react favorably to its values, let alone be persuaded to offer international political support. What the exchange programs do assert is that a government has the right, if not an obligation, to promote greater understanding about its cultural life in hopes that such familiarity will at least diminish stereotypes if not produce friendship. Charles Frankel summarizes this perspective very well.

> It may be taken for granted, then, that the promotion of "good will" and understanding among nations is a legitimate and necessary objective of United States foreign policy . . . And it is also reasonable to assume, in general, that programs to promote personal contact and communication among selected citizens of different nations are instruments that can further the achievement of this objective . . . Bad will and misunderstanding are often encouraged by the simple fact that relations between the members of different nations are not immediate and personal, but vicarious and impersonal. In such circumstances, powerful stereotypes take over . . . In this respect, there is solid warrant for the belief that educational and cultural exchanges are important instruments for the promotion of international good will and understanding.[38]

> The United States as a nation and a member of world civilization has an unquestionable interest in educational and cultural programs abroad. It has this interest in part because such programs contribute to a more favorable American "image" and make it more likely that United States political policies will succeed. But it has this interest as well because American educational, scholarly, and cultural resources can make an important contribution to the well-being and enjoyment of life of people elsewhere, and to the stability and peacefulness of their societies. And it also has this interest because other people's intellecutal and artistic achievements are

sources from which the United States can draw
strength and guidance. In this context,
international educational and cultural
programs are tools of United States national
policy.[39]

Some of the rhetoric will doubtless strike the
"tough-minded and realistic" among foreign policy
analysts as excessive if not a bit naive. But for all
the rhetoric of a "better world through better
understanding," Frankel's main argument is clear.
Cultural exchanges can create a better impression of the
United States in other nations as well as provide
valuable insights for Americans about others, and these
are important aspects of foreign policy-making. The
goal is to let others see the United States as it is.
Consequently, there is no official policy about what is
an appropriate American image as befits a culturally-
heterogeneous society.

The result is to make cultural diplomacy an
extremely sensitive activity. It must not seek to
manipulate opinion nor to pander to the most recent
political "line." This suggests less emphasis on
"telling America's story to the world" (and none of the
stridency of the 1950's "campaign for truth") and
greater emphasis on mutuality and solving common
problems. Cultural diplomats who have imersed
themselves in the language, history, art, and literature
of the country to which they are assigned should attempt
to communicate this knowldege to their colleagues in the
embassy and in Washington. Such an understanding can be
an important source of insight into matters of long-term
development. An awareness of the possible impact of
social and cultural forces, especially in non-Western
nations, is an aspect of international politics with
which foreign policy-makers seem surprisingly
unknowledgeable (at least judging by recent occurrences
in the Middle East, particularly in Iran).

The cultural diplomat can thus contribute to
framing short-range policy as well as providing a long-
range perspective. This should satisfy those who want
to see some results for the money spent on cultural
relations. But cultural diplomacy is still properly
concerned with understanding rather than political
success. The basis for exchanges is the assumption that
those who participate will come away with a better sense
of American society and institutions. They aim at
establishing a network of interconnections among
educational, cultural, and political leaders that should
be marked by mutual respect and balanced
judgments.[40] Frankel makes an interesting analogy
between trade relations and cultural relations.

When societies are tied together by extensive
commercial relations and are economically
interdependent, there is no guarantee that
they will not come into conflict with each
other. But a practical deterrent to runaway
conflict has been constructed, and modes of
cooperation have been created that may survive
the ebb and flow of emotions and events. The
potentialities of educational and cultural
cooperation in this direction are probably
even greater than the value of trade
relations.[41]

It is interesting that cultural and commercial relations
were the first steps in the normalization of relations
with China paving the way for formalized diplomatic
relations and political discussions.
     The other side of the exchange mechanism is the
value that Americans gain from exposure to the cultures
of other nations. It can produce a greater sensitivity
to other cultural values and awareness of other national
histories. "Latin American intellectuals commonly point
out, for example, how few Americans have ever had
courses in Latin-American history in school, and how
widespread are certain illusions in the United States,
for example, the popular misconception that Pancho Villa
was simply a bandit." Professor Frankel observes that
"the public opinion that makes for enlightened foreign
policy is not built out of such legends."[42] Philistine
ethnocentrism has never been one of this country's more
endearing characteristics. It is fair to observe that a
broader cultural horizon would not only benefit the
individual American but would help to defuse some of the
anti-Americanism that comes from the belief that we are
indifferent to the cultural values of other nations.
     An emphasis on the mutuality involved in a cultural
exchange would also serve to counter any
characterization of such programs as a form of "cultural
imperialism." The goal is not the Americanization of
other nations but the internationalization of
communications about education and culture. This is a
process in which the United States has as much to learn
as it has to teach. Since cultural enterprise and
awareness is not so bound by national borders or
political ideologies, it allows for a degree of
communication with different people that might not be
possible otherwise. Culture then can serve as a true
modus vivendi for facilitating understanding between and
among nations even if it does not guarantee a
commonality of interests.

THE FUTURE OF CULTURAL DIPLOMACY: SOME RECOMMENDATIONS

The administration of international cultural relations has been reorganized so many times that one draws back from suggesting yet another structural change. Moreover some of the recommendations here have been suggested by various advisory commissions but not approved or implemented. The first change is somewhat cosmetic: to change USICA's name from United States International Communication Agency to United States Information and Cultural Affairs Agency. This more accurately describes what the agency does and indicates its bureaucratic ancestry from USIA and CU. The newly named agency would also be able to keep the same initials.

A second structural change that I would recommend is anything but cosmetic and that concerns USICA's bureaucratic location. The debate over this issue has been going on ever since USIA was established as an independent agency in 1953 on the recommendation of the Rockefeller Commission. In 1958 the President's Advisory Committee on Government Organization reversed itself and advised that USIA be brought back into the State Department under an Under Secretary for International Cultural and Information Affairs who would also be responsible for the cultural exchange programs. A variation on this proposal was to have this reconstituted agency brought back into the State Department as a semi-autonomous organization headed by an administrator and reporting directly to the Secretary of State. This was the administrative status occupied by the International Cooperation Administration (now the Agency for International Development) when it returned to the State Department in 1955.[43]

Although nothing came of these reorganization schemes at the end of the Eisenhower administration, the idea to create a semi-autonomous information and cultural affairs agency was a good one. It could be done by simply introducing legislation to have the director of the International Communication Agency responsible to the Secretary of State for administrative oversight, policy-guidance, and budgetary review. USICA's director would be the Department's chief spokesman (after the Secretary) for the explanation and articulation of U.S. foreign policy and the principal adviser to the Secretary on the reactions (both probable and actual) of public opinion abroad to U.S. foreign policy decisions. The Stanton Report argued for the creation of a Deputy Under Secretary of State for Policy Information who would perform these duties but this seems to create an unnecessary official and to diminish the status of the USICA Director.

There are traditional objections that accumulating specialized agencies--AID, the Arms Control and Disarmement Agency, the proposal for USICA--would make the State Department a holding company of independent divisions and divert the Secretary from his principal task of formulating and excuting foreign policy. But the scope of foreign policy has become so great (as even John Foster Dulles, who had opposed having USIA in State, came to realize) as to require the Secretary to have control over all the instruments of diplomacy including the cultural. Moreover, it seems that a Secretary of State who wishes to maintain some parity with the Secretary of Defense and Special Assistant to the President for National Security Affairs would want to increase the State Department's powers as much as possible.

What is clear is that the functions primarily split between USIA and the State Department are better joined in the International Communication Agency. But it does not make good sense to assign "to an agency separate from and independent of the State Department" responsibility for "interpreting U.S. foreign policy to the world and advising in its formulation.⁴⁴ An autonomous status for USICA within the State Department would make better sense: by centralizing the coordination of information and cultural policy-making while allowing USICA to maintain the international administrative control necessitated by its sensitive activities.

A last area for a recommendation concerns the people who serve as cultural affairs officers. The importance of these cultural diplomats should not be underestimated. Quite apart from their regular duties that revolve around the exchange programs, cultural affairs officers are often invaluable as perhaps the only embassy personnel who are not unwelcome with intellectuals, artistic, and student groups. Cultural officers can serve as links to groups that are often very influential on public opinion and too often anti-American in their own opinions. Given the importance of such cultural postings, the long tradition of assigning prominent noncareer people might be expanded to one-third of assignments. Among those who might be seconded for two to three year terms are university professors, arts and educational administrators, journalists, trade union officials, and artists. These would be people with established reputations in their fields who could both open doors closed to regular officials and stimulate the career officers in the embassy. Additionally, career cultural affairs officers should be given opportunities to enhance not only their linquistic skills but also their skills in the languages of literature, history, science, and music found in other nations. Cultural officers must also have a thorough and continuing knowledge of American culture if they are to communicate its significance to the citizens of other nations.

It should be noted that there is a certain risk in the use of "nonprofessionals" as cultural affairs officers--that is, they are less controllable and more likely to be critical of American politics and society. There is certainly a legitimate concern that the American foreign processes must have some semblance of unity--particularly that our international objectives be intelligible, decisive, and consistent. But the Voice of America and their activities of informational diplomacy can articulate these objectives. The exchange programs allow the "voices of America" to speak. That these voices may be critical (albeit not subversive), nondisciplined (but not undisciplined) and pluralistic (although not incoherent) is the nature of a free society. The goal of cultural diplomacy is not to deny the need for a forceful vehicle to express American foreign policy abroad but to complement this with a more personal program that expresses the educational and cultural attainments of American society.

Finally, an effective cultural diplomacy must be sensitive to intellectual, religious, artistic and other "nonpolitical" devleopments abroad. By restricting our understanding of politics to governmental, military, economic and political matters, we circumscribe our intelligence about what is going on in many parts of the world. An agency responsible for an awareness of these broad-gauged cultural developments and able to communicate that awareness would go a long way toward providing American foreign policy with that necessary "fourth dimension." Educational and cultural exchanges are not the key to international understanding, nor is good will the sufficient requirement for national security, but both are necessary conditions for a more stable world order.*

*I would like to acknowledge research assistance provided by Brian Kim, Evelyn Stern, and Natalie Wanamaker and to thank my colleagues James Bolner, Cecil V. Crabb, and Adam Hayward for comments on an earlier draft of this paper. Responsibility for the final outcome is mine alone.

NOTES

[1] Charles Frankel, The Neglected Aspect of Foreign Affairs: Educational and Cultural Policy Abroad (Washington, D.C.: The Brookings Institution 1966), p.5.

[2] Ruth Emily McMurry and Muna Lee, The Cultural Approach (Chapel Hill, NC: University of North Carolina Press, 1947), pp. 9-38.

[3] Frederick C. Barghoorn, The Soviet Cultural Offensive: The Role of Cultural Diplomacy in Soviet Foreign Policy (Princeton, NJ: Princeton University Press, 1960), pp. 11-12.

[4] Ibid., p. 12. Professor Barghoorn was arrested in the Soviet Union in 1963 in espionage allegations. But this incident occurred after this book was published and, consequently, cannot explain the decidedly critical tone of the remarks quoted.

[5] Report of the Delegations of the United States of America to the Inter-American Conference for the Maintenance of Peace, Buenos Aires, Argentina, December 1-23, 1936 (Washington, DC, 1936), p. 167.

[6] J. Manuel Espinosa, Inter-American Beginnings of U.S. Cultural Diplomacy (Washington, D.C.: Department of State Publication 8854, 1976), pp. 96-97. This account is a summary of the meeting's transcript. Dr. Espinsoa was in charge of a State Department History Project documenting the International Educational and Cultural Programs. I have benefited greatly from assistance provided by Dr. Espinosa and his colleague in the History Project, James A. Donovan, Jr.

[7] Ibid., p. 103.

[8] Quoted in Henry J. Kellerman, Cultural Relations As An Instrument of U.S. Foreign Policy (Washington, D.C.: Department of State Publication 8931, 1978), p. 7.

[9] Quoted in ibid., p. 8.

[10] Quoted in Espinsoa, Inter-American Beginnings, p. 199.

[11] Kellerman, Cultural Relations, p. 9.

[12] Quoted in Espinosa, Inter-American Beginnings, pp. 319-20.

[13] Kellerman, Cultural Relations, p. 158.

[14] Ben M. Cherrington, "Ten Years After," Association of American Colleges Bulletin 34 (December 1948): 5.

[15] For a personal account of the American cultural mission to China, see Wilma Fairbank, America's Cultural Experiment in China, 1942-1949 (Washington, DC: State Department Publication 8839, 1976).

[16] Espinosa, Inter-American Beginnings, p. 188.

[17] Ibid., p. 194.

[18] Ibid., p. 193.

300

[19]Kellerman, Cultural Relations, p. 4.

[20]Ibid., pp. 10-11.

[21]Quoted in ibid., p. 21.

[22]Quoted in ibid., pp. 79-80.

[23]Ibid., p. 34.

[24]See George N. Shuster, "The Nature and Development of U.S. Cultural Relations" in Robert Blum, ed., Cultural Affairs and Foreign Relations (New York: Prentice-Hall, 1963).

[25]From 1938-43 the cultural relations program was under the direct supervision of the Under Secretary of State, Sumner Welles. In 1944-45 it was administered by the Assistant Secretary of State for Public Relations and Cultural Affairs, Archibald MacLeish. From 1945-58 the supervising official was the Assistant Secretary of State for Public Affairs.

[26]See Walter Johnson and Francis J. Colligan, The Fulbright Program: A History (Chicago, IL: University of Chicago Press, 1965).

[27]Espinosa, Inter-American Beginnings, pp. 229-30.

[28]Much of the information about these administrative changes comes from J. Manuel Espinosa, Landmark Events in the History of CU (Washington, D.C.: Bureau of Educational and Cultural Affairs, 1973).

[29]Philip H. Coombs, "The Past and Future in Perpective" in Cultural Affairs and Foreign Relations, p. 151. See also Philip H. Coombs, The Fourth Dimension of Foreign Policy: Educational and Cultural Affairs (New York: Harper and Row, 1964).

[30]Espinosa, Landmark Events in the History of CU, p. 9.

[31]Excerpts of remarks by various CU officials.

[32]This discussion is based on the Report of the Panel on International Information Education and Cultural Relations (Washington, D.C.: Center for Strategic and International Studies, 1975), pp. 4-5. This panel was chaired by Dr. Frank Stanton (formerly president of CBS Television) and is referred to hereafter as the Stanton Report.

[33]United States International Communication Agency, Fact Sheet (Washington, DC: USICA Office of Congressional and Public Liaison, 1979), p. 2. I am also grateful to Richard L. Roth, chief of ICA's Planning and Guidance Staff for much factual information.

[34]Quoted in Espinosa, Inter-American Beginnings, pp. 242-43.

[35]James H. Webb, Jr., "Cultural Attache: Scholar, Propagandist, or Bureaucrat?" South Atlantic Quarterly 71 (Summer 1972): 353. For an interesting composite protrait of the cultural affairs officer at work see Frankel, The Neglected Aspect, pp. 10-20.

[36]Ibid., p.356.

[37] Stanton Report, p. 15.

[38] Frankel, The Neglected Aspect, p. 82.

[39] Ibid., pp. 88-89.

[40] I am grateful to former Ambassador Barbara White for these insights about cultural diplomacy. However, the responsibility for how they are reported here is solely mine.

[41] Frankel, Neglected Aspect, p. 100.

[42] Ibid., p. 117.

[43] Stanton Report, pp. 69-70.

[44] Ibid., p. 41.

13
The Attack
on Public Culture:
Policy Revisionism
in a Conservative Era

Kevin V. Mulcahy

After more than a decade of benign co-existence between government and the arts, public support for culture has come under sharp attack. While war has not exactly been declared on public culture, the atmosphere is one of belligerency. The various public arts agencies have been close to the top of David Stockman's "hit list"--that doomsday book of federal government programs scheduled for budgetary cutbacks. While the proposed cuts of almost fifty percent for each of these agencies were not approved by the congressional appropriations committees, the reductions were still substantial and represent a sharp reversal of the steady budgetary growth that began in the Nixon administration. Although these revisions of existing cultural policy have been much publicized, their impact has been less often analzyed. This discussion will attempt to provide an intellectual, political, and ideological context for the attack on public culture.

WHY THE CUTS?

Public culture and the various public arts agencies have survived the Stockman onslaught--if just barely in some cases. Two things, however, need to be noted about these cuts (even as modified): first, they are off-scale--that is, disproportionately high when compared to general agency reductions; second, the appropriations involved in these budget cuts are microscopic when compared to a federal budget of $700 billion. The proposed cuts in cultural spending--even abolishing public arts agencies--would not materially reduce a projected budget deficit of $40 billion, nor would it provide even a downpayment on the $200 billion proposed for armaments spending. The combined appropriation for

public culture, which includes the National Endowment
for the Arts (NEA), National Endowment for Humanities
(NEH), Corporation for Public Broadcasting (CPB), Museum
Services Institute (MSI) as well as the Smithsonian,
National Gallery of Art, and National Trust for Historic
Preservation, was approximately $700 million in the last
year of the Carter administration: about one-tenth of a
percent of total federal government spending.

The cultural community has been in a quietly self-
congratulatory mood with the success of its congressional lobbying efforts. But it is not so surprising
that government cultural agencies which have strong
support from elite social and institutional circles
should be able to mount a successful lobbying effort.
What is more surprising is that the attack on the
cultural budget should have taken place at all. If so
little money was to be saved, why were the proposed cuts
so large?

The argument that the Office of Management and
Budget (OMB) needed to cut heavily in all non-mandated
programs to come up with its reduced budget totals is
not entirely satisfactory. Public arts agencies were
scheduled initially for the greatest percentage reductions in the budget. The attack on public culture was
motivated not only by a fiscal conservatism but by a
political conservatism that has proved itself to be
ideologically suspicious of public agencies that seek to
promote cultural diversity and availability. "These
agencies continue to be a favorite target of conservatives in Congress and of influential people in the
Reagan administration who, following the lead of the
President, ridicule them for making grants to poets who
write poems consisting of the letter U."[1] But it is
perhaps too easy to attribute all of the blame to a
Reagan philistinism--even if he has been known to remark
that government should not be in the business of subsidizing intellectual curiosity. Much of the justification for the administration's opposition to public
culture can also be found in the arguments of prominent
intellectuals.

THE ANTI-AESTHETICS OF THE INTELLECTUALS

Many intellectuals as distinct from artists, have
been suspicious of, or at least indifferent to, public
support for the arts. Universities and research, yes;
maybe even the NEH since its prime beneficiaries have
been professors and colleges. But public sponsorship of
purely cultural activities seems to strike many in the
academic community as a decidedly peripheral government

responsibility. Some of these feelings stem from a kind of "cultural populism" that is well represented by sociologist Herbert Gans. In Popular Culture and High Culture, Gans argues that much of the alleged "superiority" of the fine arts to commercial adventures is based on aesthetic judgments that are rooted in educational privilege with distinct class biases. In other words "high culture" is simply the aesthetic preferences of the upper-class and public support for the arts is a subsidy for the leisure activities of the social elite.

But this may oversimplify Gans's position. He argues further that American society is composed of a variety of "taste cultures" which have an intrinsic value for their audiences that should not be simply dismissed by participants in "higher cultures." Gans suggests that many advocates of high culture have translated these aesthetic preferences into a public policy position "which not only ignores the people's private evaluations but seeks to eliminate them all together."[2] This he says is bad public policy: "to support through public policies the welfare of the higher cultures at the expense of the lower ones."[3] "Another way of putting this would be to say," as did Tom Bethell in The Public Interest, "that arts-funding is in practice an income-transfer program for the upper-middle-class."[4]

"American society should pursue policies that would maximize educational and other opportunities for all so as to permit everyone to choose from higher taste cultures."[5] But the remedy as proposed by Gans is in fact what has been the guiding principle of public culture in the United States--at least since the chairmanship of Nancy Hanks at the NEA. Unlike public culture in Europe, which has followed a tradition of aristocratic patronage, government support in the United States has largely sought to make the arts more available and accessible, to expose people previously unaquainted with the musical and artistic heritage of Western high culture, and also to affirm the integrity of ethnic and folk arts. In short, the goal of public cultural policy has been to democratize culture, not to keep it the preserve of a literati or cognoscenti.

More militant critics of the cultural elitism allegedly practiced by public arts agencies argued that governmental efforts at democratization were a form of "cultural imperialism"--an attempt to impose alien aesthetic values. The confidence of many supporters of public culture was now badly shaken. First, they were criticized for cultural elitism, then indicted for cultural imperialism, and, finally, from within their own ranks came disaffected voices accusing a craven sellout in the form of a policy of cultural populism. Thus, Ronald Berman, NEH chairman in the 1970's, condemned public culture for "funding entertainment."

> Its principles are to spread money as far as
> it will go; to imitate the workings of HEW and
> other domestic agencies; to insist upon forms
> of equity like age, color, and sex which are
> moral and political rather than
> artistic; . . . to identify art as hobbies,
> crafts, individual pursuits, group modes of
> "participation," regional fairs, clambakes, or
> assertions of consciousness . . ."[6]

Berman is even skeptical of public support for
performing arts institutions that offer traditional
"high brow" (or at least "upper-middle brow") cultural
fare.

> The models are the Kennedy Center and Wolf
> Trap Farm, large establishments heavily
> supported by government, corporations, and
> foundations, and offering a combination of
> mass-audience programs and enough adversary
> culture to stay ahead of the media.[7]

For Ronald Berman such subsidized events amount to a
program of "cultural welfare."

With such a critical configuration, public culture
seemingly cannot win. If it is too avant-garde, it is
denounced as elitist; if it sticks to the established
repertory, it is dismissed as populist. If it produces
either kind of works from the Western European tradition, it is attacked as imperialist; if it subsidizes
largely non-European culture, it is viewed as Marxist.
So what is a public arts agency to do?

In most cases, public culture attempts to balance
competing demands and conflicting conceptions of the
cultural public interest, to represent a diversity of
artistic expressions, and even to use the cultural
budget for minority cultures and special audiences. Such
a cultural latitudinarianism is not likely to please the
doctrinaire modernist and will still be beyond the
convinced philistine. The goals of public culture in
the United States are similar to the goals of most other
public policies: to create a minimally acceptable level
of an agreed-upon public good. Public culture cannot be
too far ahead of the conventional aesthetic wisdom lest
it lose its basis of support. Nor can a public arts
agency ignore the vocal demands of cultural constituencies (majoritarian and minority) in a society where
social pluralism and group representation constitute the
public philosophy. To be excessively esoteric and
avant-garde is quite properly the preserve of the
private sector. But public culture cannot function pour

epater la bourgeoise when the middle class is taxed to
support such outrages.

The most recent attack on public culture has not
been concerned with its content (populist or elitist)
but with the very fact of subsidy itself. In Policy
Review (a publication of the Heritage Foundation),
Ernest van den Haag argues against cultural subsidies in
particular. For van den Haag, the arts must make some
special claim to justify public support. Otherwise they
are on the same footing as whiskey and religion which
also give pleasure and employment to some--but do so
unsubsidized. (Of course religion is indirectly subsidized through its tax-exempt status, and we all pay for
the ill-effects of liquor through traffic fatalities and
worker absenteeism.) "An adequate argument for federal
support of the arts must show, then, that they yield
indivisible collective benefits (as does the police
force);"8 one might also add parks and beaches--not to
mention public libraries and universities. Only if the
arts yield such benefits, and at a sufficient magnitude,
is the government justified in exacting compulsory
benefits (taxes) to provide support.

It would be difficult to determine which public
policies might measure up to van den Haag's qualifica-
tion test. Perhaps national defense and fire protection, which are really insurance policies against
disasters that we hope will not occur, measure up.
Perhaps also the police and judiciary do, although few
seem pleased with the prophylactic power of the former
or with the latter's capacity to approximate justice.
But these are also negative policies designed to
apprehend and punish transgressors against the social
contract. Public schools do not benefit the childless;
public assistance, unemployment compensation, and
medical insurance do not benefit the well-off,
fortunate, and healthy; nor do beaches and parks benefit
the sedentary, disabled, or disinterested.

Yet, one can be physically inactive on principle
and still support the opportunities for others to enjoy
the benefits of exercise--and without joining a country
club or paying admission to a park. These are, of
course, positive policies provided by government that,
while not used by everyone, benefit everyone by creating
a common good (for example, an educated citizenry); and
also policies which, while they benefit only some, are
held to be essential to notions of social responsibility
(for example, public assistance). Such commitments
reflect a society's social and political values--
including those which its citizens are willing to
support even if they are not themselves beneficiaries.
Representative democracy requires the approval of public
policy by a legislative majority--not that a majority of
the populace benefit from the policy.

Van den Haag argues further that since TV and sports prosper unsubsidized, why should the arts be different? Again, these are not unsubsidized activities--the public airwaves are leased free to private broadcasting monopolies (in exchange for certain public service programming), and sports facilities are usually constructed through bond issues or other forms of public subsidy. And what about the following assertion?

> Apart from everything else it seems hard to justify publicly subsidized TV, for it simply amounts to a tax-paid subsidy to upper-middle class viewers dissatisfied with commercial offerings addressed to the less educated.[9]

Here we have the conservative in the untypical role of popular tribune. For one thing, the best prediction of interest in the arts is education, not income. And an "unrepresentative" audience does not invalidate a public policy. Yet, van den Haag comes close to realizing the case for public culture when he wonders why New York City insists upon maintaining its own radio and TV stations. "The cost is negligible," he observes, "but why is it needed?" It is not as a symbolic subsidy for the upper-middle class but because such stations represent an alternative to commericial broadcasting and provide an outlet for viewpoints and artistic expressions not feasible in the profit sector. (And the cost is so small.)

This argument against public support is predicated upon the infallible workings of a cultural market's invisible hand. What works for pricing widgets should work for culture. Van den Haag sees the pricing mechanism as follows:

> People are willing to pay, on the average, fifteen to thirty dollars to attend a Broadway show for two hours. There is no reason to pay less to attend a museum. . . . But since museums are costless to visitors, they now attract crowds so big as to make it nearly impossible for an individual to contemplate and experience the art they display.[10]

The latter observation is reminiscent of the Duke of Wellington's opposition to public transportation on the grounds that it only encouraged the poor to travel about needlessly. And museum attendance has been found to be the most "democratic" of all cultural institutions because of low or free admissions policies--often the result of public subsidy.

Nor is the market the sole guide for cultural production (let alone for economic production). It is certainly necessary to distinguish between culture and entertainment where the latter is a pleasure-giving, profit-maximizing activity and high culture is an explicit effort to transcend the usual with new forms of expression and challenges to received ideas." This is not to say that one activity is better than the other but they are different and high culture is almost guaranteed not to be big box office. Nor is high culture necessarily the preserve of a social elite: increasing access to higher education has also broadend access to high culture. Even if fewer people choose La Giaconda over the Gong Show many more than ever before are in a position to choose; perhaps more can come to like both for their unique contributions. Interestingly, when workers' groups in Yugoslavia were given responsibility for cultural programming, they proved more likely to fund difficult artistic forms like chamber music than the cultural bureaucrats.[12] The workers seemed ready to recognize the importance of such activities even if they were themselves unfamiliar with the aesthetics involved.

Van den Haag's arguments, if wrong-headed, are clearly reasoned. There seems little reason to credit comparable standing to invectives against public culture such as Kingsley Amis's unfortunate diatribe that also appeared in Policy Review.

> . . . [Y]ou can't do that, make the arts relevant to all people in this or any other country not even to most people, who are not interested in them. Before sitting down to frame an arts policy, it's essential to understand that. It's a traditional Lefty view, the belief that anybody can enjoy art, real art, in the same way that everybody is creative. . . . The trouble with bringing art to the people is that it tends to get fatally damaged in transit. In other cases, the commodity to be brought to the people is of course not art at all but a mush of Lefty propoganda presented as art.[13]

Amis concludes that cultural subsidies only encourage "waste and irresponsibility in those who do the spending as well as self-indulgence in the artist." Further, if one is really interested in artistic quality, "one way of allowing it to improve would be to withdraw public money from the arts."[14] While there are abuses to be remedied in artistic production, the answer does not lie in abolishing government support. Nor is an unsubsidized culture more likely to be a better culture. Despite the vogue of market economics, the history of artistic activity suggests that culture has done quite well under subsidy conditions--whether royal, ecclesiastical, or aristocratic. Composers as different as Bach, Wagner, Palestrina, Verdi, Mahler, and Haydn worked under some form of subsidy. "The major modern difference is that the groups giving out the money now have a modicum of peer-group representation on the decision-making boards."[15] This is exactly what is missing in our relatively unregulated form of corporate culture (as it was also with Count Esterhazy and King Ludwig of Bavaria). If the policies of public arts agencies are politicized and mediocre, they need to be judged against the artistic decisions of boards of trustees more concerned with box-office receipts than with aesthetic innovation. Better a season of La Traviatas and Madama Butterflys and the nineteenth century symphonic repertory than riskier works which are either obscure or avant-garde.[16]

None of this is to suggest that a "state culture" would avoid the problems of "corporate culture". For all its shortcomings, the present system of public culture--essentially public support of private instiutions and individual undertakings--has offered the best hope for a democratic and autonomous arts world. The Arts Endowment, however, came in for severe criticism by the Heritage Foundation in its report to incoming President Reagan on federal government programs. Admitedly, this transition report sought to analyze these programs with an eye to recasting them in a conservative mold. Nevertheless, its judgments on the NEA were extremely harsh as the first sentence illustrates.

> Despite protestations to the contrary, under its current leadership the NEA is more concerned with politically calculated goals of social policy than with the art it was created to support.[17]

The NEA's policies are further faulted as "mere entertainment" designed to guarantee large audiences rather than supporting "the cultivation of serious culture." By seeing public culture as a social service, the NEA is judged to have sacrificed "the best" in art as part of a political tradeoff.[18]

The Heritage Foundation's report recommended that the NEA abandon its "populist" programs for an explicitly "elitist" stance. "The arts that NEA funds must support belong primarily to the area of high culture. Such culture is more than mere entertainment and is concerned with permament values beyond current tastes and wide appeal."[19] There is nothing in this declaration that is really at odds with oft-stated NEA pronouncements on the goals of public culture. What is decidedly at odds with the heretofore existing cultural consensus is the sharp criticism of government funding practices and assertions of the superiority of market-oriented cultural products.

> Contrary to present practices, the private sector, both in industry and education, must be encouraged to find its own way in support of the arts; the present exploration of the device of matching grants as a means of directing private funds to the accomplishment of government goals must be ended. And the commercial media . . . must be urged to present art under commercial sponsorship rather than be allowed, as they have in the past, to abdicate their cultural responsibilities to the public communications empire.[20]

However critical of public culture and the NEA's programs, the Heritage Foundation report urged policy reforms and a more limited scope of activity. It did not urge abolishing the federal government's support for the arts. That proposal came a bit later as the Reagan administration got under way.

THE "HIT LIST"

If the initial rumblings from the Reagan camp sounded ominous, David Stockman's budget proposals came as a preemptive strike. OMB proposed cutting the appropriations of the Arts and Humanities Endowments almost in half--from $158 million to $88 million and from $155.2 million to $85.0 million respectively. (These and other budget figures discussed here are summarized in Table 13.1.)

Stockman's proposed budgetary reductions were "premised on the notion that the (Reagan) administration should completely revamp federal policy for arts and humanities support." The Arts Endowment was sharply criticized "for promoting the notion that the federal government should be the financial patron of first resort for . . . artistic and literary pursuits."[21] OMB's working paper on the NEA further observed:

> This policy has resulted in a reduction in the historic role of private individual and corporate philanthropic support in these key areas. These reductions would be a first step toward reversing this trend.[22]

TABLE 13.1:
  Fiscal Year 1981 Budget Recommendations for the Arts
  (in millions of dollars)

Agency	FY 1981 Approp.	OMB Budget	House Approp.	Senate Approp.
National Endowment for the Arts	$158.6	$88.0	$114.0	$119.3
National Endowment for the Humanities	151.2	85.0	109.0	113.7
Institute for Museum Services	9.0	0.2	12.9	9.6
National Historic Preservation Fund	32.5	5.0	40.0	29.7

Source: Congressional Arts Caucus, August 1981.

In assuming the "probable reaction" to the drastic cuts that it would propose, OMB's officials warned that strong opposition could be expected in reaction to such cuts.

> The Arts and Humanities Endowments have broad and articulate public constituencies, ranging from university presidents to museum directors to individual artists and scholars. In addition, most artistic and cultural institutions maintain strong ties to business and corporations through honorary appointments on boards of directors.[23]

The cultural constituency is indeed a very well connected group and a member of the NEA's National Council, like Beverly Sills, can be very vocal. The response from the Endowment itself took a different tack. Instead of arguing against the normative beliefs behind the cuts in the cultural budget, NEA officials emphasized "dollars and sense" consequences. Chairman Livingston Biddle disputed David Stockman's assertions that public support for the arts militated against private funding. "I think that, from the very outset, Congress envisioned the very role of the Endowment as a catalyst. Corporate support for the arts has grown from $22 million in 1966 to more than $435 million today." Representative Sidney Yates (D-Ill.), chairman of the appropriations subcommittee responsible for the NEA and NEH, also attacked the OMB Director's assumption about cultural philanthropy.

> Mr. Stockman says that the Endowments have hindered business from contributing to arts organizations. He doesn't understand how it's worked in the past. The Endowments have been trailblazers for contributions from business, not the other way around. I think if the Endowment cut its contributions, so will business.[25]

Warnings were also forthcoming about the consequences of the budget cuts for various constituencies. The director of the NEA's Office of Federal-State Partnership, which administers the funds given to state arts agencies under statutory mandate, pointed out that a large budget cut would be particularly disadvantageous to small and rural states "where the portion the NEA gives is a large chunk of a state arts agency's budget".[26] Theodore Bikel, a member of the National Council on the Arts, also warned that the effects of the budget cuts would be hardest on small and fledgling arts organizations.

> The Los Angeles Philharmanic won't go broke. It's the small theaters, the small dance companies that depend on the federal dollar. A lot of those might simply disappear. They can't go and ask elsewhere for money unless they have that federal dollar. That federal dollar is a federal good-housekeeping seal of approval for them.[27]

One might add that these arts companies are usually artistically avant-garde and community-based organizations that involved people from outside the cultural mainstream. As with all cuts in public spending, the well-established and more financially-secure groups will be affected less than the more recently established and financially insecure.

But the Arts Endowment was not to rely on rhetorical suasion alone--however important the orchestrated appeals of supporters like Issac Stern, Maurice Abravanel, Jerome Robbins, and Eliot Feld were in getting media coverage. It also engaged in a sophisticated bit of budgetary politics of its own as it

announced program reductions for the "worst case" fifty
percent budget cut. These reductions were most
certainly not across-the-board. Rather, the cuts
followed some timeless truisms of the "politics of the
budgetary process": cut the popular and successful
programs, sacrifice some marginal programs, count on
congressional restoration in response to constituencey
group appeals.

The major programs marked for the greatest reductions were Artists-in-Education and Challenge Grant
programs. (See the comparisons of program funding
levels in Table 13.2.) Both enjoyed strong congressional support and Challenge Grants were politically
very popular since they were the means by which private
funds were raised on a three-to-one match of federal
dollars. Certain minor programs were scuttled (Fellows,
International, Partnership); Research was (as always)
considered easily dispensed with; and a controversial
Special Constituencies program (designed to make the
arts more accessible to the elderly and handicapped) was
scheduled for termination. The budgetary allocations
for administrative costs, on the other hand, was
increased moderatly--largely anticipating a constant
level of grant applications for a decidedly smaller
amount of money.

This worst case budget, according to Phil Kadis,
Special Assistant to the NEA Chairman, was "designed to
be reinflated by Congress." The cuts generally shocked
the cultural community and proposed reductions in the
arts education program disturbed congressmen; the
prospect of sharply reduced Challenge Grants was also at
odds with the Administration's stated ideological goals.
At the reconciliation stage of the budgetary process in
July 1981, the Senate approved a NEA/NEH budget of
$119.3 million and $113.7 million compared to the OMB
requests of $88.0 million and $85.0 million. The
Endowents' budgets will be less than in the Carter
administration but on the order of twenty-five percent
reductions rather than Stockman's fifty percent. Public
culture managed to fend off a major offensive in the
battle for the 1982 budget. It remains uncertain if it
can survive a future round of hostilities.

THE CONSERVATIVE "KULTURKAMPF"

Whatever the success of the Arts and Humanities
Endowments in surviving the budget battle, it is clear
that public culture is not a popular idea in the Reagan
administration. In describing the debate over arts
policy that went on among members of the Reagan

TABLE 13.2
NEA Program Funding and the "Worst Case" Budget
($ in thousands)

	FY 1981	FY 1982
Artists-in-Education	$5,254	$235
Challenge	13,450	2,500
Dance	8,992	5,810
Design Arts	5,150	3,150
Expansion Arts	9,189	5,100
Fellows (Management)	134	-0-
Folk Arts	3,000	2,275
Inter-Arts	5,136	3,000
International	287	-0-
Literature	4,813	3,310
Media Arts	12,407	5,500
Museums	12,968	7,850
Music	16,200	9,700
Opera-Musical Theater	6,193	4,000
Partnership Coordination	600	-0-
Research	1,495	-0-
Special Constituencies	431	-0-
State Programs	23,598	1,600
Theater	10,745	6,525
Visual Arts	7,218	4,780
Total Program Funds	146,660	75,335
Administrative Funds	11,900	12,665
TOTAL BUDGET	$158,560	$88,000

Source: The Cultural Post 8 (May/June 1981): 29.

transition team, Hilton Kramer reported that, among otherwise divided advisers, there was a virtually unanimous belief "that the activities of both Endowments have been profoundly compromised by politicization and an accompanying lowering of standards."[29] One faction (the radicals) would abolish the Endowments, and similar cultural agencies, altogether; the other (moderate conservatives) would define culture in more strictly "elitist" terms to preclude funding of what they would consider social activism (the special constituencies program, for example) rather than traditional high culture. In either case, the result would be the NEA's withdrawal from programs that were admittedly "populist" in their efforts at including broader segments of the American public in the cultural audience.

The Task Force on the Arts and Humanities, chaired by Charlton Heston along with Ambassador-at-large for cultural affairs Daniel J. Terra and University of Chicago president Dr. Hannah Holborn Gray, has sought to paper over some of these ideological differences. The Task Force membership is certainly meant to be reassuring with such luminaries from the world of public culture as former NEA heads Nancy Hanks and Roger Stevens, New York City Commissioner of Cultural Affairs Henry Geldzahler, Librarian of Congress Daniel Boorstin. Charlton Heston also went to great lengths to emphasize that the Reagan administration was not hostile to the arts and did not plan to terminate the federal government's commitment to the nation's cultural institutions. Yet, Heston has repeatedly said that the Task Force has "got to find some way to spend less money" on public culture, "to find ways to do more, or even as much, with less." Special Assistant to the President for Cultural Matters, Aram Bakshian, Jr., has also said that it would be incorrect to view the Reagan era as one of ill-feeling toward the arts and humanities. "The President and his wife are performing artists, and they feel very strongly about the arts." On the other hand, Bakshian also observed:

> There's a lot of special pleading in the arts. I don't see any major setback in the arts or humanities because of the cuts. . . . It wouldn't be the end of the world for any art forms or institutions if arts funding were cut. . . . Though, I'm not in favor of people starving in garrets.[30]

Despite occasional rhetorical gestures in support of public culture, distaste for the Arts Endowment's social concerns are continually expressed by members of the Reagan administration. The Expansion Arts program that finances projects for minority, working class, rural, and farm communities comes in for special criticism. Task Force Chairman Heston has suggested that such "recreational arts" would be better located in the Department of Health and Human Services (engendering a protest from Black and Hispanic community leaders).[31] Also, despite assurances to the contrary, the Reagan administration has been entertaining various proposals for restructruring the National Endowments--possibly as public corporations along the lines of the Corporation for Public Broadcasting. Moreover, the nomination of Francis Hodsoll to the NEA chairmanship and, the candidate of the neoconservatives, William Bennett, for the NEH chairmanship has the major public arts agencies headed by individuals who have expressed decided reservations about the record of public culture.

> It is also probable that the role of the reveiw panels and of the National Council in the grant awarding process will be changed. Administratively, the Endowments organization and priorities may be re-evaluated, reformed, and redirected.[32]

The more radical members of the Reagan administration seem ready to end direct government support for the arts entirely. In fairness it could be observed that the radical opposition to subsidies applies across the board (the tobacco price supports so dear to the heart of Senator Jesse Helms to the contrary notwithstanding). Nevertheless public culture has come in for a disproportionate amount of hostility--perhaps because it is symbolic of a broader commitment on the part of the government to social democracy. More moderate conservatives, on the other hand, recognize the grassroots popularity of many NEA-sponsored programs and the role that public support plays in maintaining financially hardpressed local cultural institutions. These symphonies and museums are often objects of great local pride and are traditionally supported by members of the local social elite. To oppose funding for culture often means tackling with prominent Republican businessmen and their wives, not just artists and musicians. One has only to recollect that the greatest surge in government support occurred during the Nixon administration to sense that public culture may not be as much of a straight-forward liberal/conservative issue as even opposing ideologues seem to think.

The NEA responds to these criticisms by emphasizing that it is specifically forbidden from producing art and that its concerns are with fostering, maintaining, and disseminating the nation's cultural heritage. The NEA would also cite the greater numbers of arts organizations, the growth in audience size, and the increase in private of support of the arts. Some examples will suffice.[33]

> --In the decade prior to the Endowment's establishment, private support for the arts rose 3 percent; since 1965 this support has shown a 13-fold increase (corporate giving grew at the fastest rate--a 20-fold increase).

--In 1965 there were about one million tickets sold for dance performances, principally in New York; today, there are about 16 million ticket-buyers, 90 percent of whom live outside of New York; the orchestral audience has risen from 10 million to 23 million; annual museum attendance has risen from 22 million to over 43 million.

--Since 1965 the number of professional arts organizations has grown by almost 700 percent. Professional orchestras have increased from 58 to 145; professional opera companies from 31 to 109; professional dance companies from 35 to 250; professional theater companies from 40 to 500.

This is an impressive record of cultural growth--even if the question of quality is not answered by the data alone--and the NEA can rightly claim credit for contributing to this success. Much of the cultural growth sponsored by public arts agencies has been dismissed as subsidizing mass entertainment and criticized for draining off needed funds from elite arts organizations. Put crudely (but not untypically), the NEA has been funding "cultural clambakes" at the expense of "national treasures." The NEA responds that for the past decade "6.2 percent of the nation's arts organizations received 51.6 percent of the Endowment's dollars."[34] (Such an admission will doubtless fuel the fires of the Endowment's populist critics.) What the NEA has sought to accomplish involves two broad objectives: supporting established institutions (while also funding touring and satellite companies to serve grass-roots cultural constitutents); and, promoting the broad dissemination of quality cultural resources (thus aiding the creative activities of artists and expanding the cultural horizons of the population as a whole).[35] The policy goal is not to attempt to realize cultural equality but to approximate some form of cultural equity.

Since NEA policies have not been simply "distributive" (not all arts organizations or cultural forms have benefited equally), they have necessarily proved controversial as the Endowment has sought ends that were "redistributive" (for instance, through geographic representation and Expansion Arts programs) and by means of "incentives" (monetary inducement for arts organizations to act in certain ways). But the NEA has not engaged in a "regulative" cultural policy (dictating aesthetic standards by deciding which arts organizations are allowed to survive).[36] The NEA's cultural policies have been traditionally liberal in their emphasis on increased access, broader equality of cultural opportunity, and the encouragement of private artistic production. In sum, public culture has also reflected the broader pluralism of American society in the distinctly minority role played by government in the arts world. Public support for the arts has been important, even crucial--but, it has not been decisive.

By its own admission, a primary purpose of the Endowment "has been to get the arts to the people." Government support for the arts can hardly be characterized as a "transfer payment for the upper-middle class" (Tom Bethell and Ernest van den Haag), nor is it a form of "cultural imperialism" (as Herbert Gans might put it) that threatens the artistic autonomy and cultural vitality of "non-high cultural taste publics."

> The responses of those without high-school diplomas to cross-sectional survey questions indicate that a sizable group of Americans are, in fact, cultural dropouts, individuals with no apparent artistic or cultural interests . . . Cultural deprivation then is not a matter of choosing performances or hobbies that diverge from upper-middle-class norms, rather, it consists of having no creative or expressive pastimes, enjoying no performances of any kind, and being equally immune to the claims of galleries, zoos, or public parks.[38]

It is this forgotten cultural constituency to whom the Endowment has addressed much of its efforts through out-reach programs and support for community-based cultural activities. The NEA thus seeks to reconcile high culture with mass publics. It should also be clear that such small, non-establishmentarian arts groups will be badly, if not mortally, wounded by any further attacks on public culture. As already noted the Los Angeles Philharmonic will surivive all but an out-right war, as will the Metropolitan Museums and San Francisco Operas of the country. Rich patrons--or more likely an oil company taking advantage of a tax writeoff--could underwrite their continued survival if public support were abolished or dramatically reduced. What are unlikely to survive are community-based and minority-oriented institutions that depend almost solely on NEA or NEA-generated, funds. This would be a decided step back from past public commitments to artistic pluralism and cultural democracy. It might do well to recollect the preamble to the enabling legislation of the national foundation for the Arts and Humanities (P.L. 89-209).

> . . . [W]hile no government can call a great
> artist or scholar into existence, it is
> necessary and appropriate for the federal
> government to help create and sustain not only
> a climate encouraging freedom of thought,
> imagination, and inquiry, but also the
> material conditions facilitating the release
> of this creative talent . . .

These words are more than platitudes; they express a
legislative intent for a policy of government support of
the arts that has yet to be repealed by Congress.*

*I would like to thank my colleagues Jim Bolner, Cecil
Eubanks, and Adam Hayward for their help in preparing
this discussion.

NOTES

[1] Irvin Molotsky, "The President, the Congress and the Arts," New York Times, August 9, 1981, sec. 2, p.1.

[2] Herbert Gans, Popular Culture and High Culture (New York: Basic Books, 1979), p. 121.

[3] Ibid., p. 128.

[4] Tom Bethell, "Welfare Arts," The Public Interest 53 (Fall 1978): 136.

[5] Gans, Popular Culture, p. 128.

[6] Ronald Berman, "Letter to the Editor," Commentary (March 1980), p. 12.

[7] Ronald Berman, "Art vs. the Arts," Commentary (November 1979), p. 49.

[8] Ernest van den Haag, "Should the Government Subsidize the Arts?" Policy Review 10 (Fall 1979): 64.

[9] Ibid., p. 69.

[10] Ibid., p. 72.

[11] See George Clack, "Art in the Marketplace," Cultural Post 7 (September/October 1981): 13-17.

[12] Bogdan Denitch, "What is Socialism?" Dissent, (Summer 1978), p. 354.

[13] Kingsley Amis, "An Arts Policy?" Policy Review 11 (Fall 1980): 85.

[14] Ibid.: 89.

[15] Bruce Jackson, "Letter to the Editor," New York Times, September 15, 1980, sec. A, p. 2.

[16] For a strongly critical discussion of the cultural values of members of orchestra boards, see Edward Arian, Bach, Beethoven, and Bureaucracy (University, AL: University of Alabama Press, 1971).

[17] "Report on the National Endowment for the Arts," in Charles L. Heatherly, ed., Mandate for Leadership (Washington, DC: Heritage Foundation, 1980), p. 1051.

[18] Ibid., p. 1053.

[19] Ibid., p. 1055.

[20] Ibid., p. 1056.

[21] U.S. House of Representatives, Democratic Study Group, "Special Report: The Stockman Hit List" (mimeograph, February 7, 1981), p. 35.

[22] Ibid.

[23] Ibid., p. 37.

[24] Washington Post, February 14, 1981, sec. D, p. 1.

[25] Washington Post, February 2, 1981, sec. B, p. 5.

[26] Ibid. By federal law the NEA is required to give at least twenty percent of its budget to state arts agencies as a basic operating grant.

[27] Washington Post, February 18, 1981, sec. D, p. 11.

[28] Quoted in Margaret J. Wyszomirski, "The Reagan Administration and the Arts: Early Indications," paper presented at the Annual Meeting of the American Political Science Association, New York, September 3-6, 1981, pp. 18-19.

[29]New York Times, November 26, 1980, sec. C, p. 1.

[30]New York Times, August 9, 1981, sec. B, p. 16.

[31]New York Times, April 23, 1981, p. 23.

[32]Wyszomirski, "Reagan Administration and the Arts," p. 27.

[33]The following data are from "Advancing the Arts in America," Cultural Post 7 (September/October 1981): 20, 22. (This is a summary of a report which the National Council on the Arts submitted on July 23, 1981 to the Presidential Task Force on the Arts and Humanities.)

[34]Ibid., pp. 22-23.

[35]These points were suggested by Margaret J. Wyszomirski, "Arts Policy-making and Interest-Group Policies" in "Government and the Arts: A Symposium," Kevin V. Mulcahy, ed., Journal of Aesthetic Education 14 (October 1980): 32.

[36]This typology is taken from Theodore Lowi, "American Business, Public Policy: Case Studies and Political Theory," World Politics 16 (July 1964): 689-91.

[37]"Advancing the Arts," p. 21.

[38]Paul DiMaggio and Michael Useem, "The Arts and Cultural Participation," Journal of Aesthetic Education 14 (October 1980): 65.

Contributors

Derral Cheatwood (Ph.D., Ohio State) teaches sociology at the University of Baltimore. He has published articles on visual sociology, the sociology of art, and is currently doing research on prison films and correctional practice. He is the co-founder of the Conference on Social Theory and the Arts and is co-editor of the Journal of Qualitative Sociology.

Milton C. Cummings, Jr. (Ph.D., Harvard) teaches political science at The Johns Hopkins University. He is the author, co-author, or editor of several books including Congressmen and the Electorate, The Image of the Federal Science, (with Franklin P. Kilpatrick and M. Kent Jennings), The National Elections of 1964, and Democracy Under Pressure (with David Wise.) He is the president of the Conference Group on Government and the Arts and is currently working on a book about government policies in the United States that affect the arts.

David Cwi (Ph.D., Johns Hopkins) directs the Cultural Policy Institute. For ten years he was a senior research associate at The Johns Hopkins University Center for Metropolitan Planning and Reasearch. He has published widely on the economics of arts activities including Economic Impact of Arts and Cultural Institutions.

Richard S. Katz, (Ph.D., Yale) teaches political science at The Johns Hopkins University. He is the author of A Theory of Parties and Electoral System and of American Votes (with Kevin V. Mulcahy). He has published articles in Europe and the United States on comparative policies and cultural policymaking and is the executive secretary of the Conference Group on Government and the Arts.

Lawrence Mankin (Ph.D., Illinois) teaches at the Center for Public Affairs of Arizona State University where he is also associate dean of the Graduate School. He has published articles on public administration and arts policy and is currently finishing a book entitled The National Government and the Arts.

Kevin V. Mulcahy (Ph.D., Brown) teaches public policy and administration at Louisiana State University where he is also director of the Institute of Government. He serves as a consultant to the Speaker of the Louisiana House of Representatives and is the co-founder of the Conference Group on Government and the Arts. He has written America Votes (with Richard S. Katz) and is

323

currently working on a book entitled <u>White House</u>
<u>Government: Presidential Management and Public</u>
<u>Policymaking</u>.

C. Richard Swaim (Ph.D., University of Colorado)
teaches political science at the University of
Baltimore. He is a former administrative intern at the
National Endowment for the Arts and at the Office on
Aging of the U.S. Department of Health and Human
Services. He is currently finishing a book on the
politics and administration of the National Arts
Endowment.

Arthur Svenson (Ph.D., University of California at
Santa Barbara) teaches political science at the
University of Redlands. He has published articles on
cultural politics and done research on a National
Science Foundation study of earthquake preparedness.
He is a performing artist and has played violin with
several community orchestras including the Santa
Barbara Symphony.

Margaret J. Wyszomirski (Ph.D., Cornell) teaches
political science at Douglas College-Rutgers and has
been an administrative intern at the National Endowment
for the Arts. She is also a student of the American
presidency and is currently writing a book on
presidential advisory systems.

Index

332